RYAN **PARROTT** • RACHEL **WAGNER** • FRANCESCO **MORTARINO** • MOISÉS **HIDALGO**

POWER RANGERS

VOLUME THREE

SERIES DESIGNER
SCOTT NEWMAN

COLLECTION DESIGNER
**CHELSEA ROBERTS
& MARIE KRUPINA**

ASSISTANT EDITOR
GWEN WALLER

EDITOR
DAFNA PLEBAN

HASBRO SPECIAL THANKS
ED LANE, **BETH ARTALE**,
AND **MICHAEL KELLY**

Ross Richie Chairman & Founder
Jen Harned CFO
Matt Gagnon Editor-in-Chief
Filip Sablik President, Publishing & Marketing
Stephen Christy President, Development
Lance Kreiter Vice President, Licensing & Merchandising
Bryce Carlson Vice President, Editorial & Creative Strategy
Hunter Gorinson Vice President, Business Development
Kate Henning Director, Operations
Ryan Matsunaga Director, Marketing
Elyse Strandberg Manager, Finance
Michelle Ankley Manager, Production Design
Sierra Hahn Executive Editor
Dafna Pleban Senior Editor
Eric Harburn Senior Editor
Elizabeth Brei Editor
Kathleen Wisneski Editor
Sophie Philips-Roberts Editor
Jonathan Manning Associate Editor
Allyson Gronowitz Associate Editor
Gavin Gronenthal Assistant Editor
Gwen Waller Assistant Editor
Ramiro Portnoy Assistant Editor
Kenzie Rzonca Assistant Editor
Rey Netschke Editorial Assistant
Marie Krupina Design Lead
Grace Park Design Coordinator
Madison Goyette Production Designer
Crystal White Production Designer
Veronica Gutierrez Production Designer
Samantha Knapp Production Design Assistant
Esther Kim Marketing Lead
Breanna Sarpy Marketing Lead, Digital
Amanda Lawson Marketing Coordinator
Alex Lorenzen Marketing Coordinator, Copywriter
Grecia Martinez Marketing Assistant, Digital
José Meza Consumer Sales Lead
Ashley Troub Consumer Sales Coordinator
Morgan Perry Retail Sales Lead
Harley Salbacka Sales Coordinator
Megan Christopher Operations Coordinator
Rodrigo Hernandez Operations Coordinator
Zipporah Smith Operations Coordinator
Jason Lee Senior Accountant
Sabrina Lesin Accounting Assistant
Lauren Alexander Administrative Assistant

Licensed by:

WRITTEN BY
RYAN PARROTT
& RACHEL WAGNER (CHAPTER 10)

ILLUSTRATED BY
FRANCESCO MORTARINO
& MOISÉS HIDALGO (CHAPTERS 9 - 10)

COLORS BY
RAÚL ANGULO
WITH COLOR ASSISTANCE BY **JOSE ENRIQUE FERNÁNDEZ**

LETTERS BY
ED DUKESHIRE

COVER BY
MATTEO SCALERA
WITH COLORS BY **MORENO DINISIO**

FERAL DRAKKON, EMPYREALS, AND ELTARIAN
CHARACTER DESIGNS BY
DAN MORA

CHAPTER
NINE

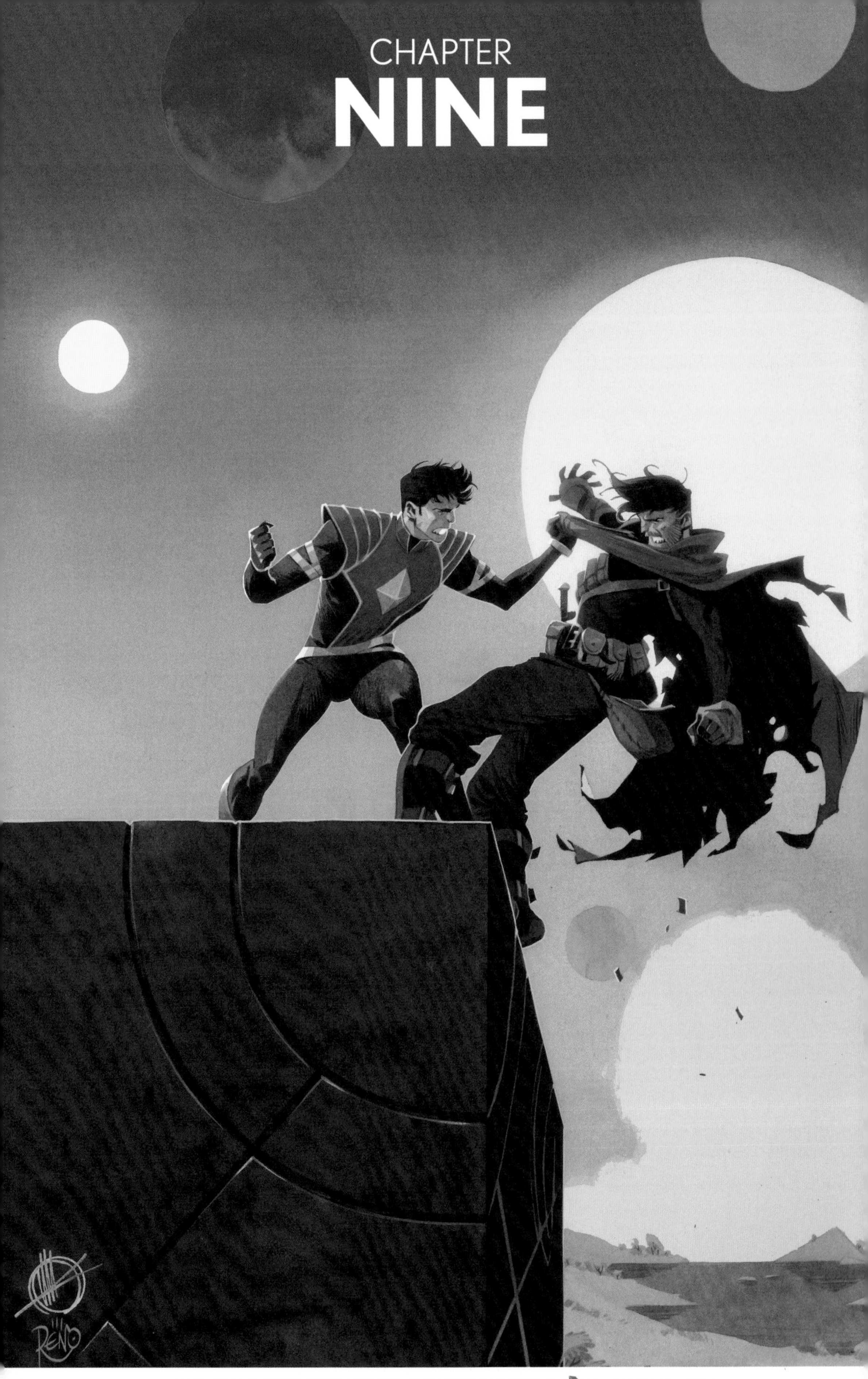

MATTEO SCALERA WITH COLORS BY **MORENO DINISIO** ISSUE NINE COVER

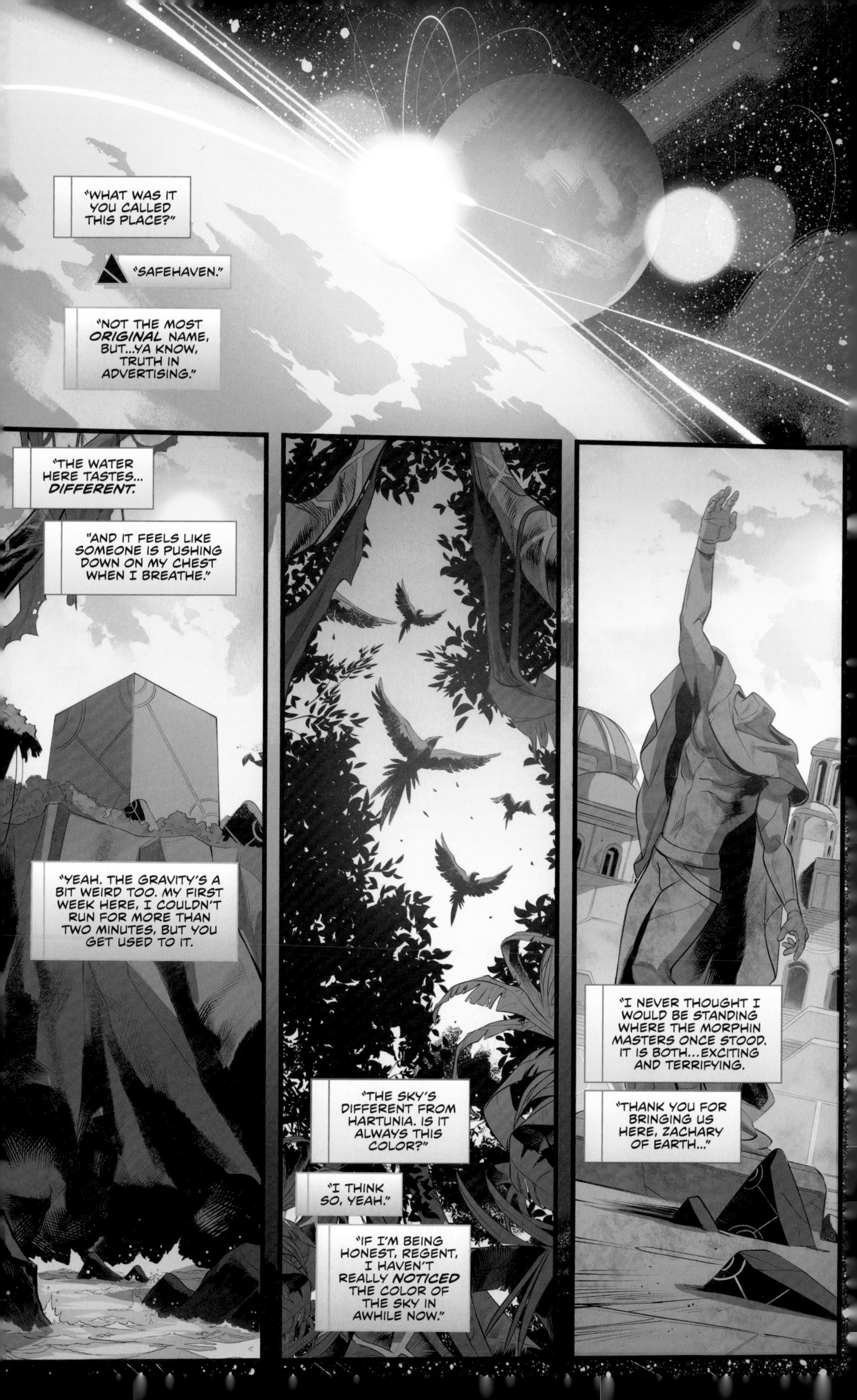
"WHAT WAS IT YOU CALLED THIS PLACE?"
"SAFEHAVEN."
"NOT THE MOST ORIGINAL NAME, BUT...YA KNOW, TRUTH IN ADVERTISING."
"THE WATER HERE TASTES... DIFFERENT.
"AND IT FEELS LIKE SOMEONE IS PUSHING DOWN ON MY CHEST WHEN I BREATHE."
"YEAH. THE GRAVITY'S A BIT WEIRD TOO. MY FIRST WEEK HERE, I COULDN'T RUN FOR MORE THAN TWO MINUTES, BUT YOU GET USED TO IT.
"THE SKY'S DIFFERENT FROM HARTUNIA. IS IT ALWAYS THIS COLOR?"
"I THINK SO, YEAH."
"IF I'M BEING HONEST, REGENT, I HAVEN'T REALLY NOTICED THE COLOR OF THE SKY IN AWHILE NOW."
"I NEVER THOUGHT I WOULD BE STANDING WHERE THE MORPHIN MASTERS ONCE STOOD. IT IS BOTH...EXCITING AND TERRIFYING.
"THANK YOU FOR BRINGING US HERE, ZACHARY OF EARTH..."

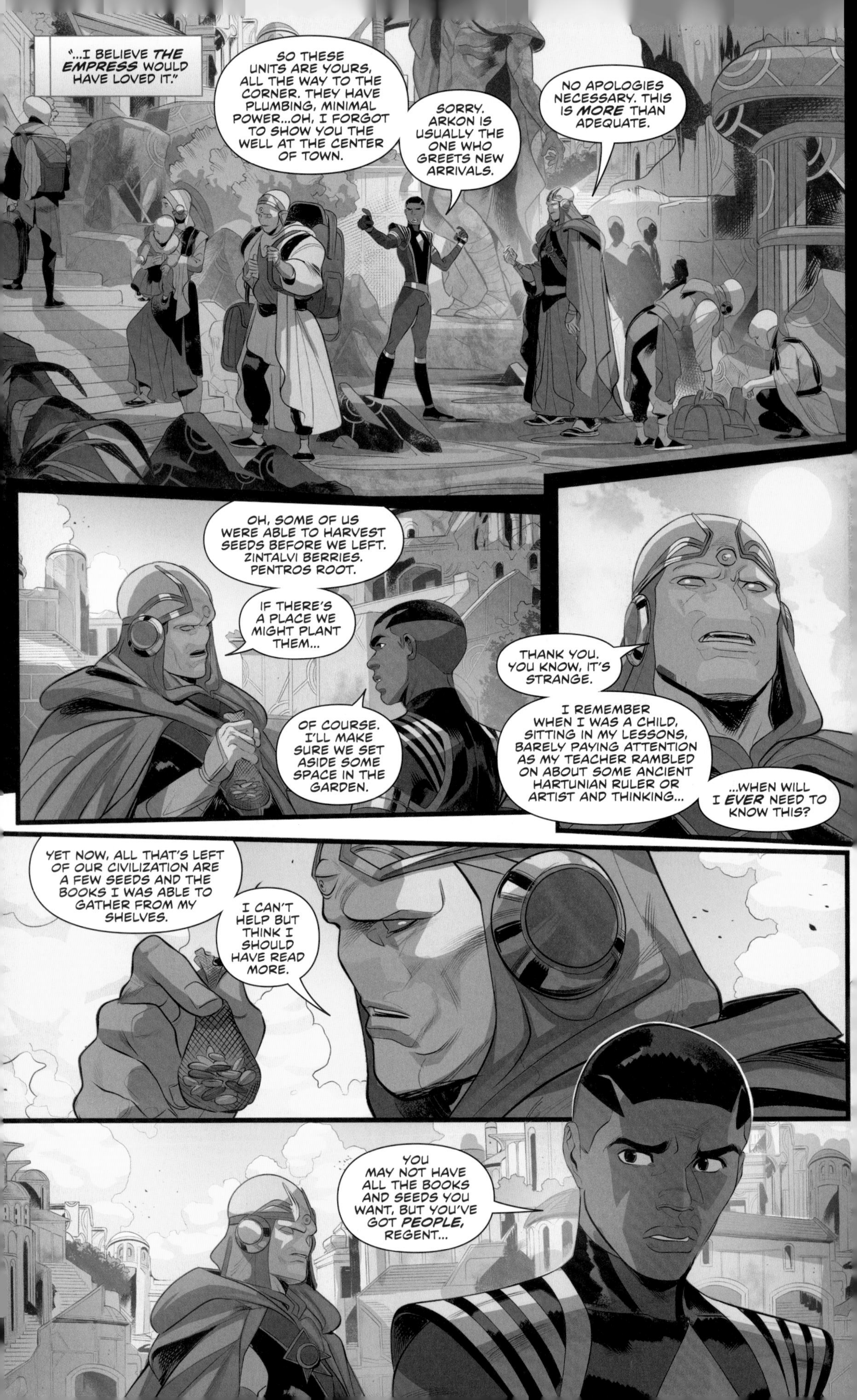
"...I BELIEVE THE EMPRESS WOULD HAVE LOVED IT."
SO THESE UNITS ARE YOURS, ALL THE WAY TO THE CORNER. THEY HAVE PLUMBING, MINIMAL POWER...OH, I FORGOT TO SHOW YOU THE WELL AT THE CENTER OF TOWN.
SORRY. ARKON IS USUALLY THE ONE WHO GREETS NEW ARRIVALS.
NO APOLOGIES NECESSARY. THIS IS MORE THAN ADEQUATE.
OH, SOME OF US WERE ABLE TO HARVEST SEEDS BEFORE WE LEFT. ZINTALVI BERRIES. PENTROS ROOT.
IF THERE'S A PLACE WE MIGHT PLANT THEM...
OF COURSE. I'LL MAKE SURE WE SET ASIDE SOME SPACE IN THE GARDEN.
THANK YOU. YOU KNOW, IT'S STRANGE.
I REMEMBER WHEN I WAS A CHILD, SITTING IN MY LESSONS, BARELY PAYING ATTENTION AS MY TEACHER RAMBLED ON ABOUT SOME ANCIENT HARTUNIAN RULER OR ARTIST AND THINKING...
...WHEN WILL I EVER NEED TO KNOW THIS?
YET NOW, ALL THAT'S LEFT OF OUR CIVILIZATION ARE A FEW SEEDS AND THE BOOKS I WAS ABLE TO GATHER FROM MY SHELVES.
I CAN'T HELP BUT THINK I SHOULD HAVE READ MORE.
YOU MAY NOT HAVE ALL THE BOOKS AND SEEDS YOU WANT, BUT YOU'VE GOT PEOPLE, REGENT...

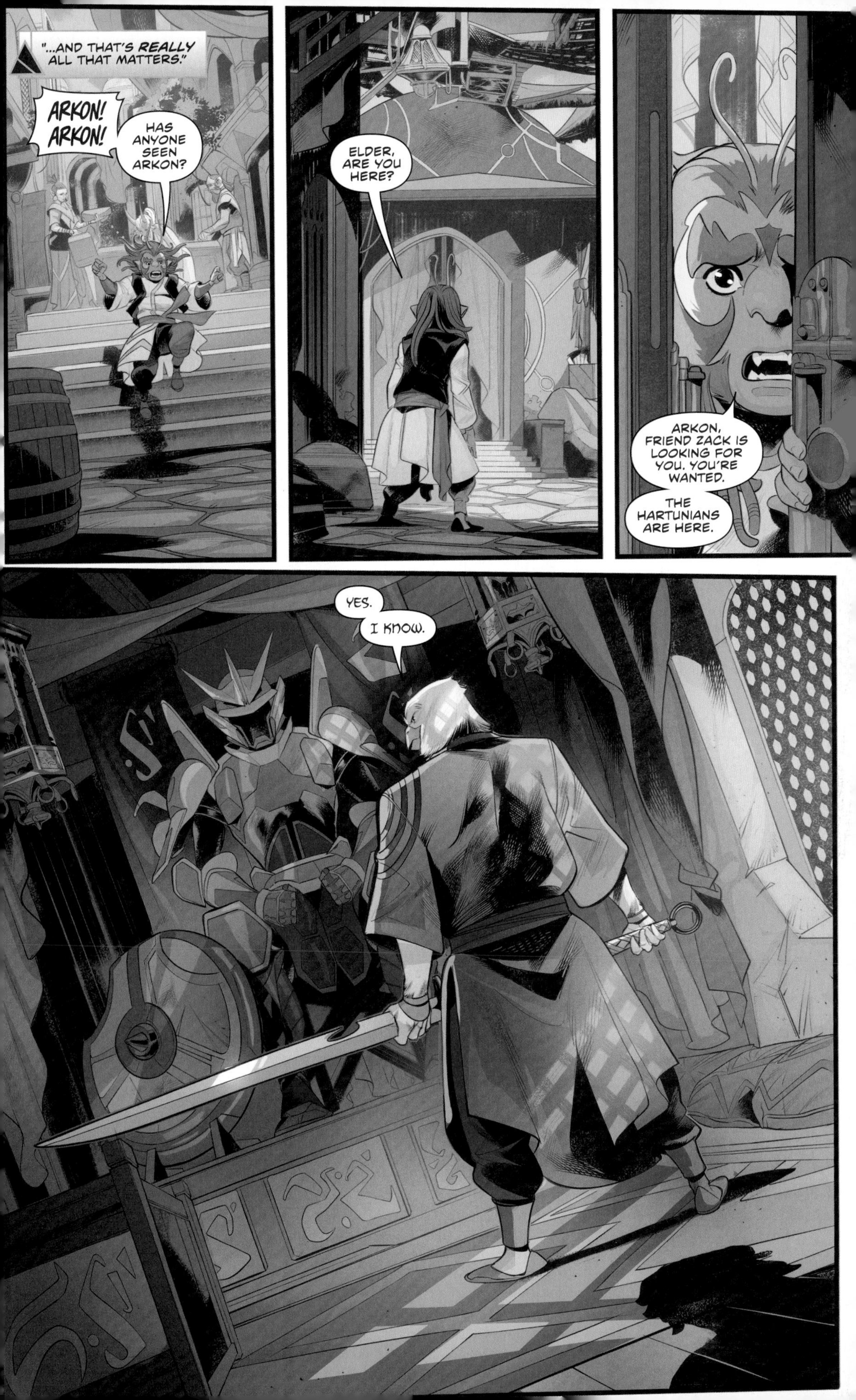
"...AND THAT'S REALLY ALL THAT MATTERS."
ARKON! ARKON!
HAS ANYONE SEEN ARKON?
ELDER, ARE YOU HERE?
ARKON, FRIEND ZACK IS LOOKING FOR YOU. YOU'RE WANTED.
THE HARTUNIANS ARE HERE.
YES.
I KNOW.

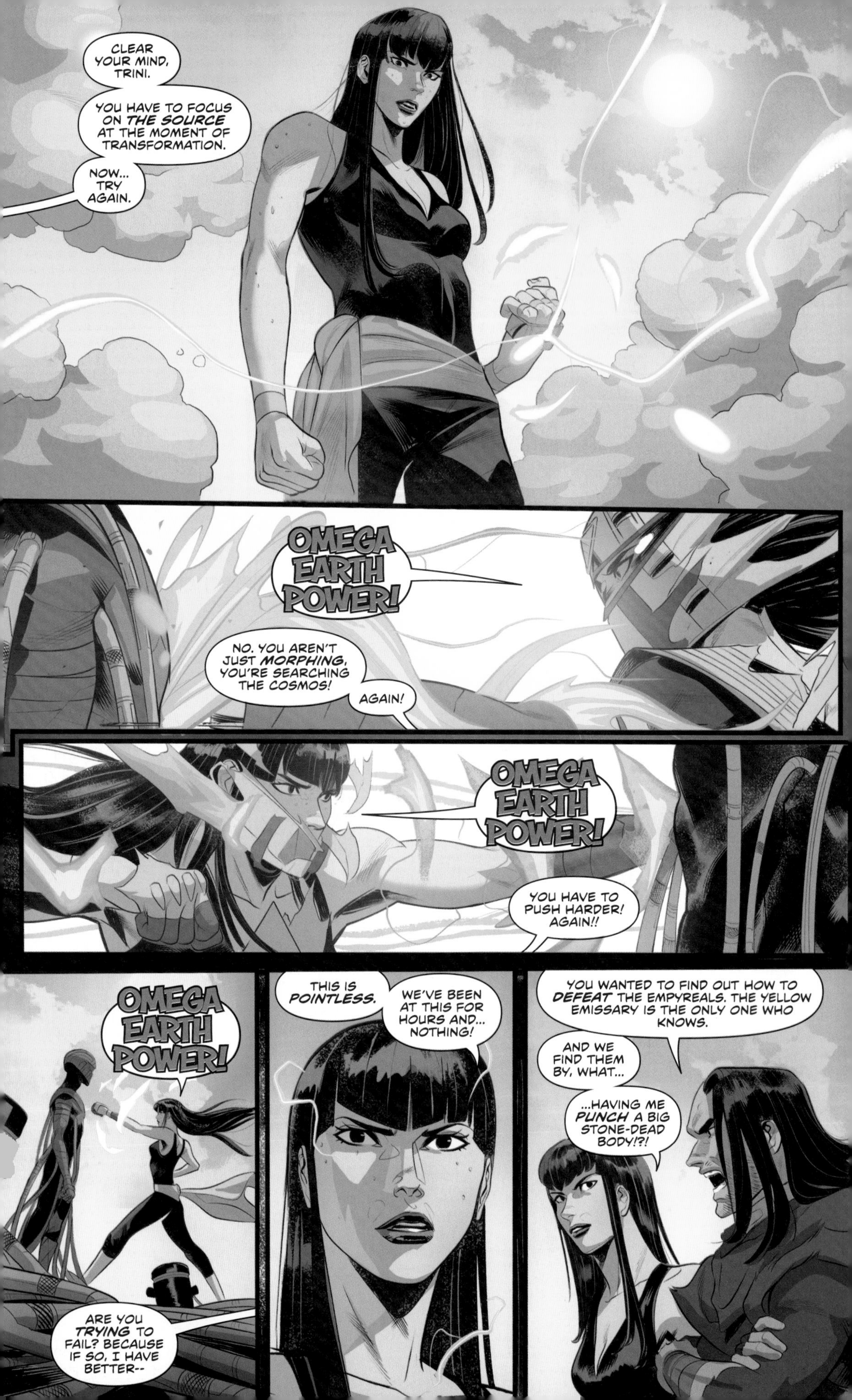
CLEAR YOUR MIND, TRINI.
YOU HAVE TO FOCUS ON *THE SOURCE* AT THE MOMENT OF TRANSFORMATION.
NOW... TRY AGAIN.
OMEGA EARTH POWER!
NO. YOU AREN'T JUST *MORPHING*, YOU'RE SEARCHING THE COSMOS!
AGAIN!
OMEGA EARTH POWER!
YOU HAVE TO PUSH HARDER! AGAIN!!
OMEGA EARTH POWER!
ARE YOU *TRYING* TO FAIL? BECAUSE IF SO, I HAVE BETTER--
THIS IS *POINTLESS.*
WE'VE BEEN AT THIS FOR HOURS AND... NOTHING!
YOU WANTED TO FIND OUT HOW TO *DEFEAT* THE EMPYREALS. THE YELLOW EMISSARY IS THE ONLY ONE WHO KNOWS.
AND WE FIND THEM BY, WHAT...
...HAVING ME *PUNCH* A BIG STONE-DEAD BODY!?!

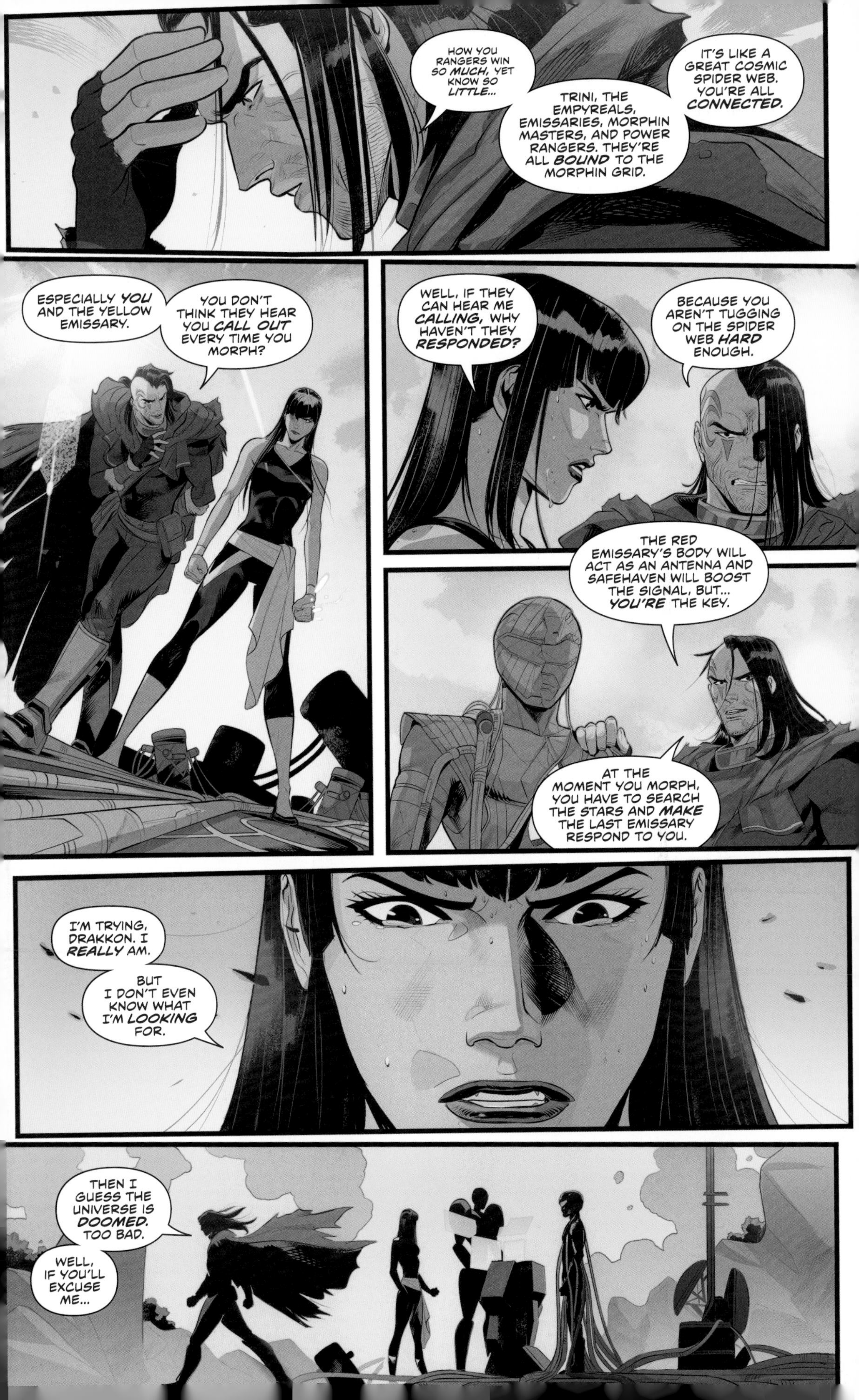
HOW YOU RANGERS WIN SO MUCH, YET KNOW SO LITTLE...
TRINI, THE EMPYREALS, EMISSARIES, MORPHIN MASTERS, AND POWER RANGERS. THEY'RE ALL BOUND TO THE MORPHIN GRID.
IT'S LIKE A GREAT COSMIC SPIDER WEB. YOU'RE ALL CONNECTED.
ESPECIALLY YOU AND THE YELLOW EMISSARY.
YOU DON'T THINK THEY HEAR YOU CALL OUT EVERY TIME YOU MORPH?
WELL, IF THEY CAN HEAR ME CALLING, WHY HAVEN'T THEY RESPONDED?
BECAUSE YOU AREN'T TUGGING ON THE SPIDER WEB HARD ENOUGH.
THE RED EMISSARY'S BODY WILL ACT AS AN ANTENNA AND SAFEHAVEN WILL BOOST THE SIGNAL, BUT... YOU'RE THE KEY.
AT THE MOMENT YOU MORPH, YOU HAVE TO SEARCH THE STARS AND MAKE THE LAST EMISSARY RESPOND TO YOU.
I'M TRYING, DRAKKON. I REALLY AM.
BUT I DON'T EVEN KNOW WHAT I'M LOOKING FOR.
THEN I GUESS THE UNIVERSE IS DOOMED. TOO BAD.
WELL, IF YOU'LL EXCUSE ME...

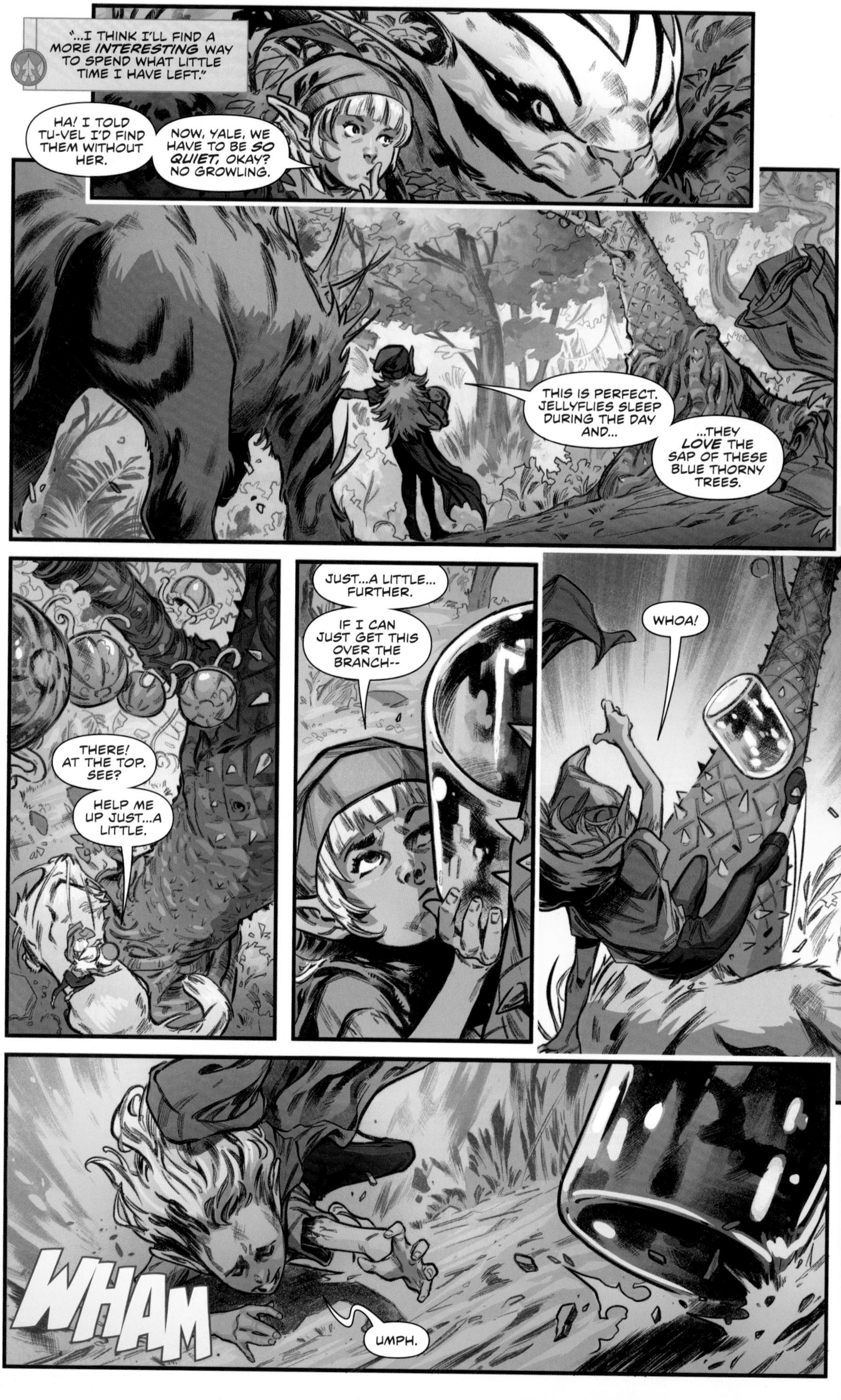
"...I THINK I'LL FIND A MORE INTERESTING WAY TO SPEND WHAT LITTLE TIME I HAVE LEFT."
HA! I TOLD TU-VEL I'D FIND THEM WITHOUT HER.
NOW, YALE, WE HAVE TO BE SO QUIET, OKAY? NO GROWLING.
THIS IS PERFECT. JELLYFLIES SLEEP DURING THE DAY AND...
...THEY LOVE THE SAP OF THESE BLUE THORNY TREES.
THERE! AT THE TOP. SEE?
HELP ME UP JUST...A LITTLE.
JUST...A LITTLE... FURTHER.
IF I CAN JUST GET THIS OVER THE BRANCH--
WHOA!
WHAM
UMPH.

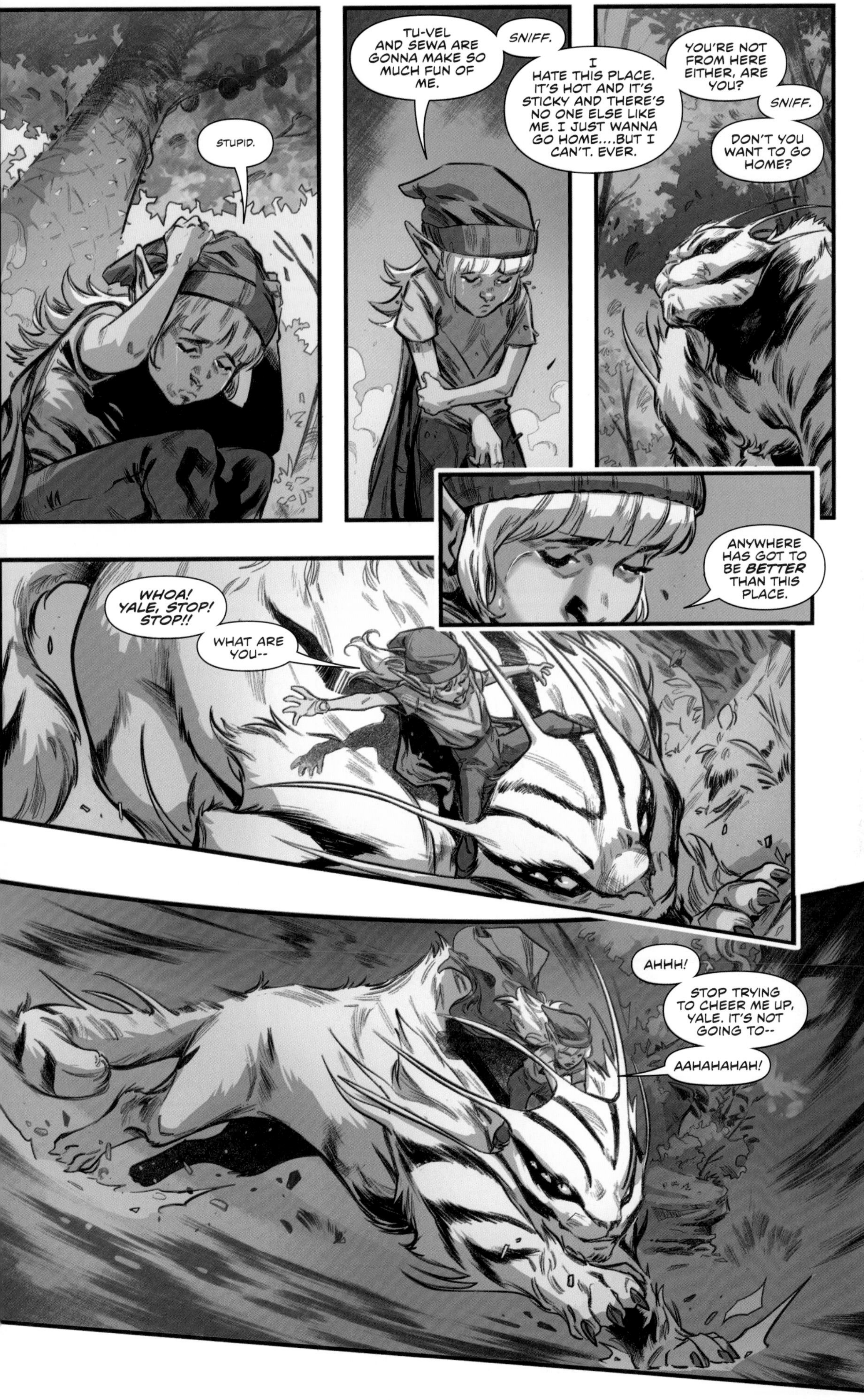
STUPID.
TU-VEL AND SEWA ARE GONNA MAKE SO MUCH FUN OF ME.
SNIFF.
I HATE THIS PLACE. IT'S HOT AND IT'S STICKY AND THERE'S NO ONE ELSE LIKE ME. I JUST WANNA GO HOME....BUT I CAN'T. EVER.
YOU'RE NOT FROM HERE EITHER, ARE YOU?
SNIFF.
DON'T YOU WANT TO GO HOME?
ANYWHERE HAS GOT TO BE BETTER THAN THIS PLACE.
WHOA! YALE, STOP! STOP!!
WHAT ARE YOU--
AHHH!
STOP TRYING TO CHEER ME UP, YALE. IT'S NOT GOING TO--
AAHAHAHAH!

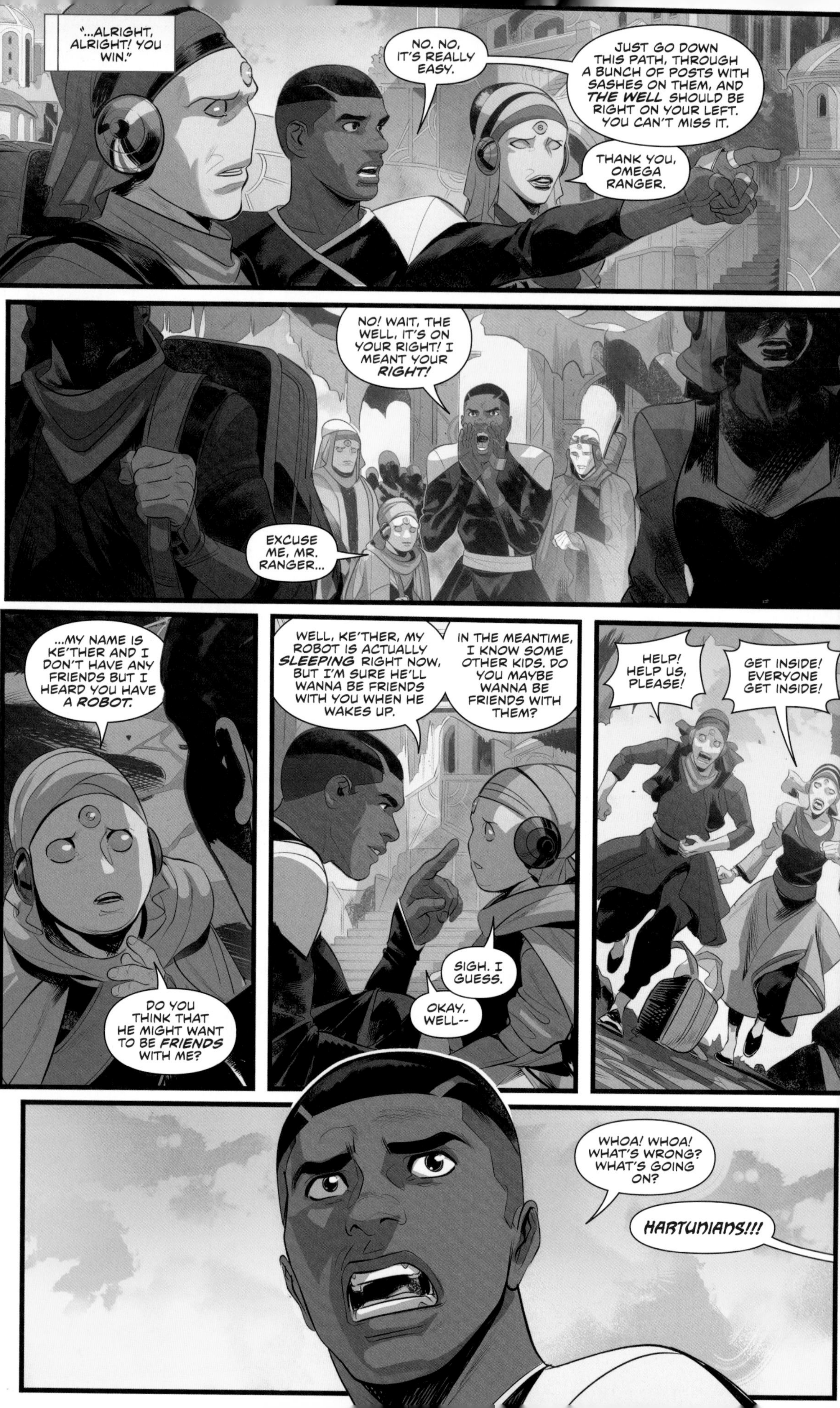
"...ALRIGHT, ALRIGHT! YOU WIN."
NO. NO, IT'S REALLY EASY.
JUST GO DOWN THIS PATH, THROUGH A BUNCH OF POSTS WITH SASHES ON THEM, AND THE WELL SHOULD BE RIGHT ON YOUR LEFT. YOU CAN'T MISS IT.
THANK YOU, OMEGA RANGER.
NO! WAIT, THE WELL, IT'S ON YOUR RIGHT! I MEANT YOUR RIGHT!
EXCUSE ME, MR. RANGER...
...MY NAME IS KE'THER AND I DON'T HAVE ANY FRIENDS BUT I HEARD YOU HAVE A ROBOT.
DO YOU THINK THAT HE MIGHT WANT TO BE FRIENDS WITH ME?
WELL, KE'THER, MY ROBOT IS ACTUALLY SLEEPING RIGHT NOW, BUT I'M SURE HE'LL WANNA BE FRIENDS WITH YOU WHEN HE WAKES UP.
IN THE MEANTIME, I KNOW SOME OTHER KIDS. DO YOU MAYBE WANNA BE FRIENDS WITH THEM?
SIGH. I GUESS.
OKAY, WELL--
HELP! HELP US, PLEASE!
GET INSIDE! EVERYONE GET INSIDE!
WHOA! WHOA! WHAT'S WRONG? WHAT'S GOING ON?
HARTUNIANS!!!

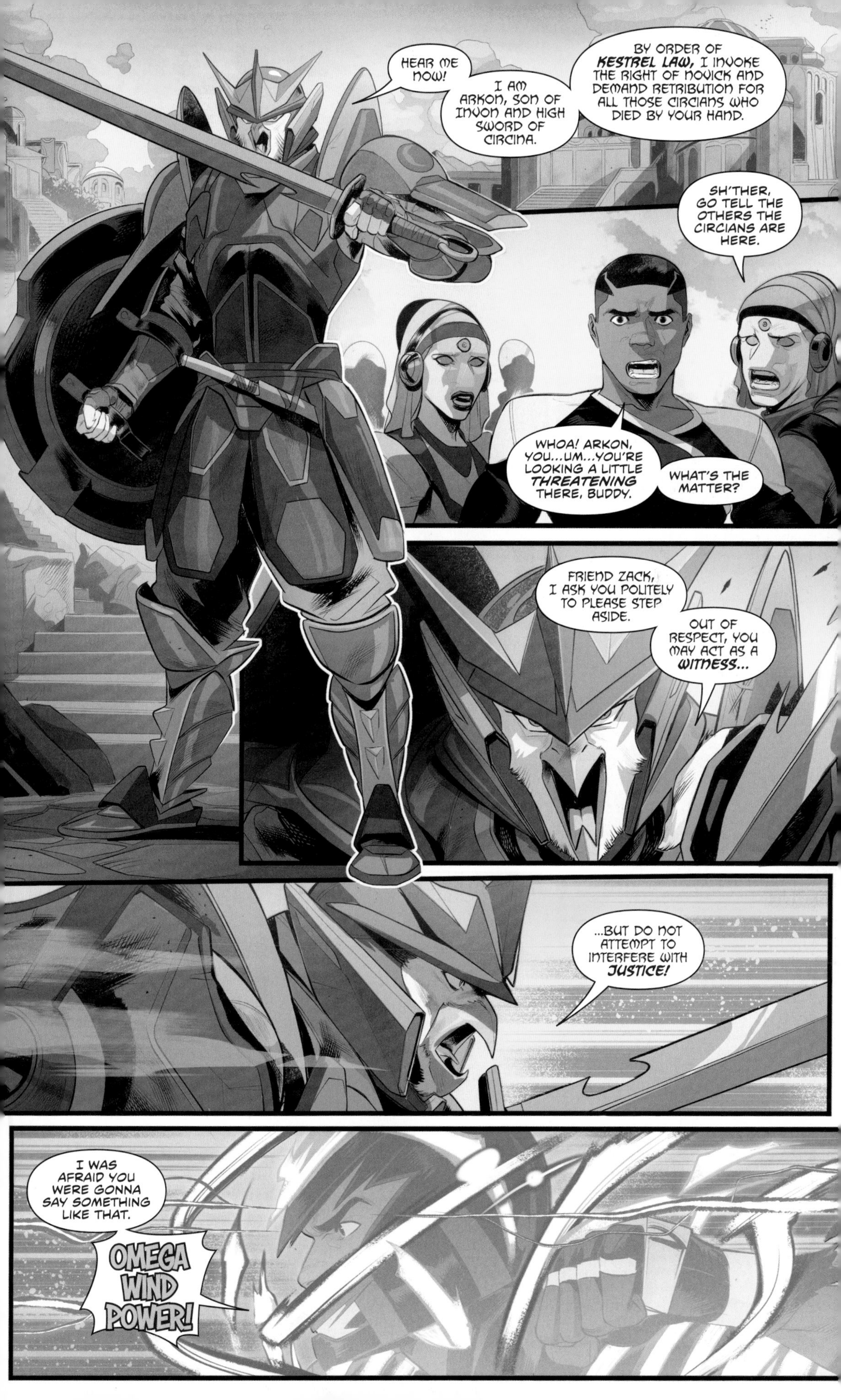

HEAR ME NOW!
I AM ARKON, SON OF INVON AND HIGH SWORD OF CIRCINA.
BY ORDER OF KESTREL LAW, I INVOKE THE RIGHT OF NOVICK AND DEMAND RETRIBUTION FOR ALL THOSE CIRCIANS WHO DIED BY YOUR HAND.
SH'THER, GO TELL THE OTHERS THE CIRCIANS ARE HERE.
WHOA! ARKON, YOU...UM...YOU'RE LOOKING A LITTLE THREATENING THERE, BUDDY.
WHAT'S THE MATTER?
FRIEND ZACK, I ASK YOU POLITELY TO PLEASE STEP ASIDE.
OUT OF RESPECT, YOU MAY ACT AS A WITNESS...
...BUT DO NOT ATTEMPT TO INTERFERE WITH JUSTICE!
I WAS AFRAID YOU WERE GONNA SAY SOMETHING LIKE THAT.
OMEGA WIND POWER!

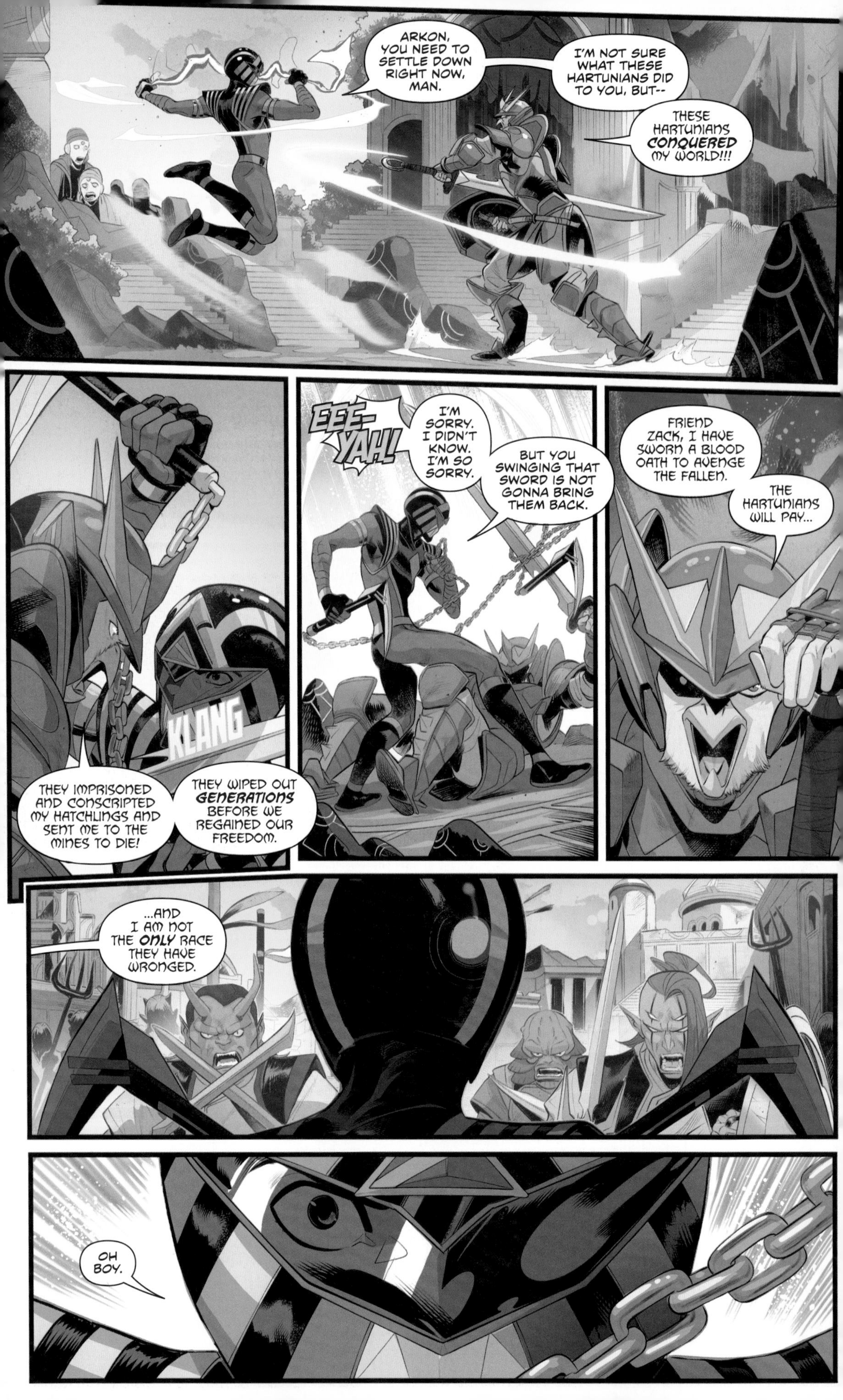
ARKON, YOU NEED TO SETTLE DOWN RIGHT NOW, MAN.
I'M NOT SURE WHAT THESE HARTUNIANS DID TO YOU, BUT--
THESE HARTUNIANS CONQUERED MY WORLD!!!
KLANG
THEY IMPRISONED AND CONSCRIPTED MY HATCHLINGS AND SENT ME TO THE MINES TO DIE!
THEY WIPED OUT GENERATIONS BEFORE WE REGAINED OUR FREEDOM.
EEE-YAH!
I'M SORRY. I DIDN'T KNOW. I'M SO SORRY.
BUT YOU SWINGING THAT SWORD IS NOT GONNA BRING THEM BACK.
FRIEND ZACK, I HAVE SWORN A BLOOD OATH TO AVENGE THE FALLEN.
THE HARTUNIANS WILL PAY...
...AND I AM NOT THE ONLY RACE THEY HAVE WRONGED.
OH BOY.

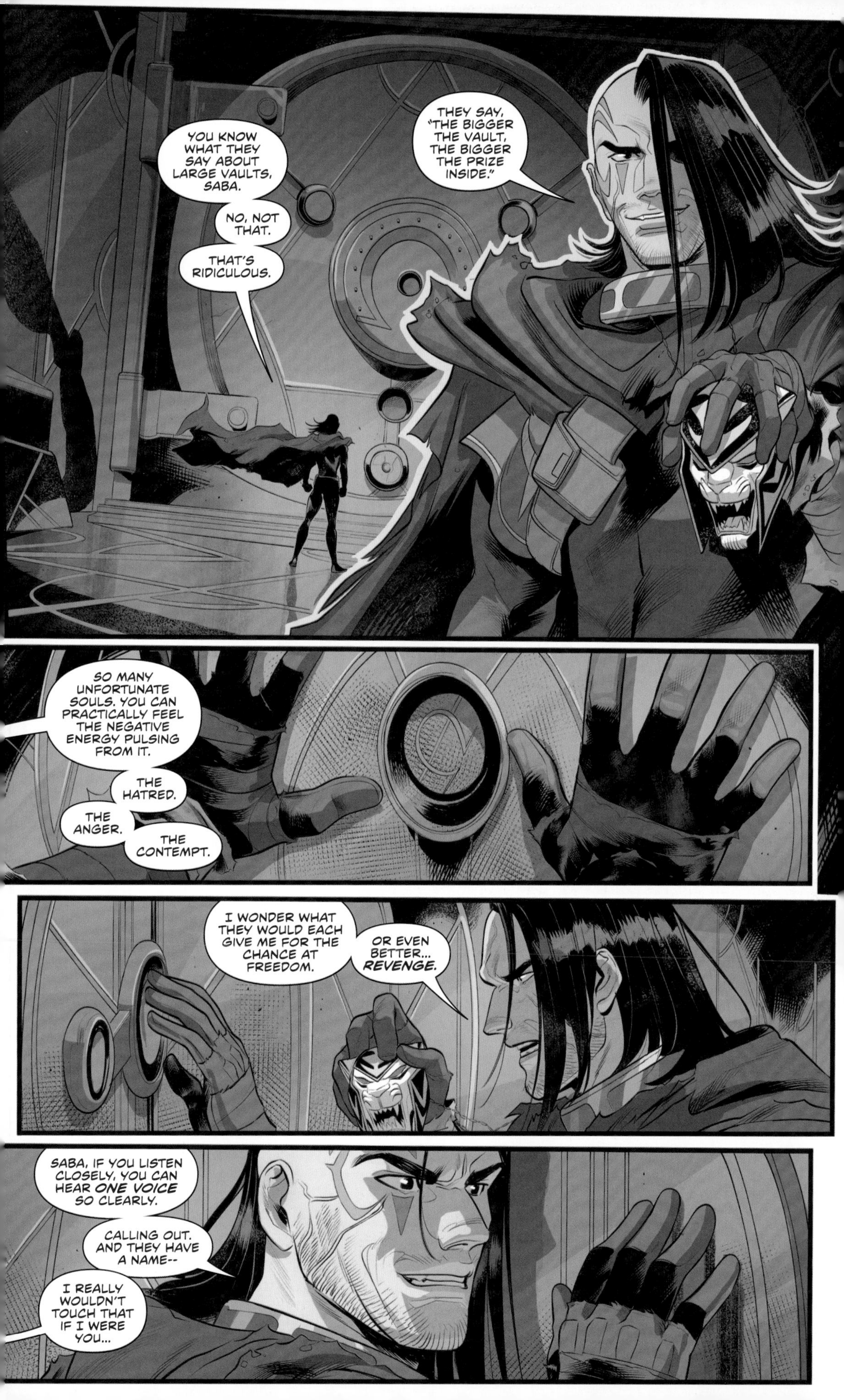
YOU KNOW WHAT THEY SAY ABOUT LARGE VAULTS, SABA.
NO, NOT THAT.
THAT'S RIDICULOUS.
THEY SAY, "THE BIGGER THE VAULT, THE BIGGER THE PRIZE INSIDE."
SO MANY UNFORTUNATE SOULS. YOU CAN PRACTICALLY FEEL THE NEGATIVE ENERGY PULSING FROM IT.
THE HATRED.
THE ANGER.
THE CONTEMPT.
I WONDER WHAT THEY WOULD EACH GIVE ME FOR THE CHANCE AT FREEDOM.
OR EVEN BETTER... *REVENGE.*
SABA, IF YOU LISTEN CLOSELY, YOU CAN HEAR *ONE VOICE* SO CLEARLY.
CALLING OUT. AND THEY HAVE A NAME--
I REALLY WOULDN'T TOUCH THAT IF I WERE YOU...

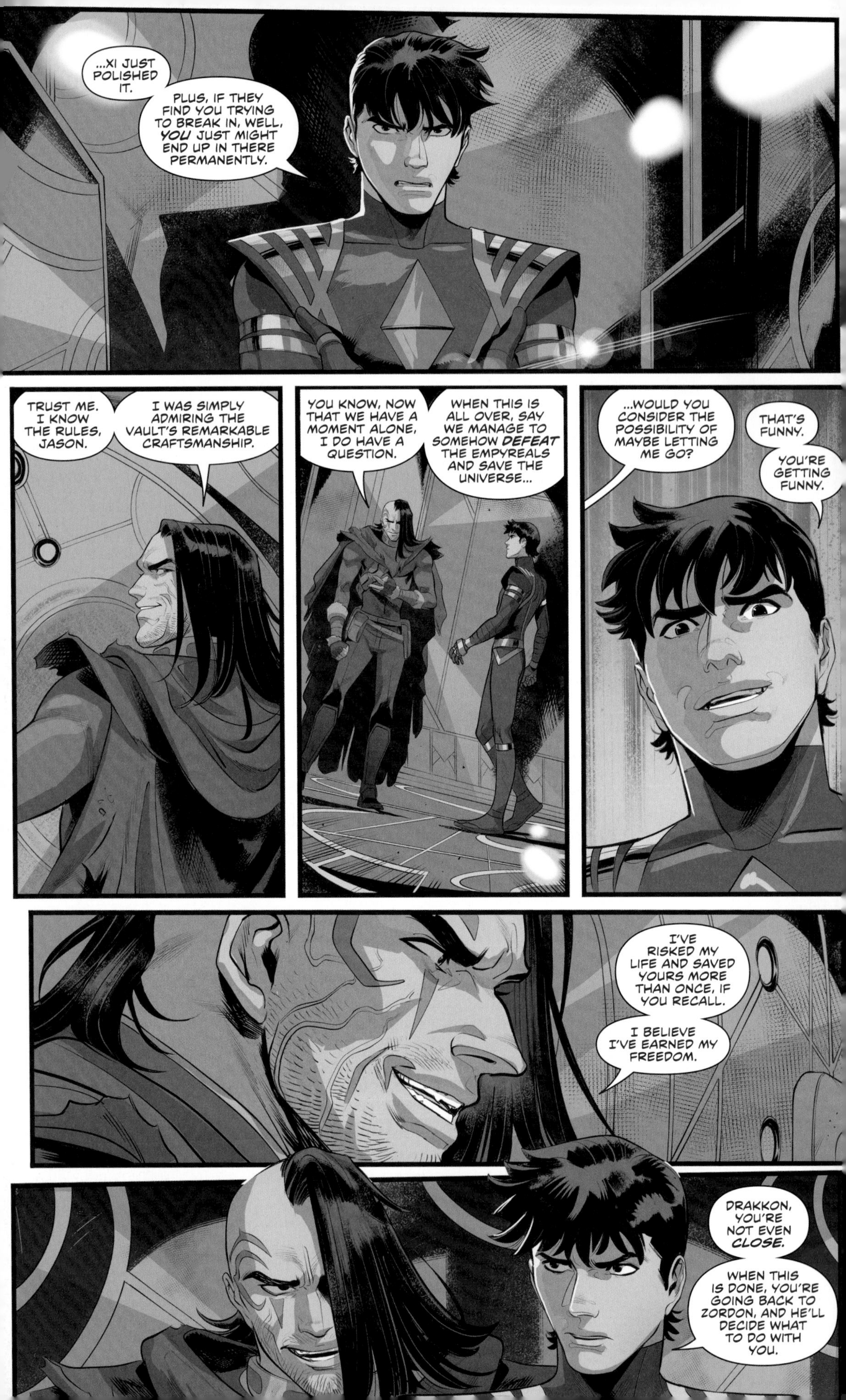
...XI JUST POLISHED IT.
PLUS, IF THEY FIND YOU TRYING TO BREAK IN, WELL, YOU JUST MIGHT END UP IN THERE PERMANENTLY.
TRUST ME. I KNOW THE RULES, JASON.
I WAS SIMPLY ADMIRING THE VAULT'S REMARKABLE CRAFTSMANSHIP.
YOU KNOW, NOW THAT WE HAVE A MOMENT ALONE, I DO HAVE A QUESTION.
WHEN THIS IS ALL OVER, SAY WE MANAGE TO SOMEHOW DEFEAT THE EMPYREALS AND SAVE THE UNIVERSE...
...WOULD YOU CONSIDER THE POSSIBILITY OF MAYBE LETTING ME GO?
THAT'S FUNNY.
YOU'RE GETTING FUNNY.
I'VE RISKED MY LIFE AND SAVED YOURS MORE THAN ONCE, IF YOU RECALL.
I BELIEVE I'VE EARNED MY FREEDOM.
DRAKKON, YOU'RE NOT EVEN CLOSE.
WHEN THIS IS DONE, YOU'RE GOING BACK TO ZORDON, AND HE'LL DECIDE WHAT TO DO WITH YOU.

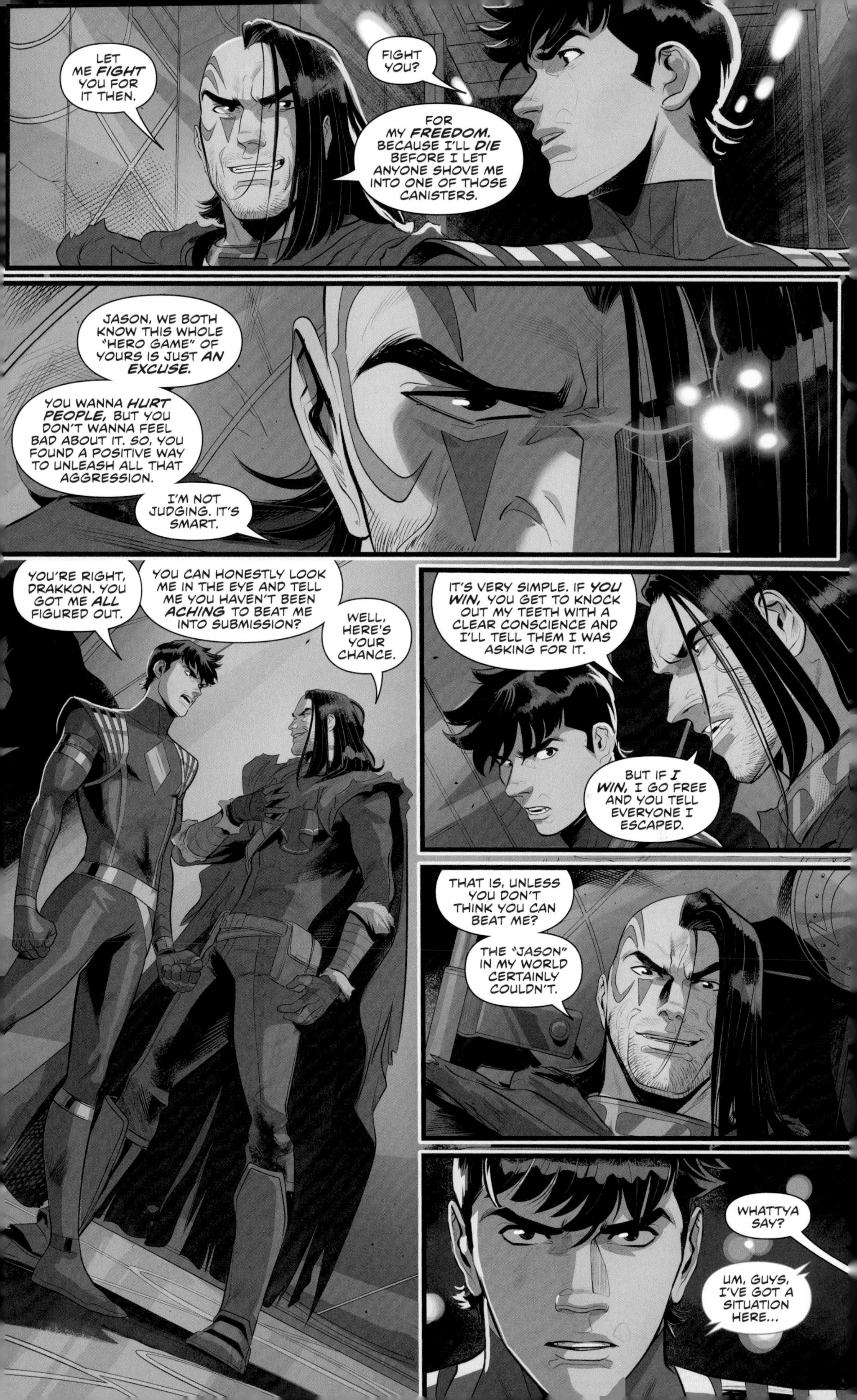
LET ME FIGHT YOU FOR IT THEN.
FIGHT YOU?
FOR MY FREEDOM. BECAUSE I'LL DIE BEFORE I LET ANYONE SHOVE ME INTO ONE OF THOSE CANISTERS.
JASON, WE BOTH KNOW THIS WHOLE "HERO GAME" OF YOURS IS JUST AN EXCUSE.
YOU WANNA HURT PEOPLE, BUT YOU DON'T WANNA FEEL BAD ABOUT IT. SO, YOU FOUND A POSITIVE WAY TO UNLEASH ALL THAT AGGRESSION.
I'M NOT JUDGING. IT'S SMART.
YOU'RE RIGHT, DRAKKON. YOU GOT ME ALL FIGURED OUT.
YOU CAN HONESTLY LOOK ME IN THE EYE AND TELL ME YOU HAVEN'T BEEN ACHING TO BEAT ME INTO SUBMISSION?
WELL, HERE'S YOUR CHANCE.
IT'S VERY SIMPLE. IF YOU WIN, YOU GET TO KNOCK OUT MY TEETH WITH A CLEAR CONSCIENCE AND I'LL TELL THEM I WAS ASKING FOR IT.
BUT IF I WIN, I GO FREE AND YOU TELL EVERYONE I ESCAPED.
THAT IS, UNLESS YOU DON'T THINK YOU CAN BEAT ME?
THE "JASON" IN MY WORLD CERTAINLY COULDN'T.
WHATTYA SAY?
UM, GUYS, I'VE GOT A SITUATION HERE...

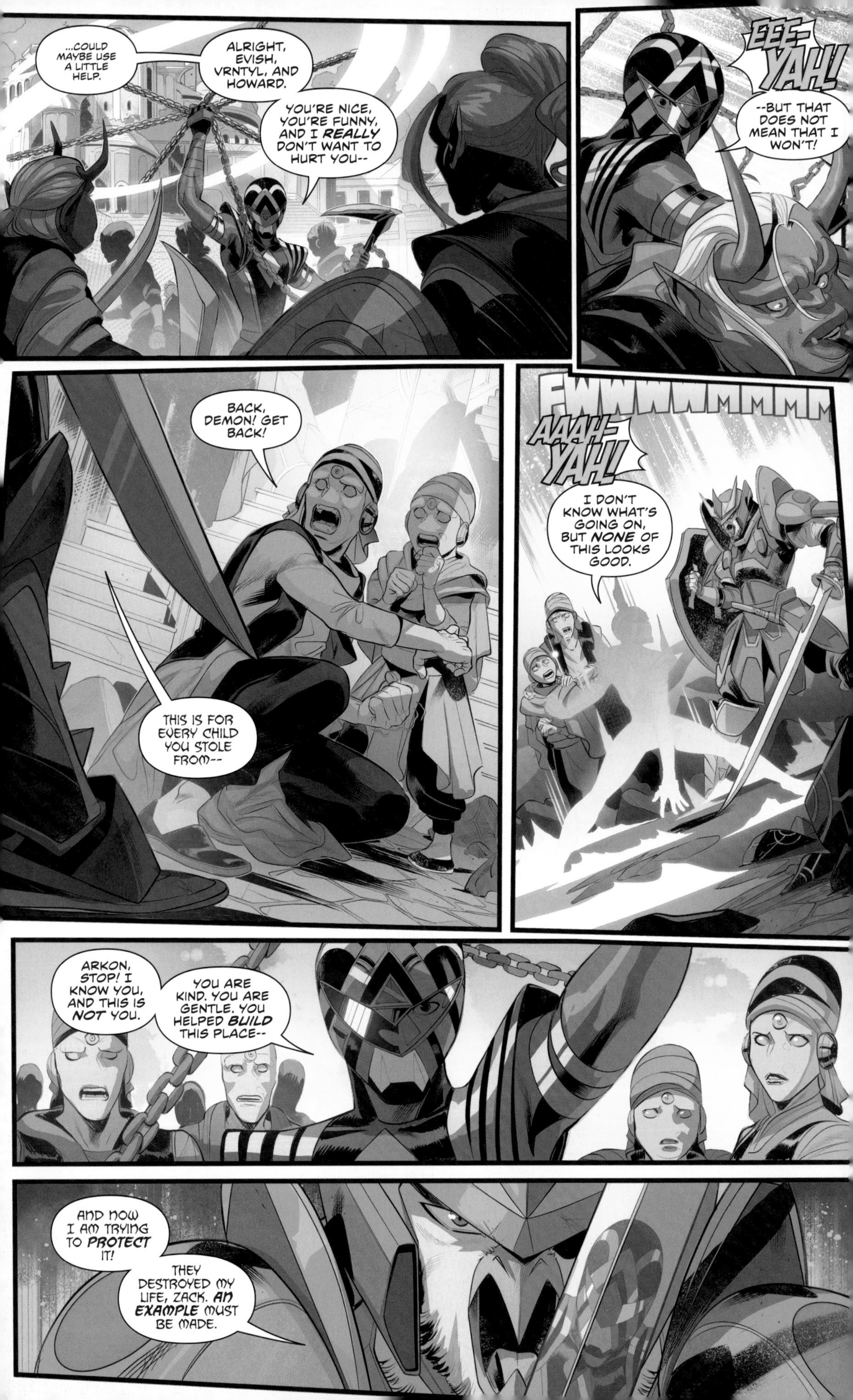
...COULD MAYBE USE A LITTLE HELP.
ALRIGHT, EVISH, VRNTYL, AND HOWARD.
YOU'RE NICE, YOU'RE FUNNY, AND I REALLY DON'T WANT TO HURT YOU--
EEE-YAH!
--BUT THAT DOES NOT MEAN THAT I WON'T!
BACK, DEMON! GET BACK!
THIS IS FOR EVERY CHILD YOU STOLE FROM--
FWWWWMMMMM
AAAH-YAH!
I DON'T KNOW WHAT'S GOING ON, BUT NONE OF THIS LOOKS GOOD.
ARKON, STOP! I KNOW YOU, AND THIS IS NOT YOU.
YOU ARE KIND. YOU ARE GENTLE. YOU HELPED BUILD THIS PLACE--
AND NOW I AM TRYING TO PROTECT IT!
THEY DESTROYED MY LIFE, ZACK. AN EXAMPLE MUST BE MADE.

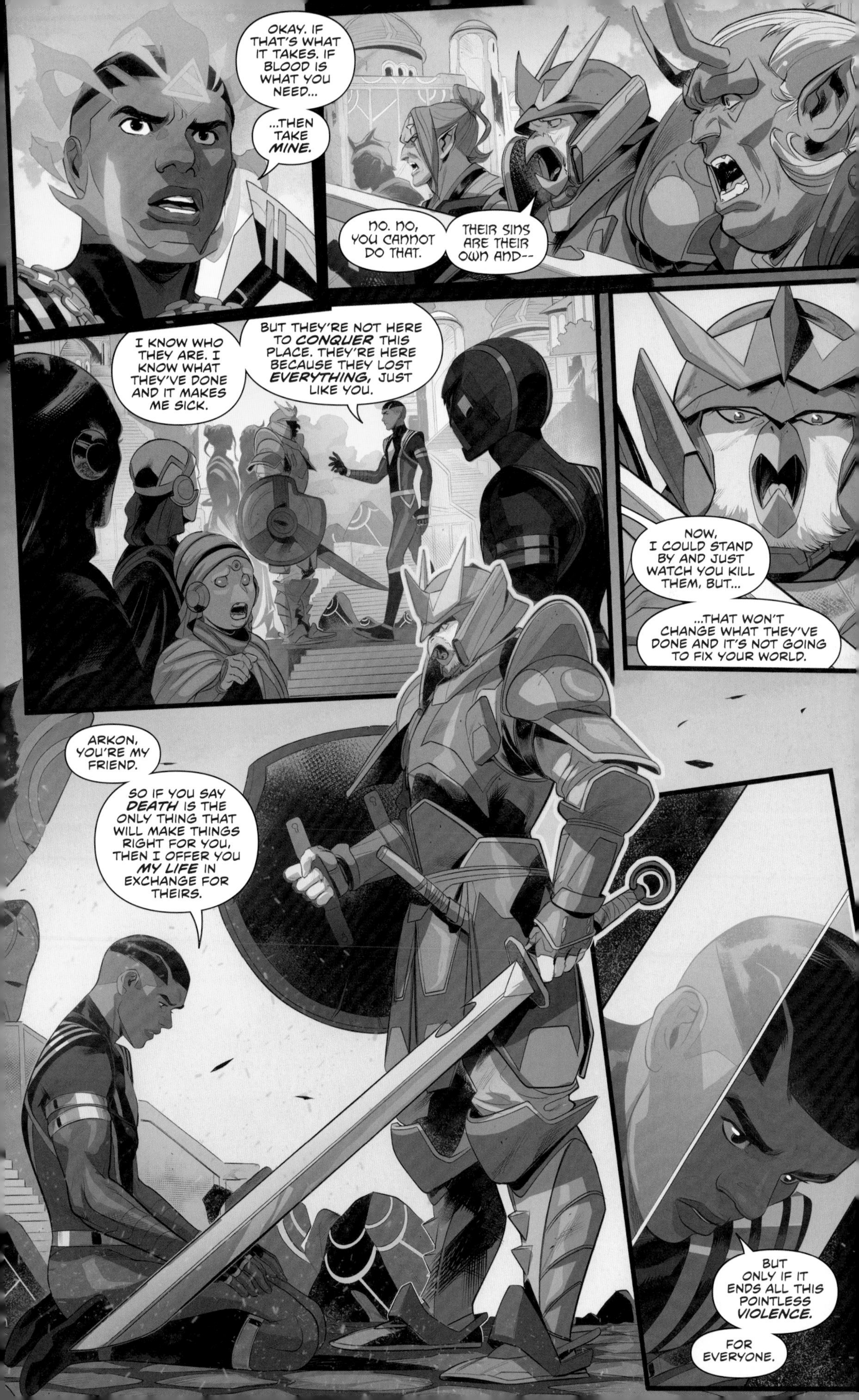
OKAY. IF THAT'S WHAT IT TAKES. IF BLOOD IS WHAT YOU NEED...
...THEN TAKE MINE.
NO. NO, YOU CANNOT DO THAT.
THEIR SINS ARE THEIR OWN AND--
I KNOW WHO THEY ARE. I KNOW WHAT THEY'VE DONE AND IT MAKES ME SICK.
BUT THEY'RE NOT HERE TO CONQUER THIS PLACE. THEY'RE HERE BECAUSE THEY LOST EVERYTHING, JUST LIKE YOU.
NOW, I COULD STAND BY AND JUST WATCH YOU KILL THEM, BUT...
...THAT WON'T CHANGE WHAT THEY'VE DONE AND IT'S NOT GOING TO FIX YOUR WORLD.
ARKON, YOU'RE MY FRIEND.
SO IF YOU SAY DEATH IS THE ONLY THING THAT WILL MAKE THINGS RIGHT FOR YOU, THEN I OFFER YOU MY LIFE IN EXCHANGE FOR THEIRS.
BUT ONLY IF IT ENDS ALL THIS POINTLESS VIOLENCE.
FOR EVERYONE.

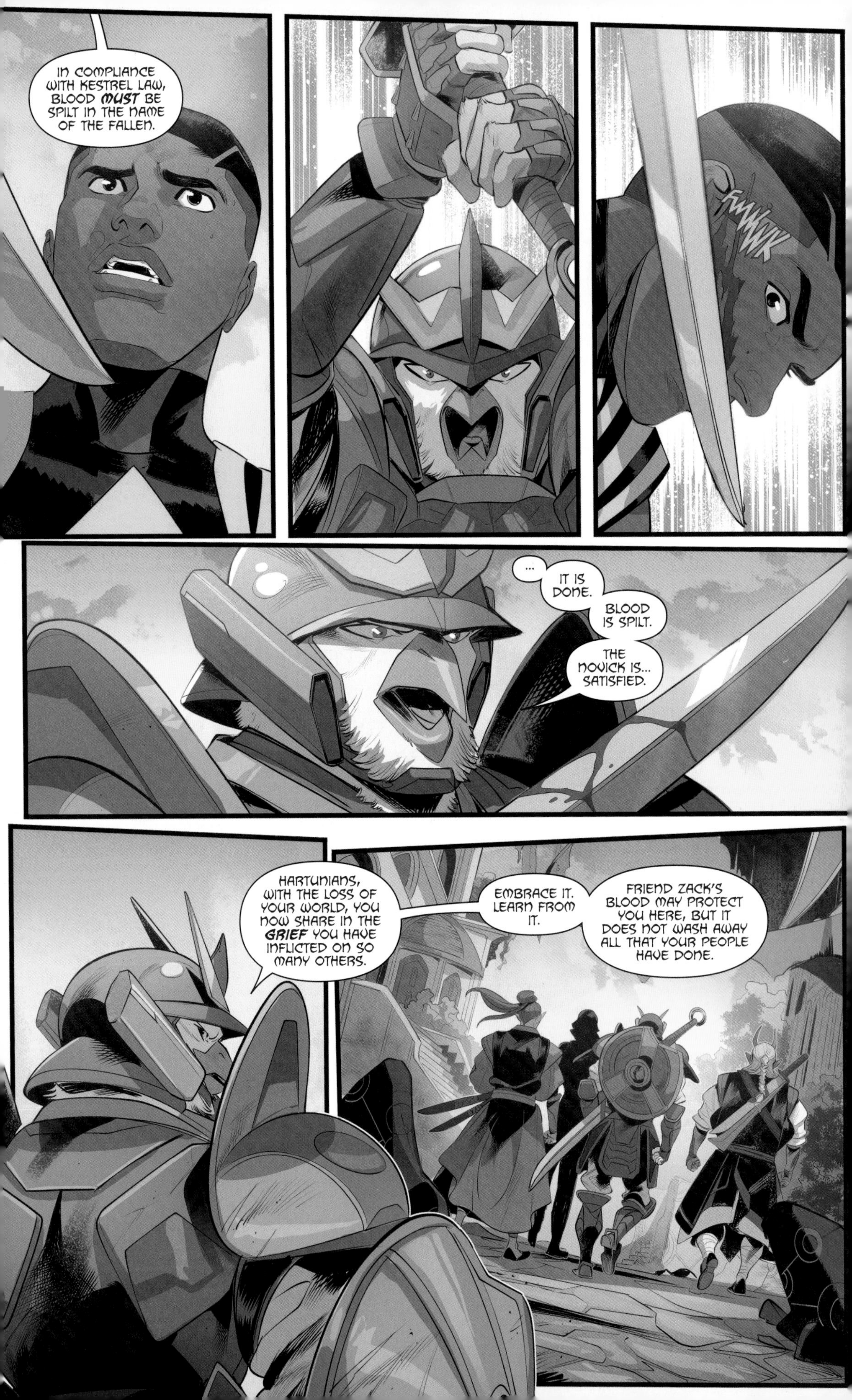
IN COMPLIANCE WITH KESTREL LAW, BLOOD MUST BE SPILT IN THE NAME OF THE FALLEN.
FWAWK
...
IT IS DONE.
BLOOD IS SPILT.
THE NOVICK IS... SATISFIED.
HARTUNIANS, WITH THE LOSS OF YOUR WORLD, YOU NOW SHARE IN THE GRIEF YOU HAVE INFLICTED ON SO MANY OTHERS.
EMBRACE IT. LEARN FROM IT.
FRIEND ZACK'S BLOOD MAY PROTECT YOU HERE, BUT IT DOES NOT WASH AWAY ALL THAT YOUR PEOPLE HAVE DONE.

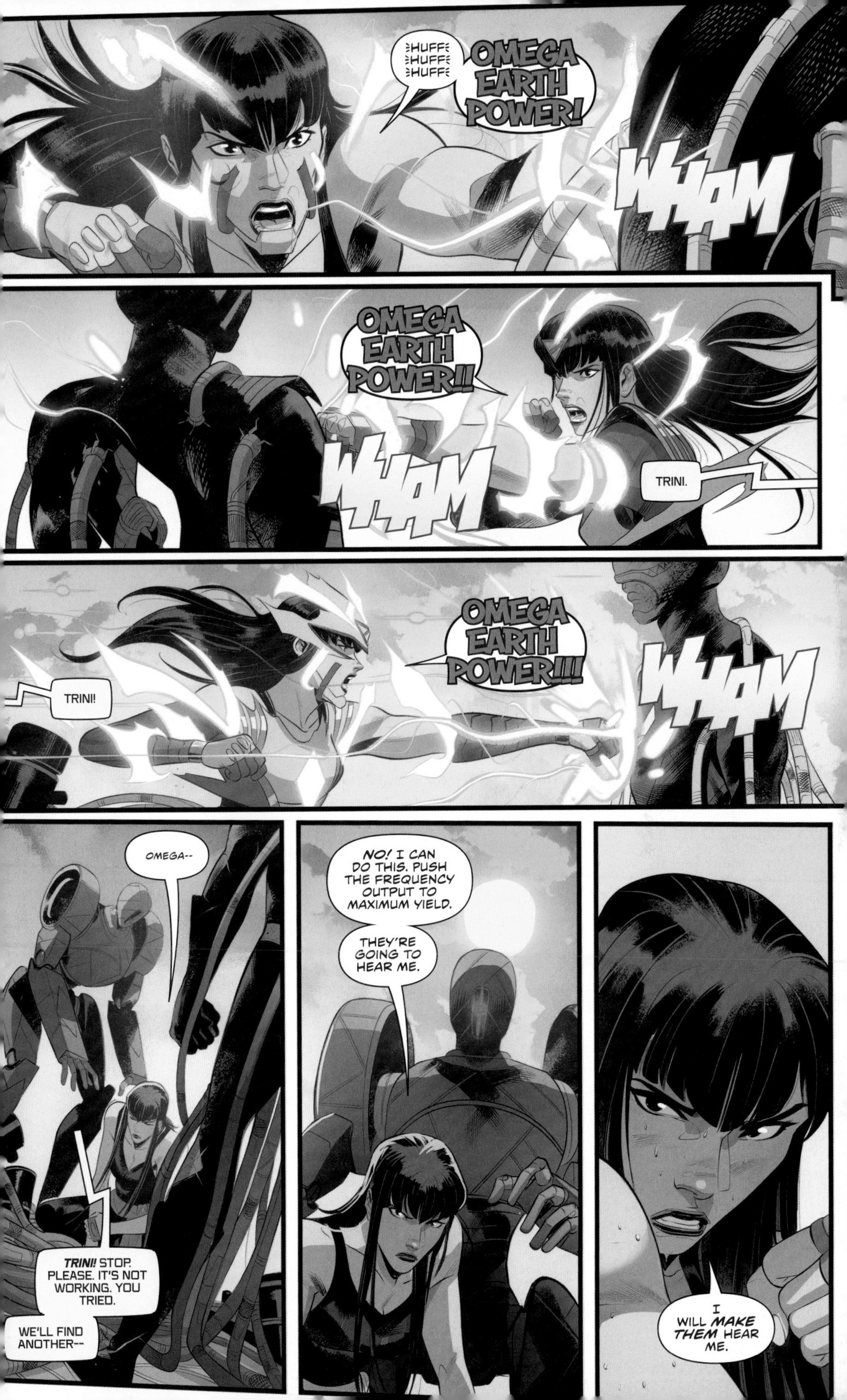
HUFF HUFF HUFF
OMEGA EARTH POWER!
WHAM
OMEGA EARTH POWER!!
WHAM
TRINI.
OMEGA EARTH POWER!!!
TRINI!
WHAM
OMEGA--
TRINI!! STOP. PLEASE. IT'S NOT WORKING. YOU TRIED.
WE'LL FIND ANOTHER--
NO! I CAN DO THIS. PUSH THE FREQUENCY OUTPUT TO MAXIMUM YIELD.
THEY'RE GOING TO HEAR ME.
I WILL MAKE THEM HEAR ME.

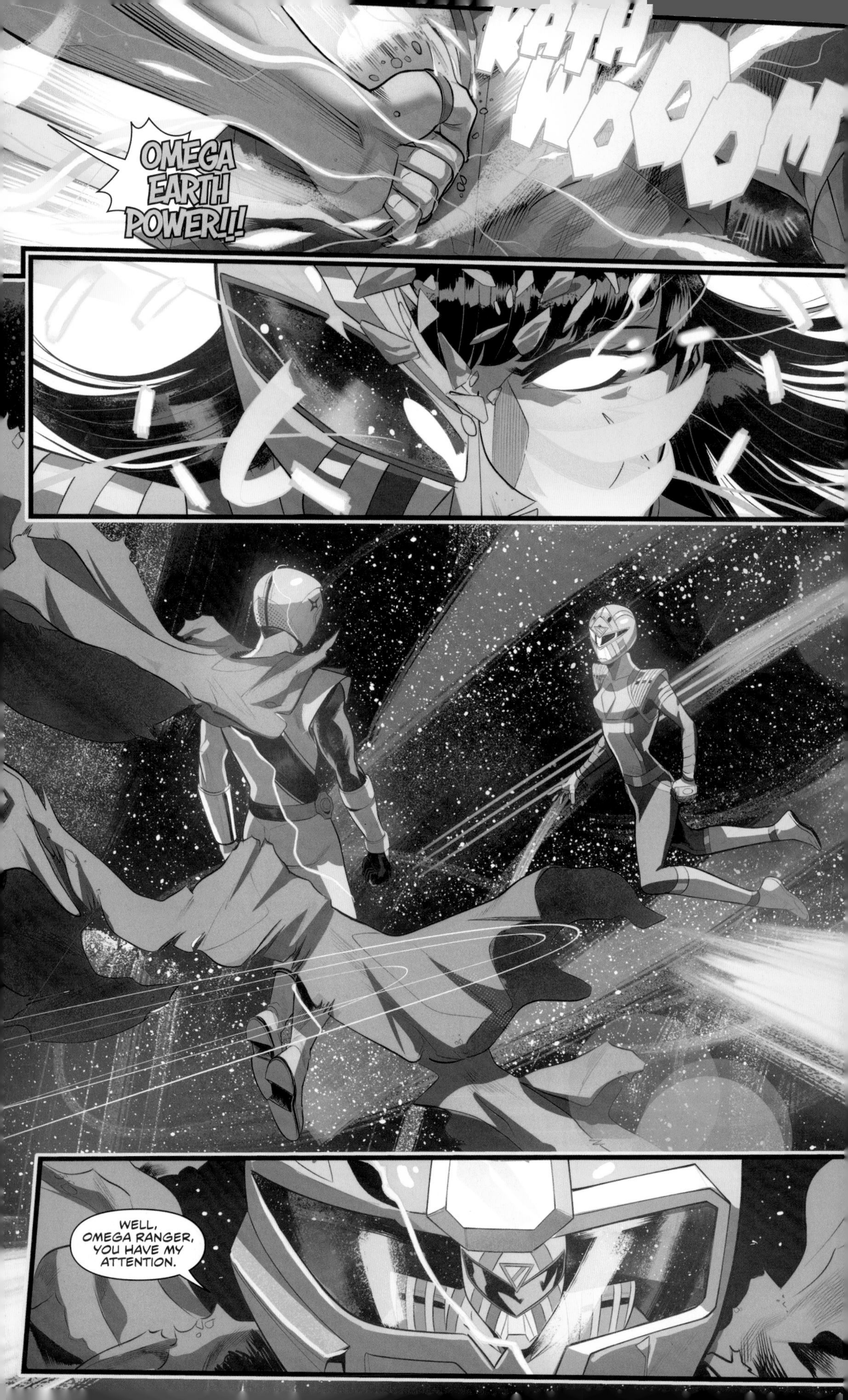
KATH-WOOOM
OMEGA EARTH POWER!!!
WELL, OMEGA RANGER, YOU HAVE MY ATTENTION.

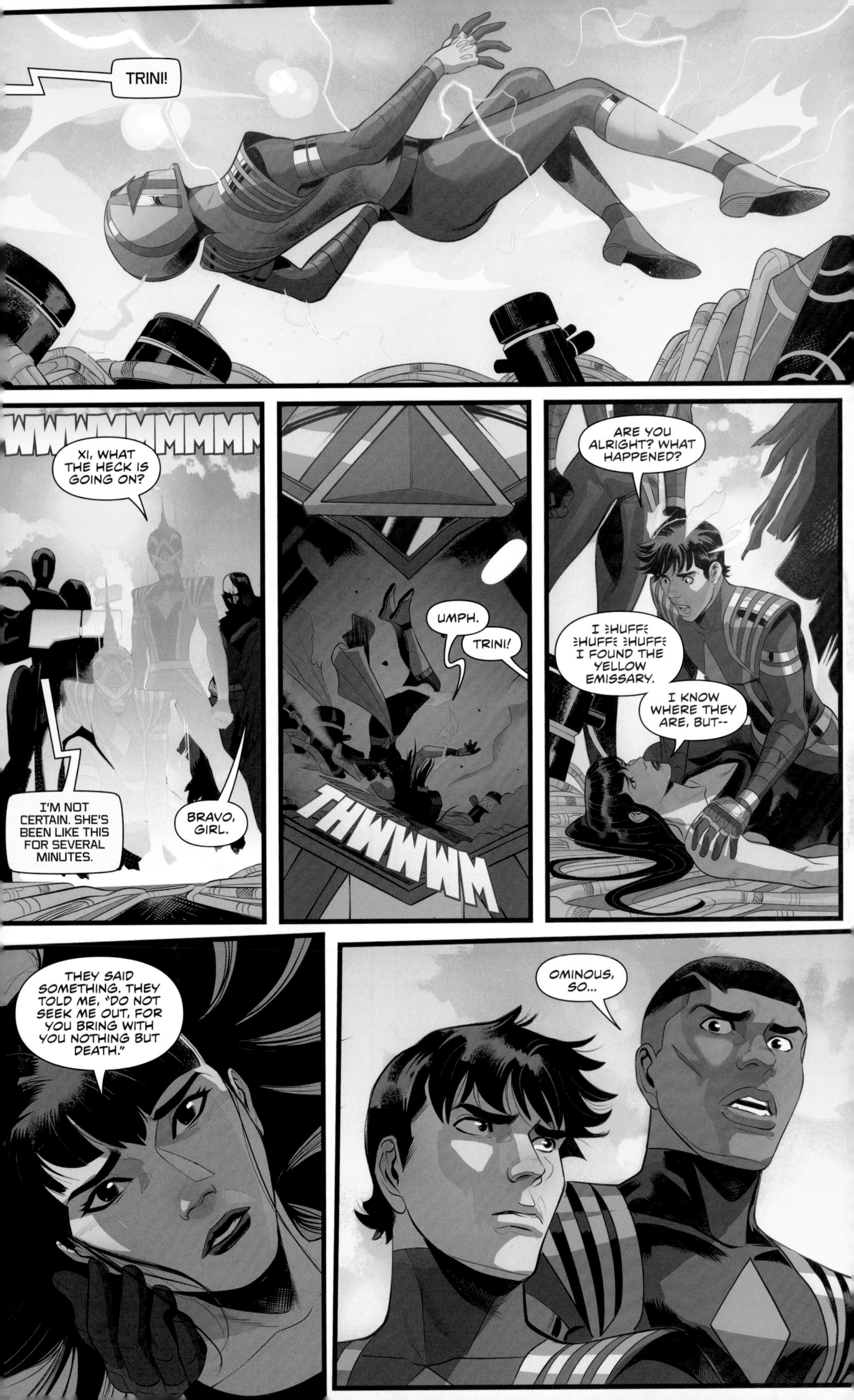
TRINI!
WWWMMMMMM
XI, WHAT THE HECK IS GOING ON?
I'M NOT CERTAIN. SHE'S BEEN LIKE THIS FOR SEVERAL MINUTES.
BRAVO, GIRL.
UMPH.
TRINI!
THWWWM
ARE YOU ALRIGHT? WHAT HAPPENED?
I *HUFF* *HUFF* *HUFF* I FOUND THE YELLOW EMISSARY.
I KNOW WHERE THEY ARE, BUT--
THEY SAID SOMETHING. THEY TOLD ME, "DO NOT SEEK ME OUT, FOR YOU BRING WITH YOU NOTHING BUT DEATH."
OMINOUS, SO...

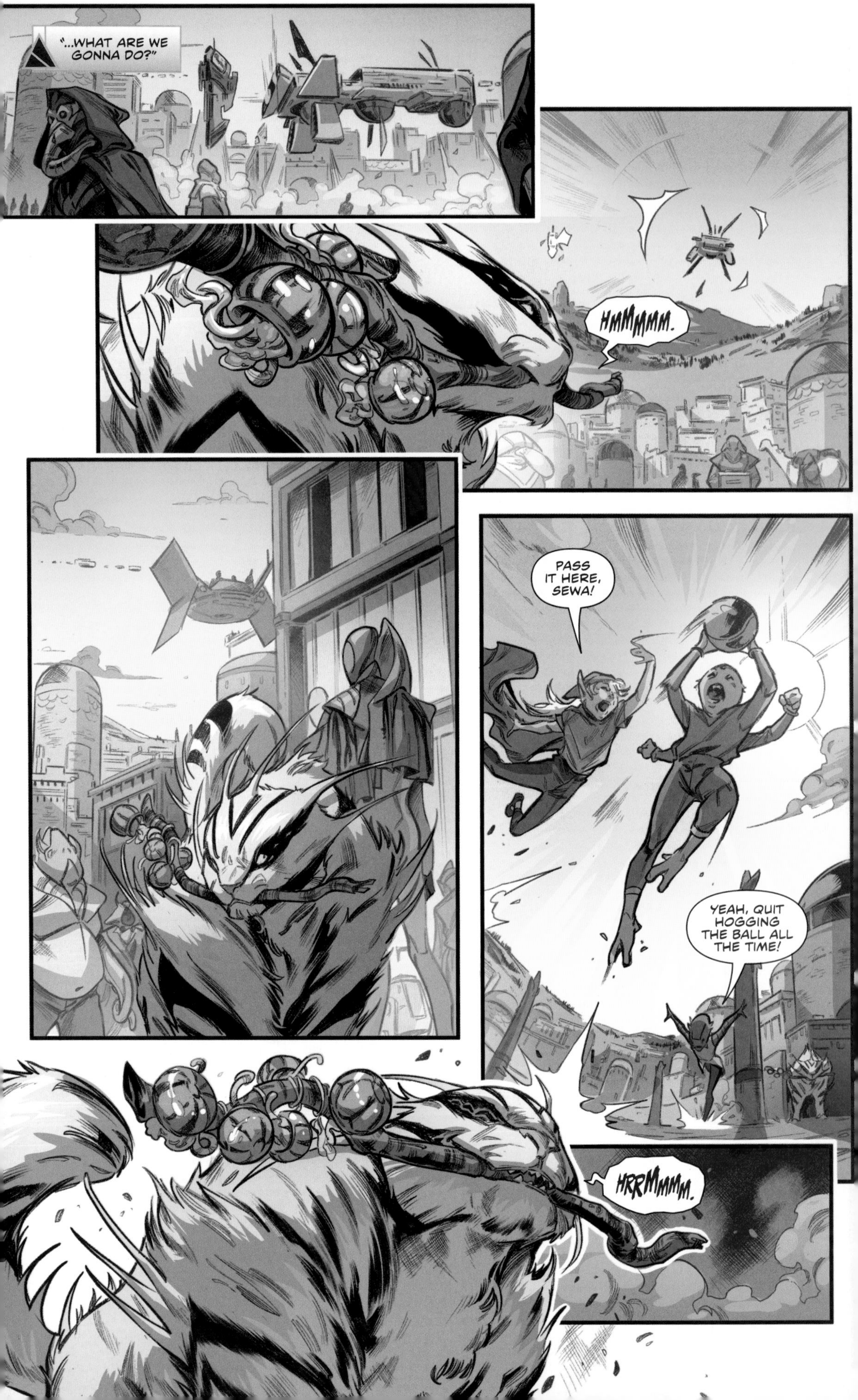
"...WHAT ARE WE GONNA DO?"
HMMMMM.
PASS IT HERE, SEWA!
YEAH, QUIT HOGGING THE BALL ALL THE TIME!
HRRMMMM.

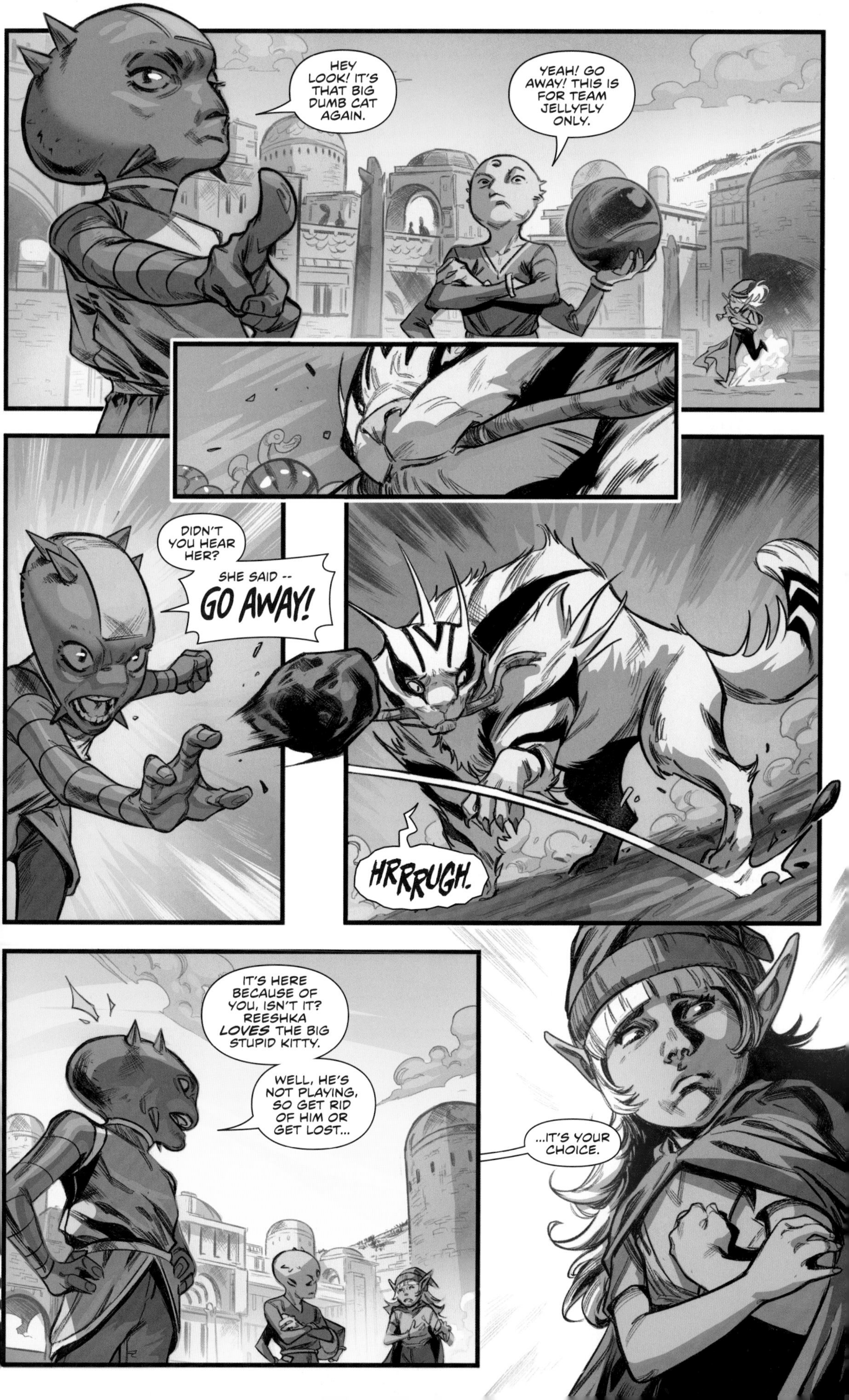
HEY LOOK! IT'S THAT BIG DUMB CAT AGAIN.
YEAH! GO AWAY! THIS IS FOR TEAM JELLYFLY ONLY.
DIDN'T YOU HEAR HER?
SHE SAID -- GO AWAY!
HRRRUGH.
IT'S HERE BECAUSE OF YOU, ISN'T IT? REESHKA LOVES THE BIG STUPID KITTY.
WELL, HE'S NOT PLAYING, SO GET RID OF HIM OR GET LOST...
...IT'S YOUR CHOICE.

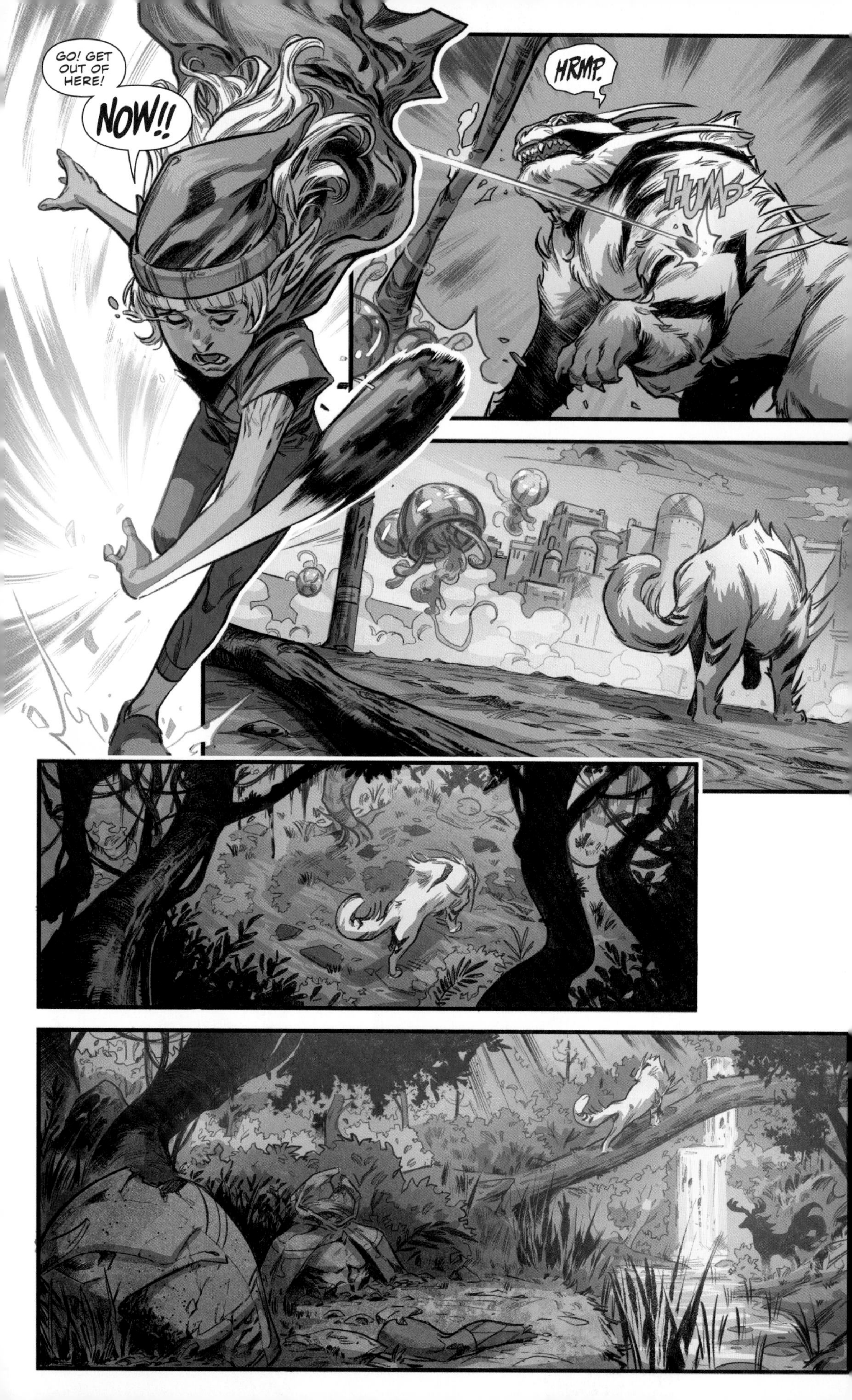
GO! GET OUT OF HERE!
NOW!!
HRMP.
THUMP

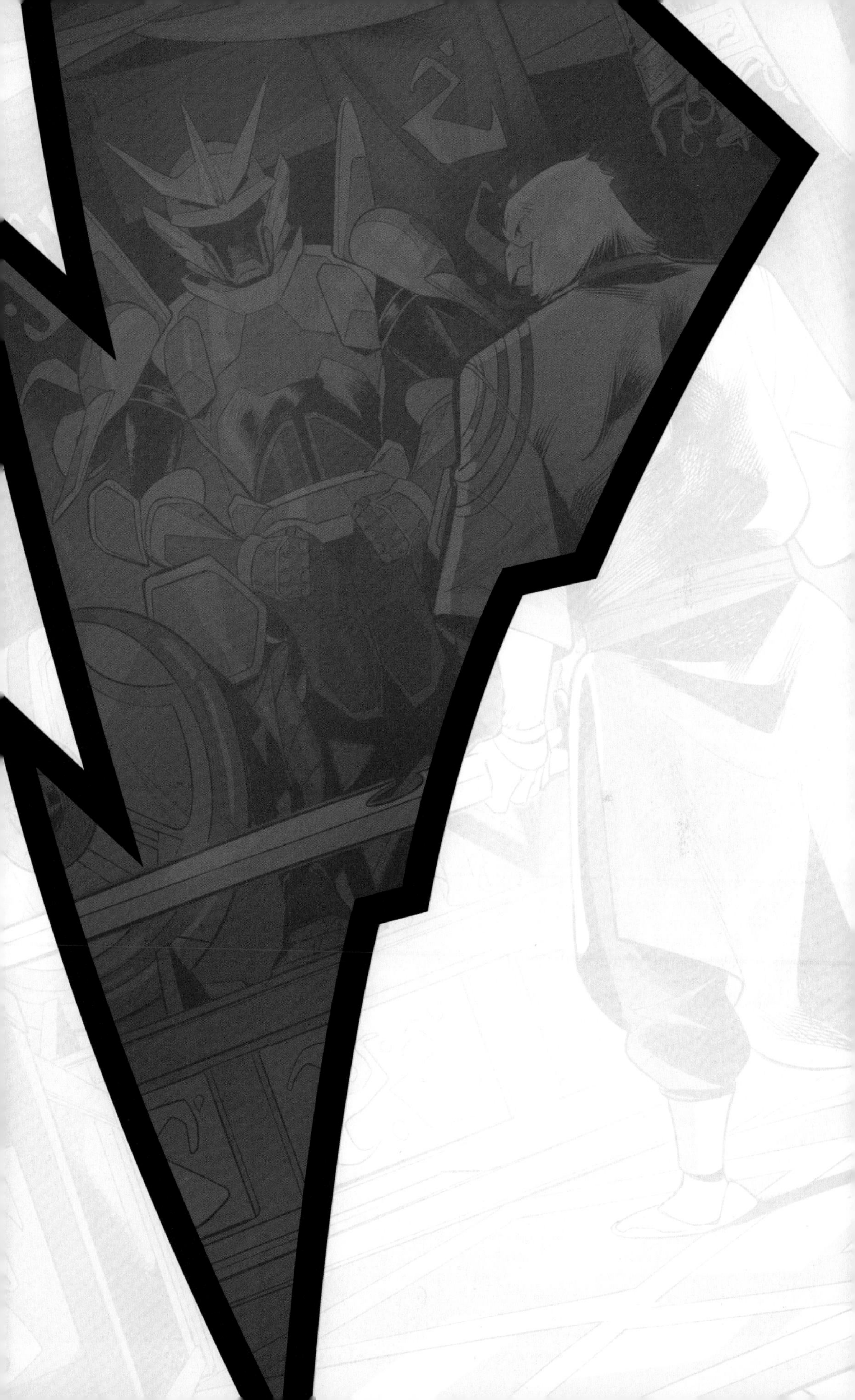

CHAPTER
TEN

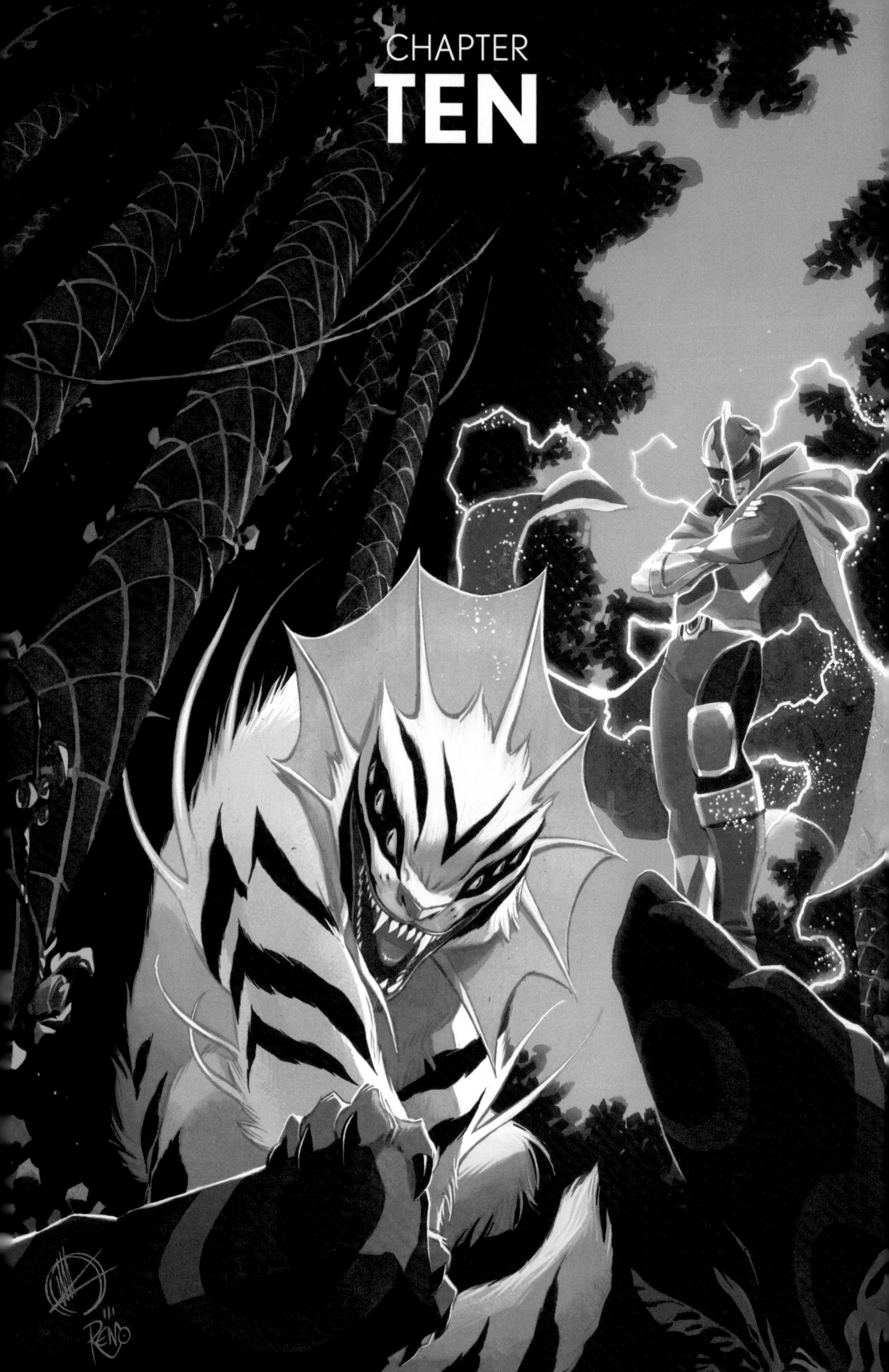

MATTEO SCALERA WITH COLORS BY **MORENO DINISIO** ISSUE TEN COVER

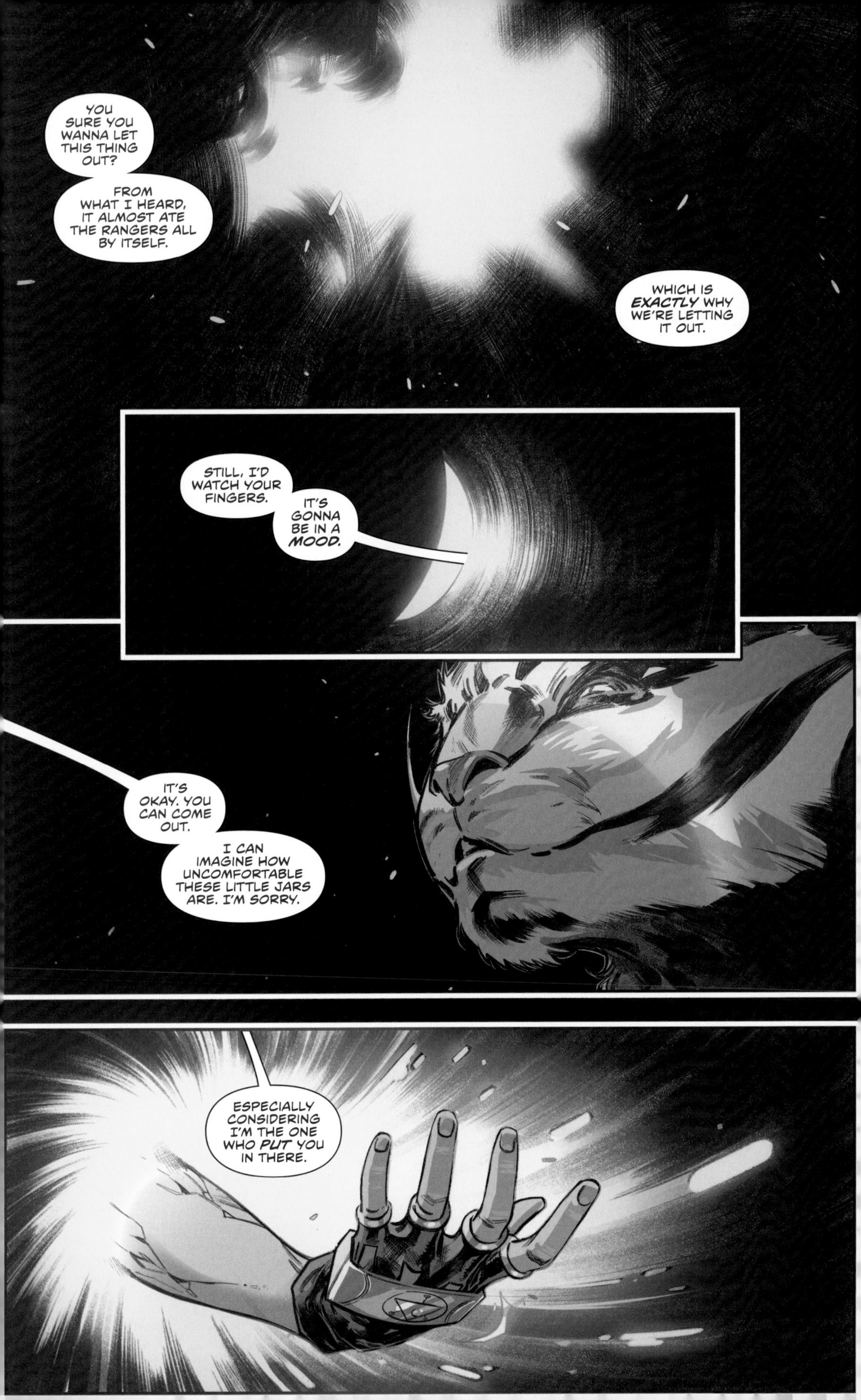
YOU SURE YOU WANNA LET THIS THING OUT?
FROM WHAT I HEARD, IT ALMOST ATE THE RANGERS ALL BY ITSELF.
WHICH IS *EXACTLY* WHY WE'RE LETTING IT OUT.
STILL, I'D WATCH YOUR FINGERS.
IT'S GONNA BE IN A *MOOD.*
IT'S OKAY. YOU CAN COME OUT.
I CAN IMAGINE HOW UNCOMFORTABLE THESE LITTLE JARS ARE. I'M SORRY.
ESPECIALLY CONSIDERING I'M THE ONE WHO *PUT* YOU IN THERE.

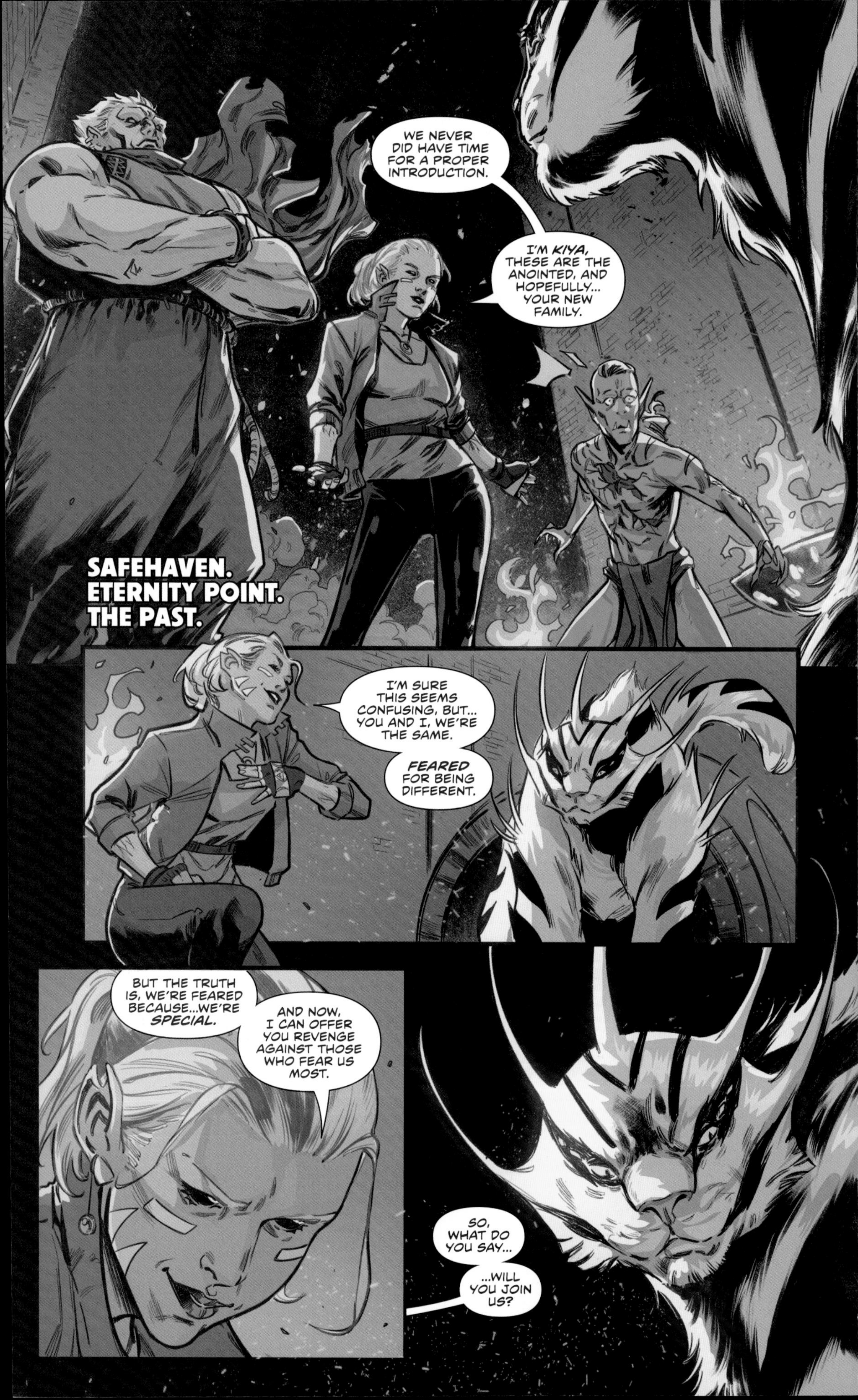
WE NEVER DID HAVE TIME FOR A PROPER INTRODUCTION.
I'M *KIYA*, THESE ARE THE ANOINTED, AND HOPEFULLY... YOUR NEW FAMILY.
SAFEHAVEN. ETERNITY POINT. THE PAST.
I'M SURE THIS SEEMS CONFUSING, BUT... YOU AND I, WE'RE THE SAME.
FEARED FOR BEING DIFFERENT.
BUT THE TRUTH IS, WE'RE FEARED BECAUSE...WE'RE *SPECIAL*.
AND NOW, I CAN OFFER YOU REVENGE AGAINST THOSE WHO FEAR US MOST.
SO, WHAT DO YOU SAY...
...WILL YOU JOIN US?

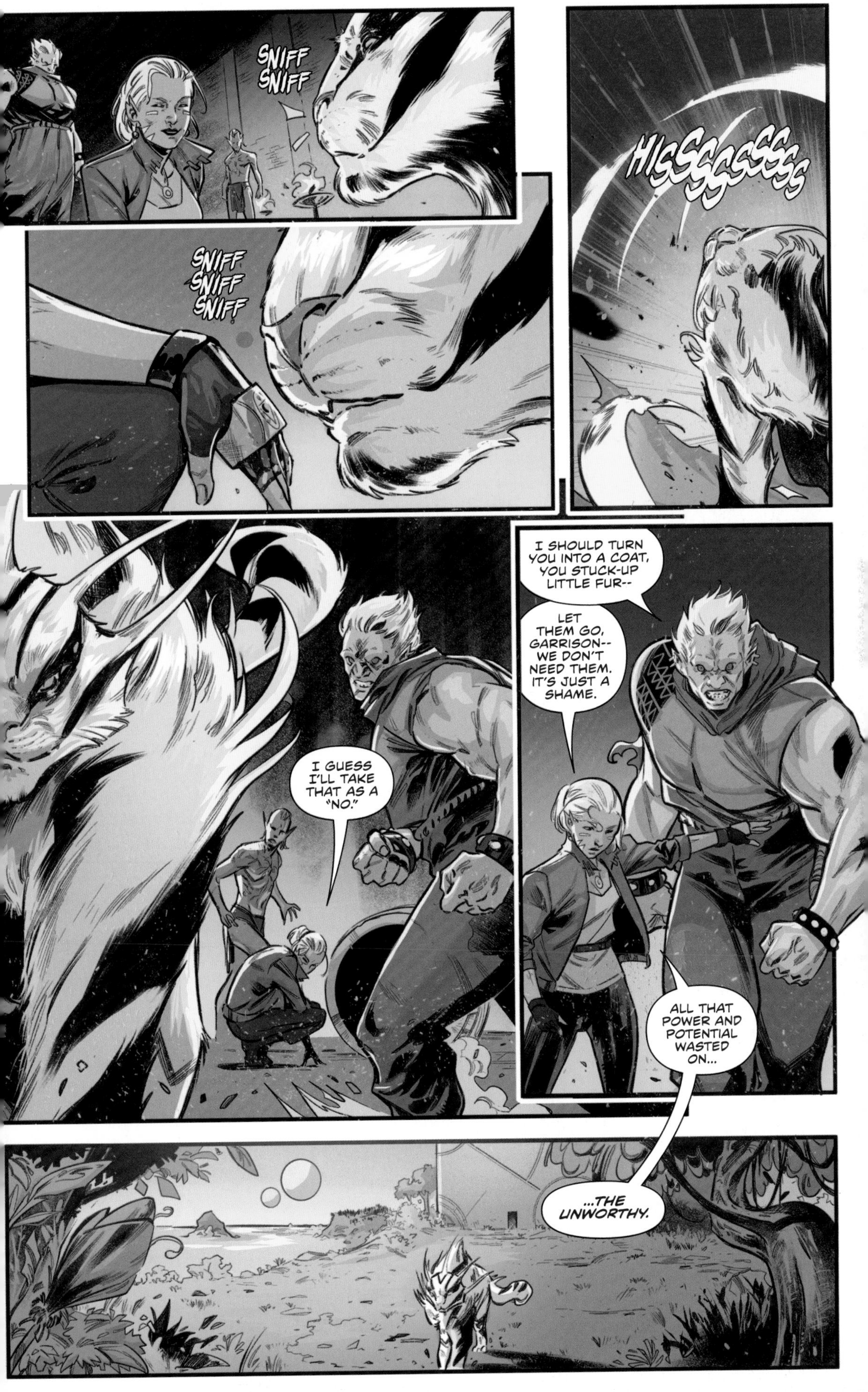
SNIFF SNIFF
SNIFF SNIFF SNIFF
HISSSSSSSSS
I GUESS I'LL TAKE THAT AS A "NO."
I SHOULD TURN YOU INTO A COAT, YOU STUCK-UP LITTLE FUR--
LET THEM GO, GARRISON-- WE DON'T NEED THEM. IT'S JUST A SHAME.
ALL THAT POWER AND POTENTIAL WASTED ON...
...THE UNWORTHY.

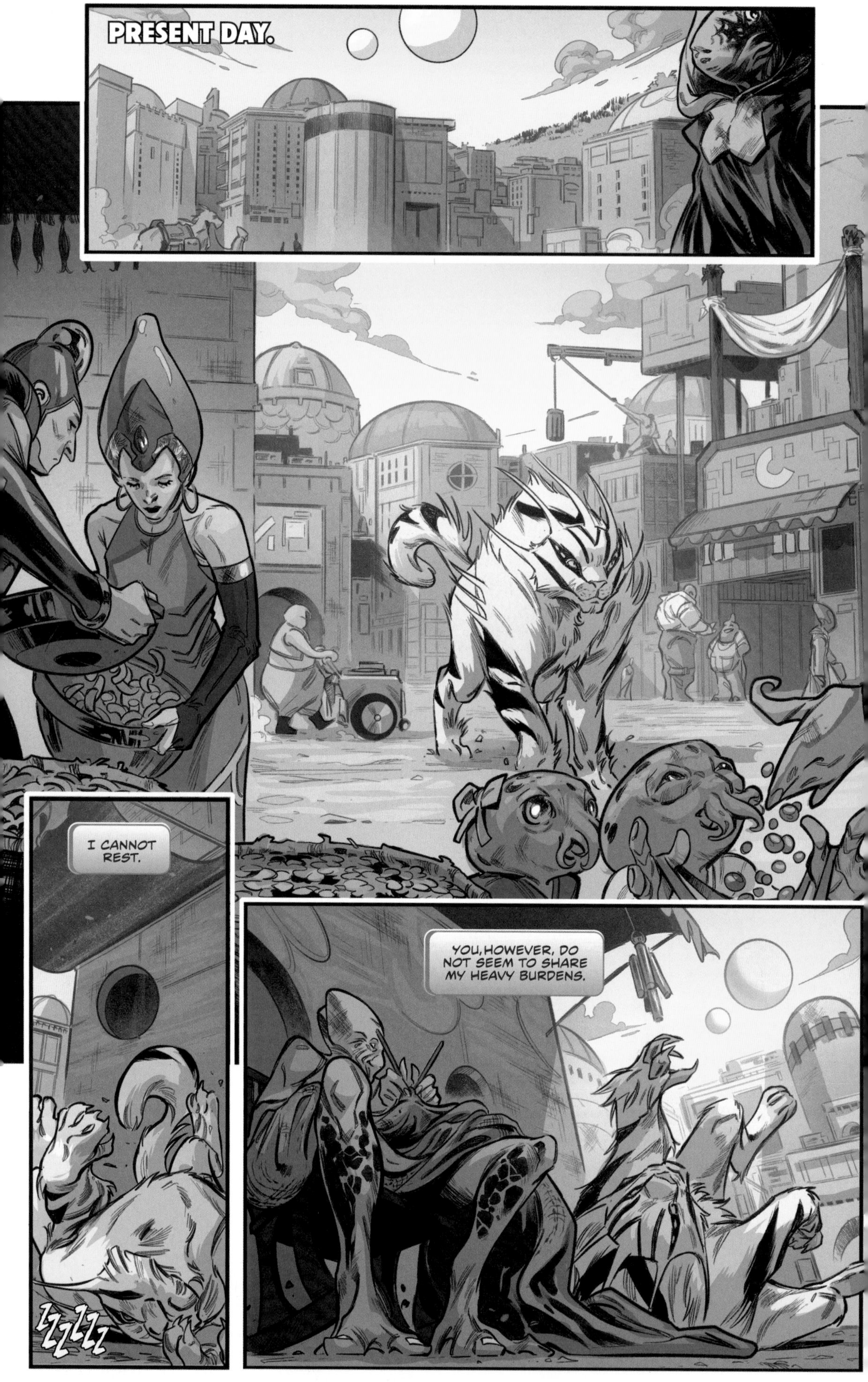
PRESENT DAY.
I CANNOT REST.
YOU, HOWEVER, DO NOT SEEM TO SHARE MY HEAVY BURDENS.
ZZZZZZ

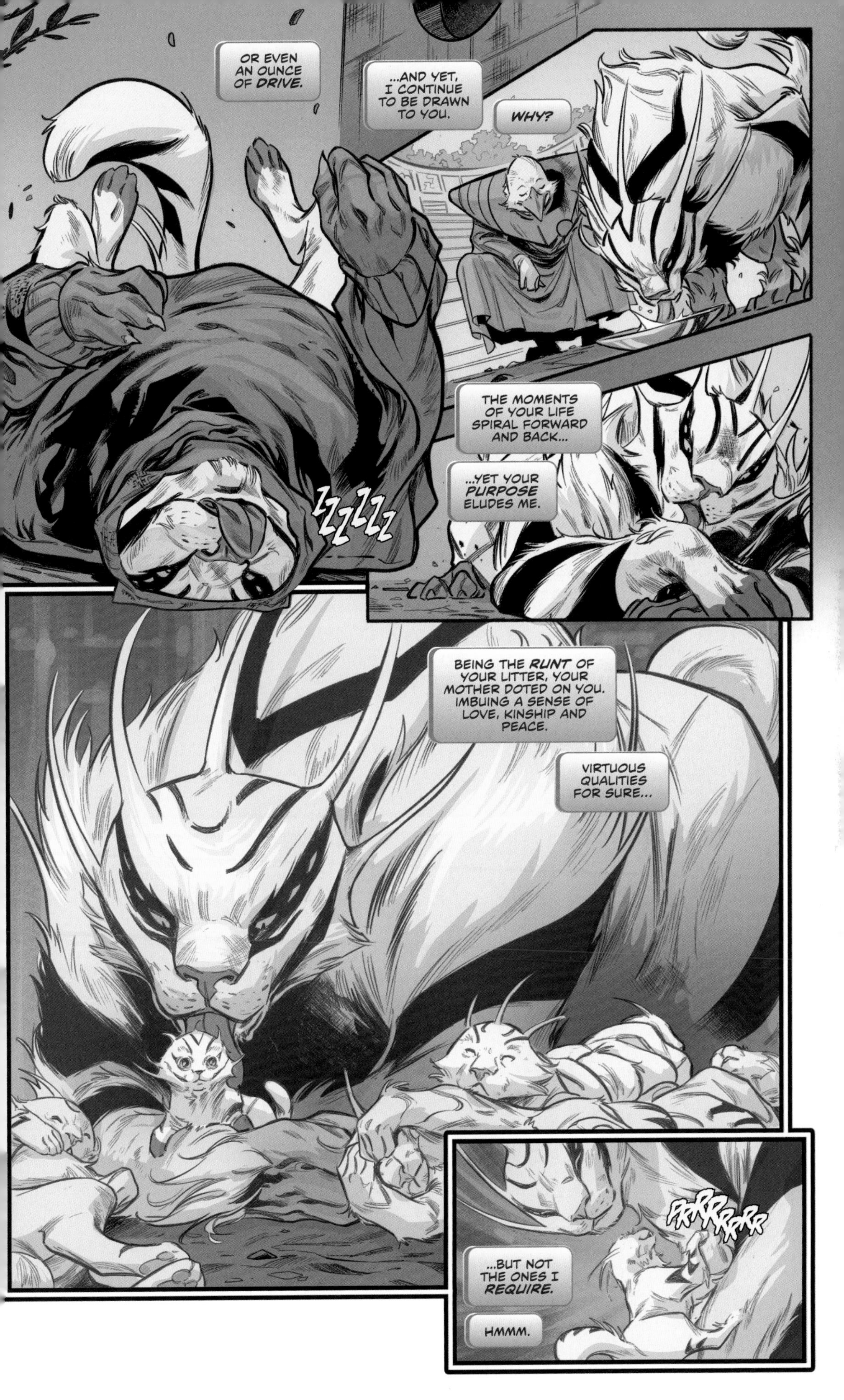
OR EVEN AN OUNCE OF *DRIVE.*
...AND YET, I CONTINUE TO BE DRAWN TO YOU.
WHY?
ZZZZZZ
THE MOMENTS OF YOUR LIFE SPIRAL FORWARD AND BACK...
...YET YOUR *PURPOSE* ELUDES ME.
BEING THE *RUNT* OF YOUR LITTER, YOUR MOTHER DOTED ON YOU. IMBUING A SENSE OF LOVE, KINSHIP AND PEACE.
VIRTUOUS QUALITIES FOR SURE...
PRRRRRRRR
...BUT NOT THE ONES I *REQUIRE.*
HMMM.

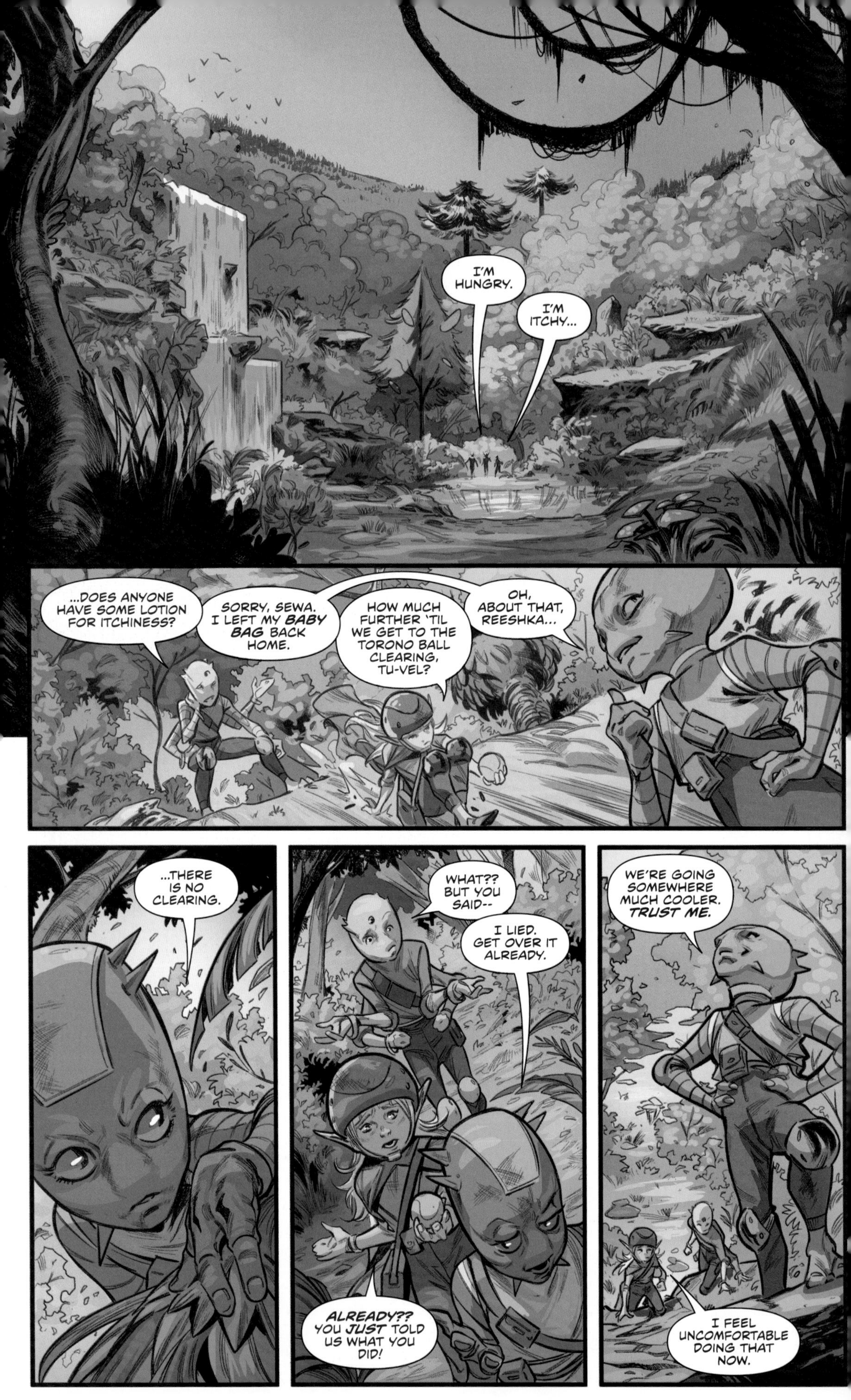
I'M HUNGRY.
I'M ITCHY...
...DOES ANYONE HAVE SOME LOTION FOR ITCHINESS?
SORRY, SEWA. I LEFT MY BABY BAG BACK HOME.
HOW MUCH FURTHER 'TIL WE GET TO THE TORONO BALL CLEARING, TU-VEL?
OH, ABOUT THAT, REESHKA...
...THERE IS NO CLEARING.
WHAT?? BUT YOU SAID--
I LIED. GET OVER IT ALREADY.
ALREADY?? YOU JUST TOLD US WHAT YOU DID!
WE'RE GOING SOMEWHERE MUCH COOLER. TRUST ME.
I FEEL UNCOMFORTABLE DOING THAT NOW.

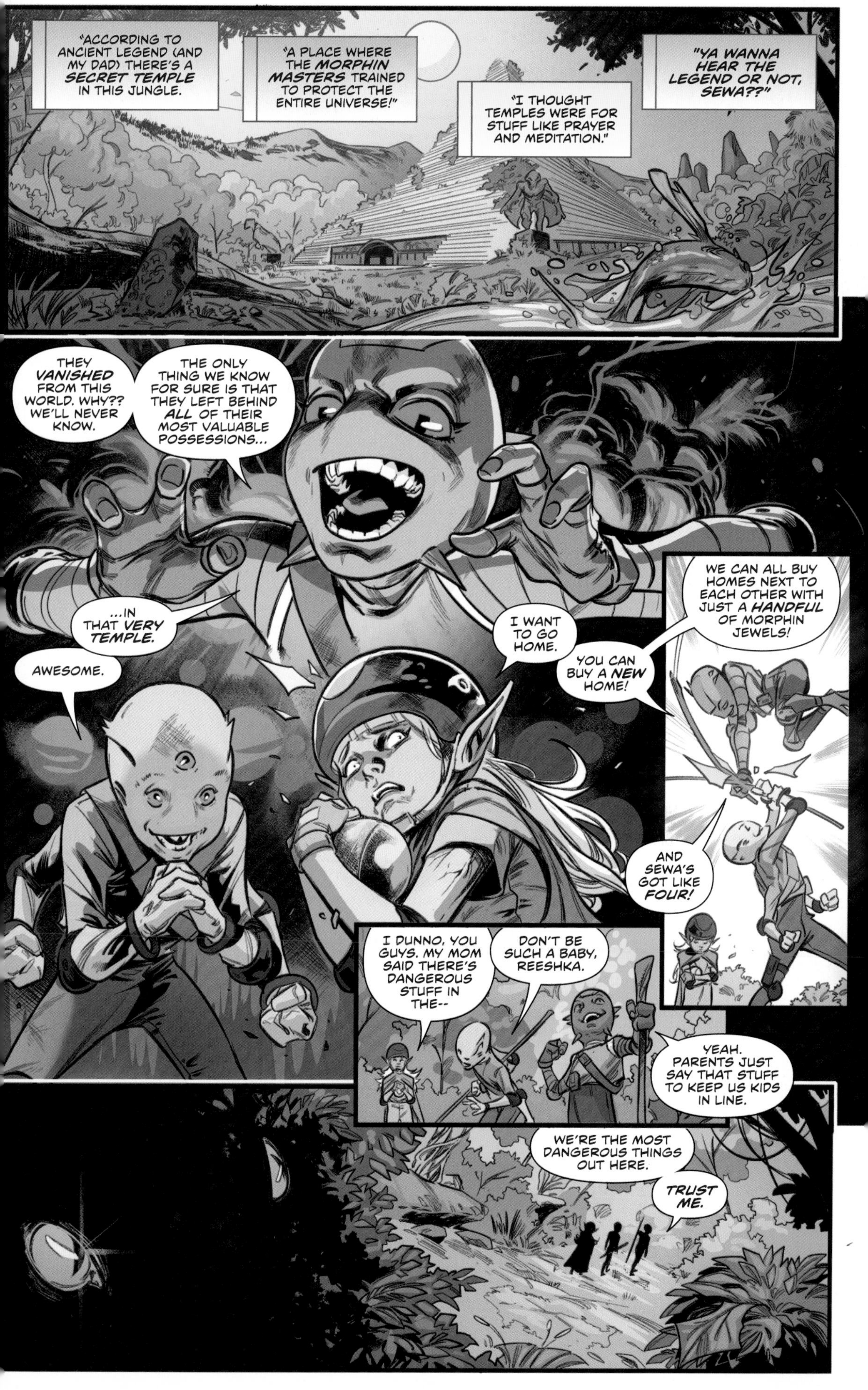
"ACCORDING TO ANCIENT LEGEND (AND MY DAD) THERE'S A SECRET TEMPLE IN THIS JUNGLE.
"A PLACE WHERE THE MORPHIN MASTERS TRAINED TO PROTECT THE ENTIRE UNIVERSE!"
"I THOUGHT TEMPLES WERE FOR STUFF LIKE PRAYER AND MEDITATION."
"YA WANNA HEAR THE LEGEND OR NOT, SEWA??"
THEY VANISHED FROM THIS WORLD. WHY?? WE'LL NEVER KNOW.
THE ONLY THING WE KNOW FOR SURE IS THAT THEY LEFT BEHIND ALL OF THEIR MOST VALUABLE POSSESSIONS...
...IN THAT VERY TEMPLE.
AWESOME.
I WANT TO GO HOME.
YOU CAN BUY A NEW HOME!
WE CAN ALL BUY HOMES NEXT TO EACH OTHER WITH JUST A HANDFUL OF MORPHIN JEWELS!
AND SEWA'S GOT LIKE FOUR!
I DUNNO, YOU GUYS. MY MOM SAID THERE'S DANGEROUS STUFF IN THE--
DON'T BE SUCH A BABY, REESHKA.
YEAH. PARENTS JUST SAY THAT STUFF TO KEEP US KIDS IN LINE.
WE'RE THE MOST DANGEROUS THINGS OUT HERE.
TRUST ME.

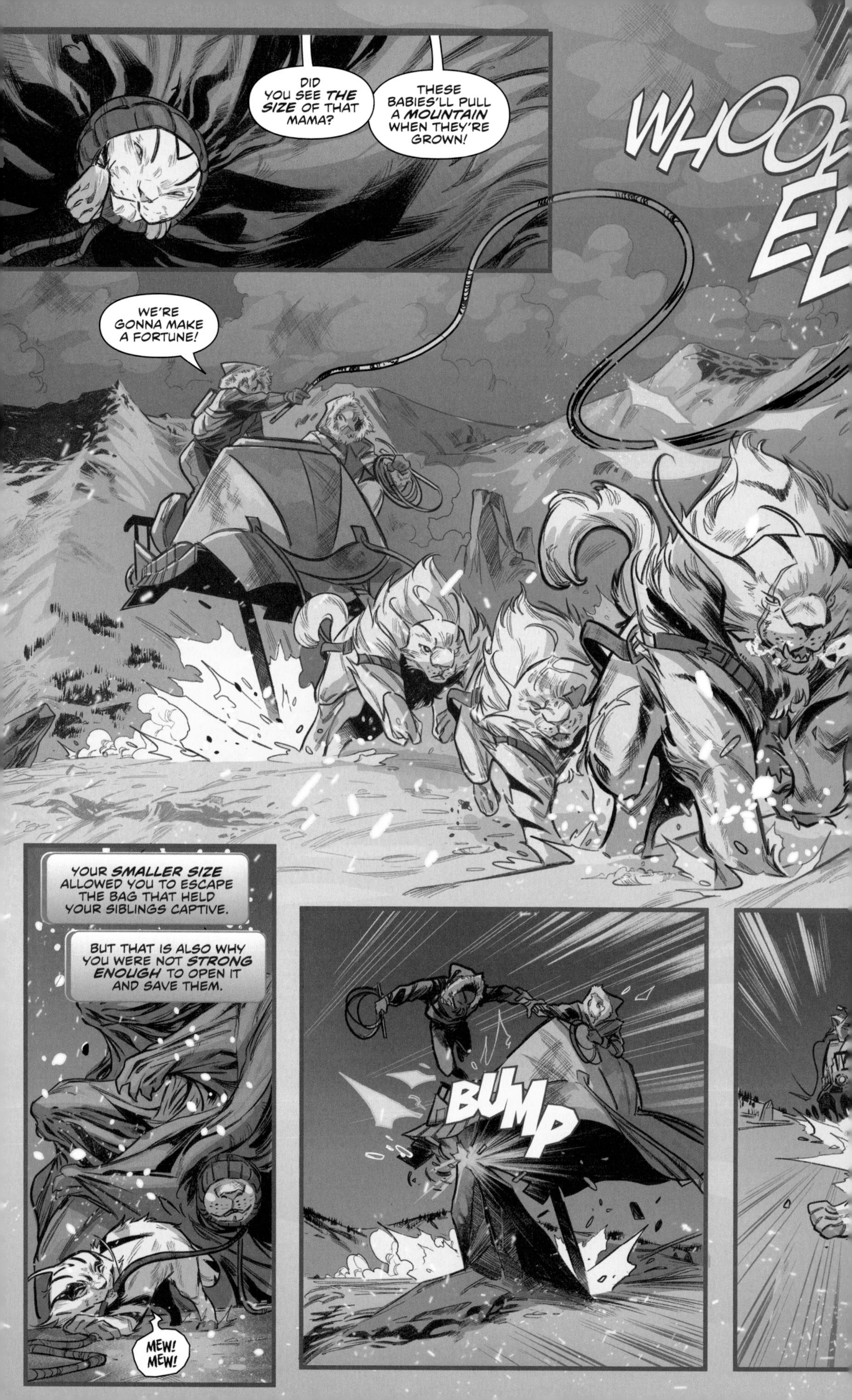
DID YOU SEE THE SIZE OF THAT MAMA?
THESE BABIES'LL PULL A MOUNTAIN WHEN THEY'RE GROWN!
WHOO
EE
WE'RE GONNA MAKE A FORTUNE!
YOUR SMALLER SIZE ALLOWED YOU TO ESCAPE THE BAG THAT HELD YOUR SIBLINGS CAPTIVE.
BUT THAT IS ALSO WHY YOU WERE NOT STRONG ENOUGH TO OPEN IT AND SAVE THEM.
MEW! MEW!
BUMP

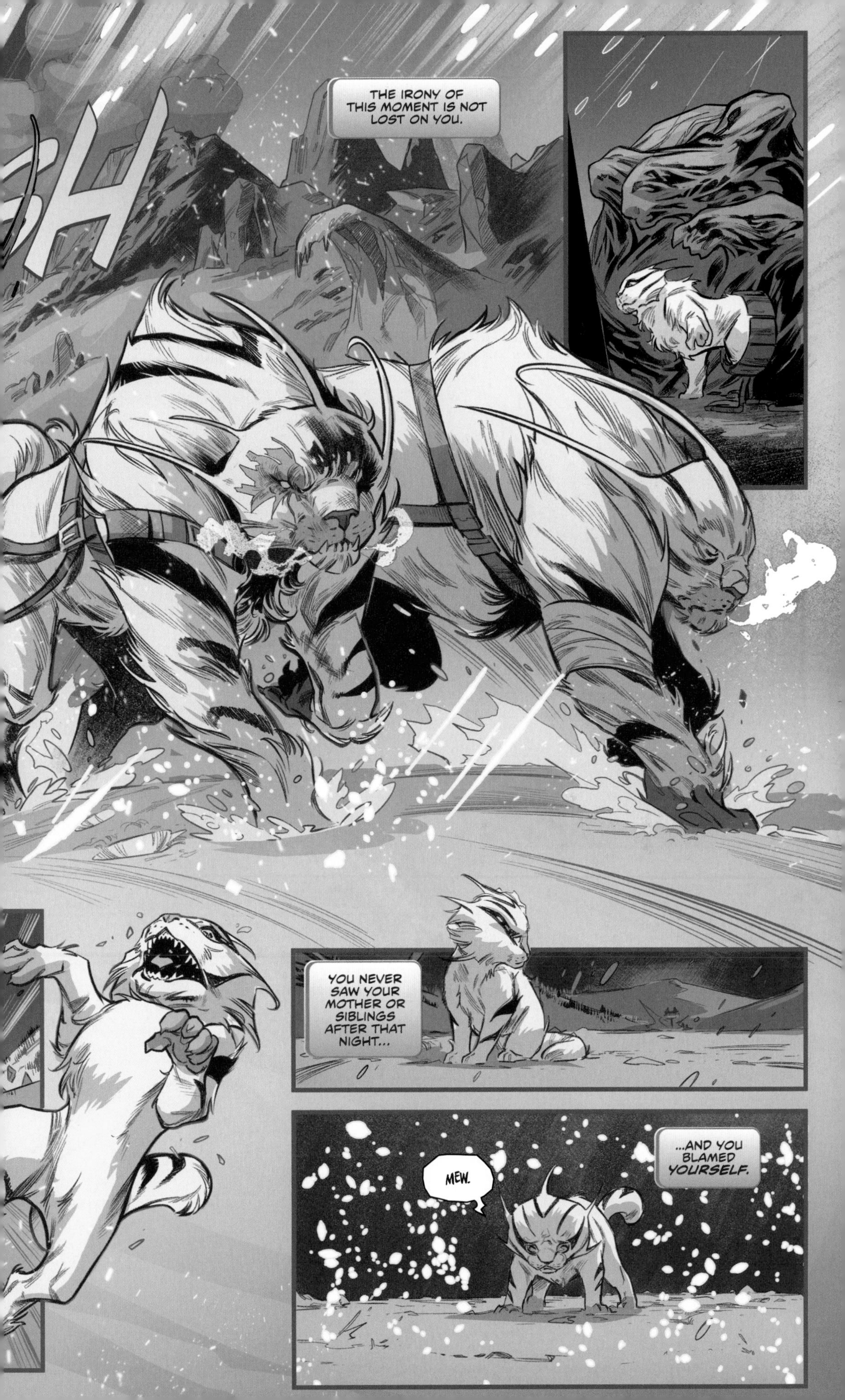

THE IRONY OF THIS MOMENT IS NOT LOST ON YOU.
YOU NEVER SAW YOUR MOTHER OR SIBLINGS AFTER THAT NIGHT...
MEW.
...AND YOU BLAMED YOURSELF.

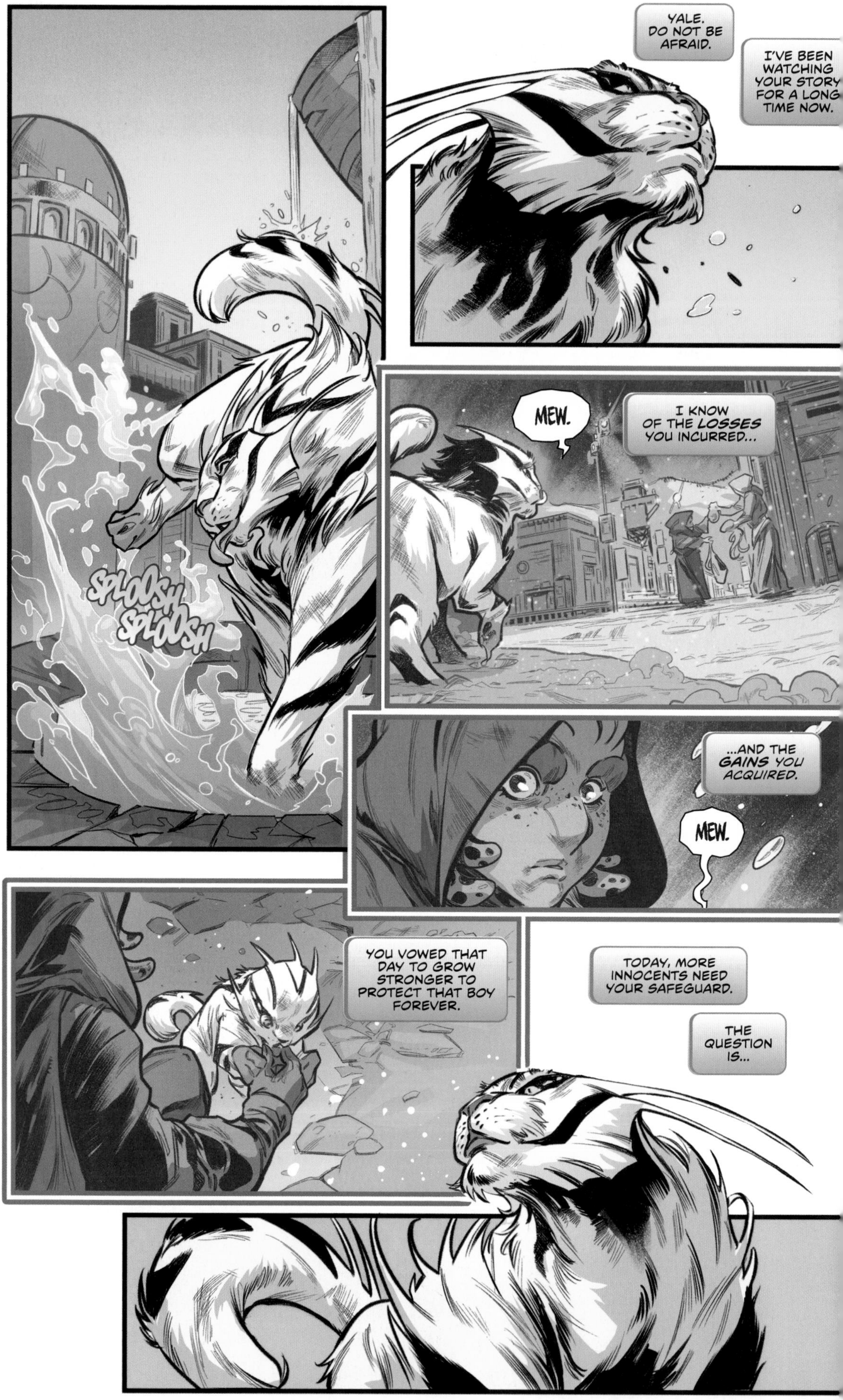

YALE. DO NOT BE AFRAID.
I'VE BEEN WATCHING YOUR STORY FOR A LONG TIME NOW.
SPLOOSH
SPLOOSH
MEW.
I KNOW OF THE LOSSES YOU INCURRED...
...AND THE GAINS YOU ACQUIRED.
MEW.
YOU VOWED THAT DAY TO GROW STRONGER TO PROTECT THAT BOY FOREVER.
TODAY, MORE INNOCENTS NEED YOUR SAFEGUARD.
THE QUESTION IS...

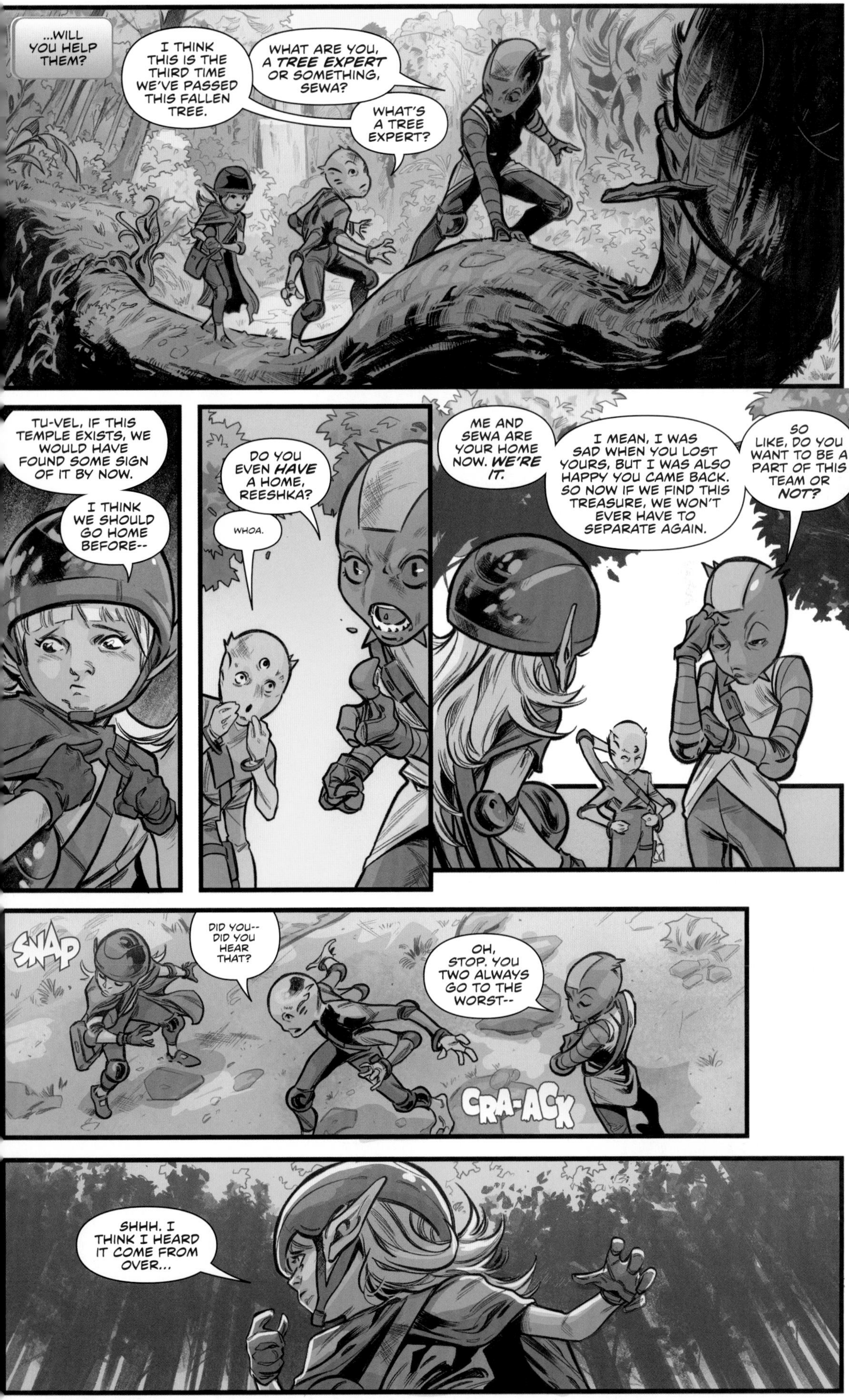
...WILL YOU HELP THEM?
I THINK THIS IS THE THIRD TIME WE'VE PASSED THIS FALLEN TREE.
WHAT ARE YOU, A ***TREE EXPERT*** OR SOMETHING, SEWA?
WHAT'S A TREE EXPERT?
TU-VEL, IF THIS TEMPLE EXISTS, WE WOULD HAVE FOUND SOME SIGN OF IT BY NOW.
I THINK WE SHOULD GO HOME BEFORE--
DO YOU EVEN ***HAVE*** A HOME, REESHKA?
WHOA.
ME AND SEWA ARE YOUR HOME NOW. ***WE'RE IT.***
I MEAN, I WAS SAD WHEN YOU LOST YOURS, BUT I WAS ALSO HAPPY YOU CAME BACK. SO NOW IF WE FIND THIS TREASURE, WE WON'T EVER HAVE TO SEPARATE AGAIN.
SO LIKE, DO YOU WANT TO BE A PART OF THIS TEAM OR ***NOT?***
SNAP
DID YOU-- DID YOU HEAR THAT?
OH, STOP. YOU TWO ALWAYS GO TO THE WORST--
CRA-ACK
SHHH. I THINK I HEARD IT COME FROM OVER...

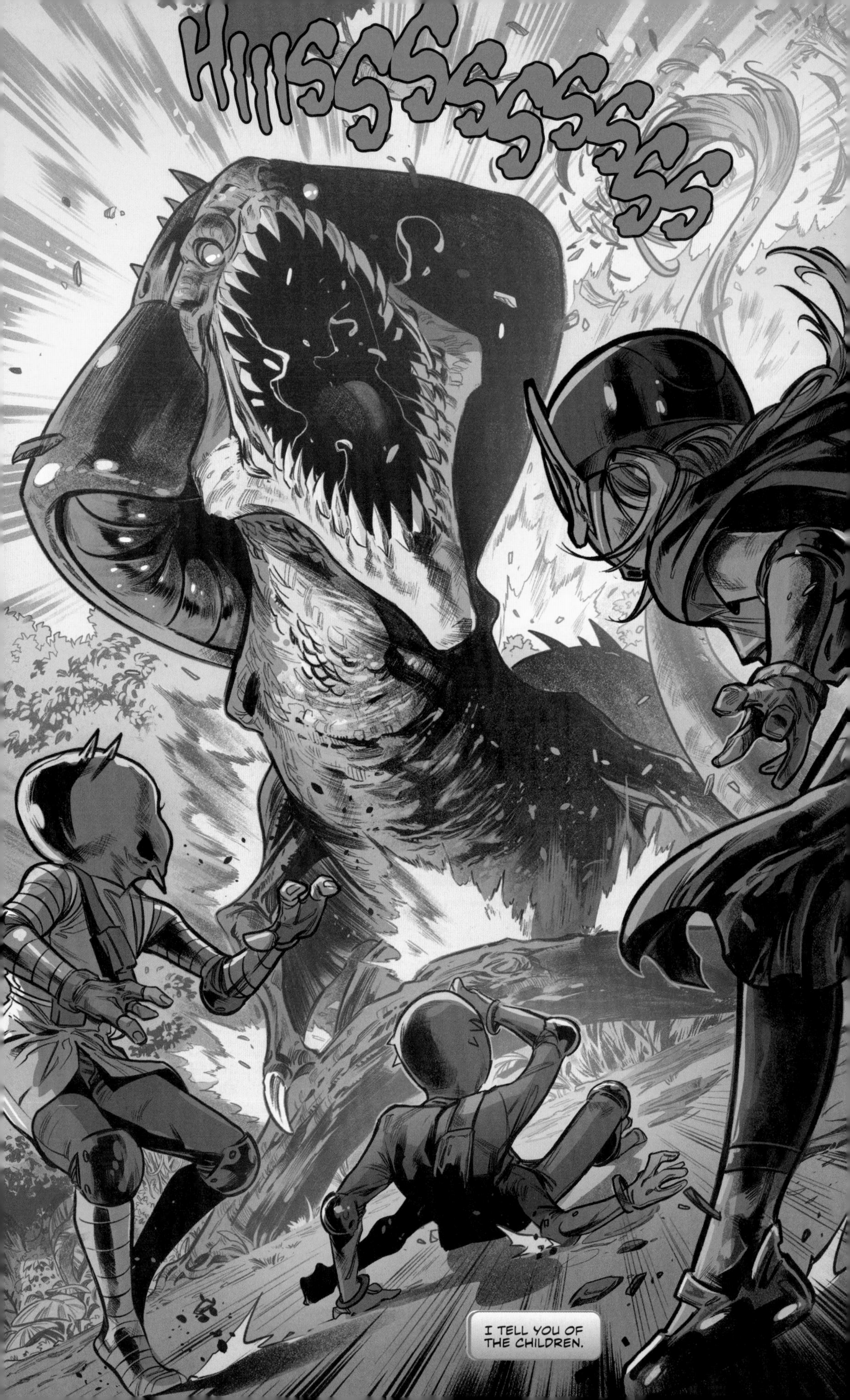
HIIISSSSSSSS
I TELL YOU OF THE CHILDREN.

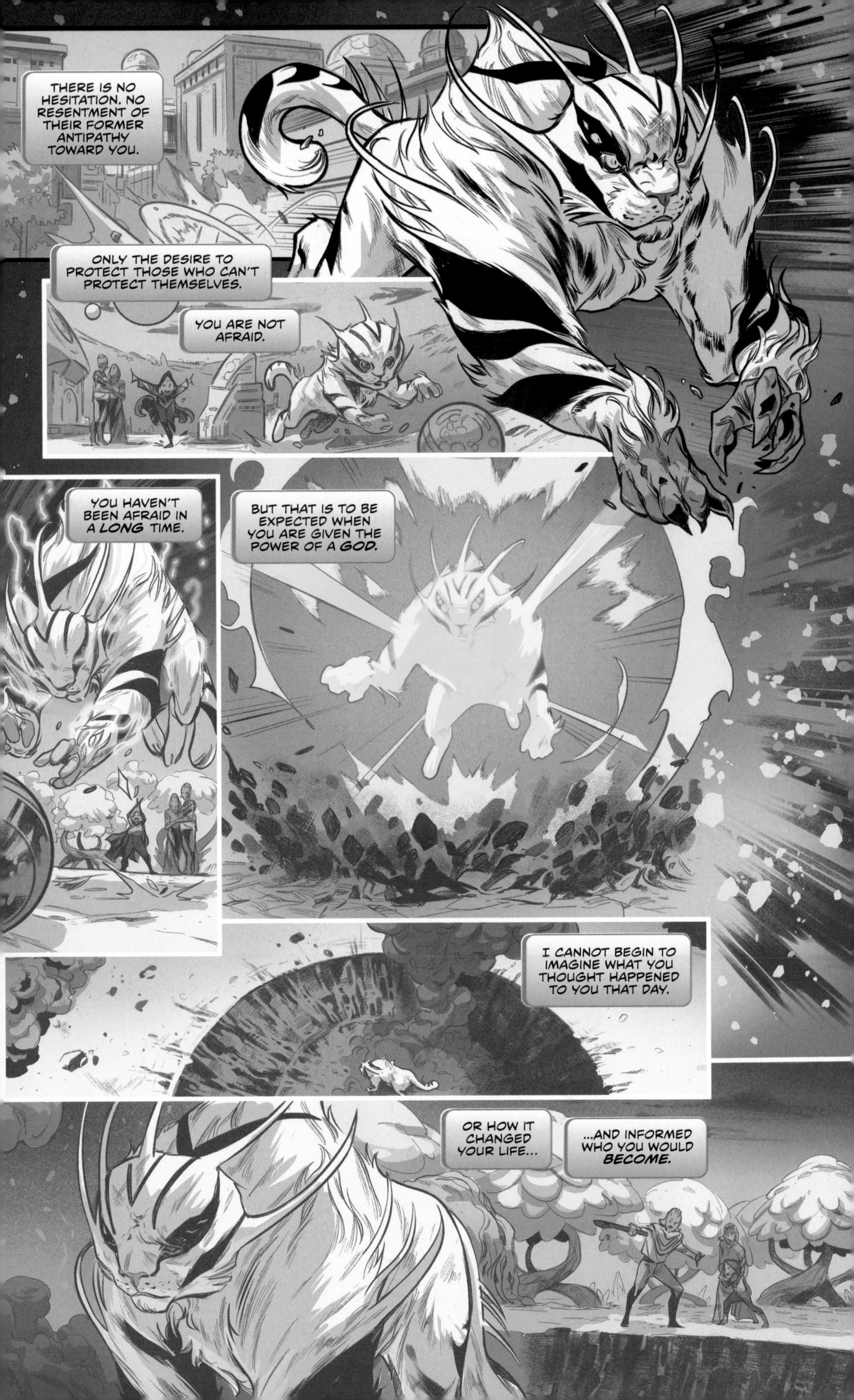
THERE IS NO HESITATION. NO RESENTMENT OF THEIR FORMER ANTIPATHY TOWARD YOU.
ONLY THE DESIRE TO PROTECT THOSE WHO CAN'T PROTECT THEMSELVES.
YOU ARE NOT AFRAID.
YOU HAVEN'T BEEN AFRAID IN A *LONG* TIME.
BUT THAT IS TO BE EXPECTED WHEN YOU ARE GIVEN THE POWER OF A *GOD*.
I CANNOT BEGIN TO IMAGINE WHAT YOU THOUGHT HAPPENED TO YOU THAT DAY.
OR HOW IT CHANGED YOUR LIFE...
...AND INFORMED WHO YOU WOULD *BECOME*.

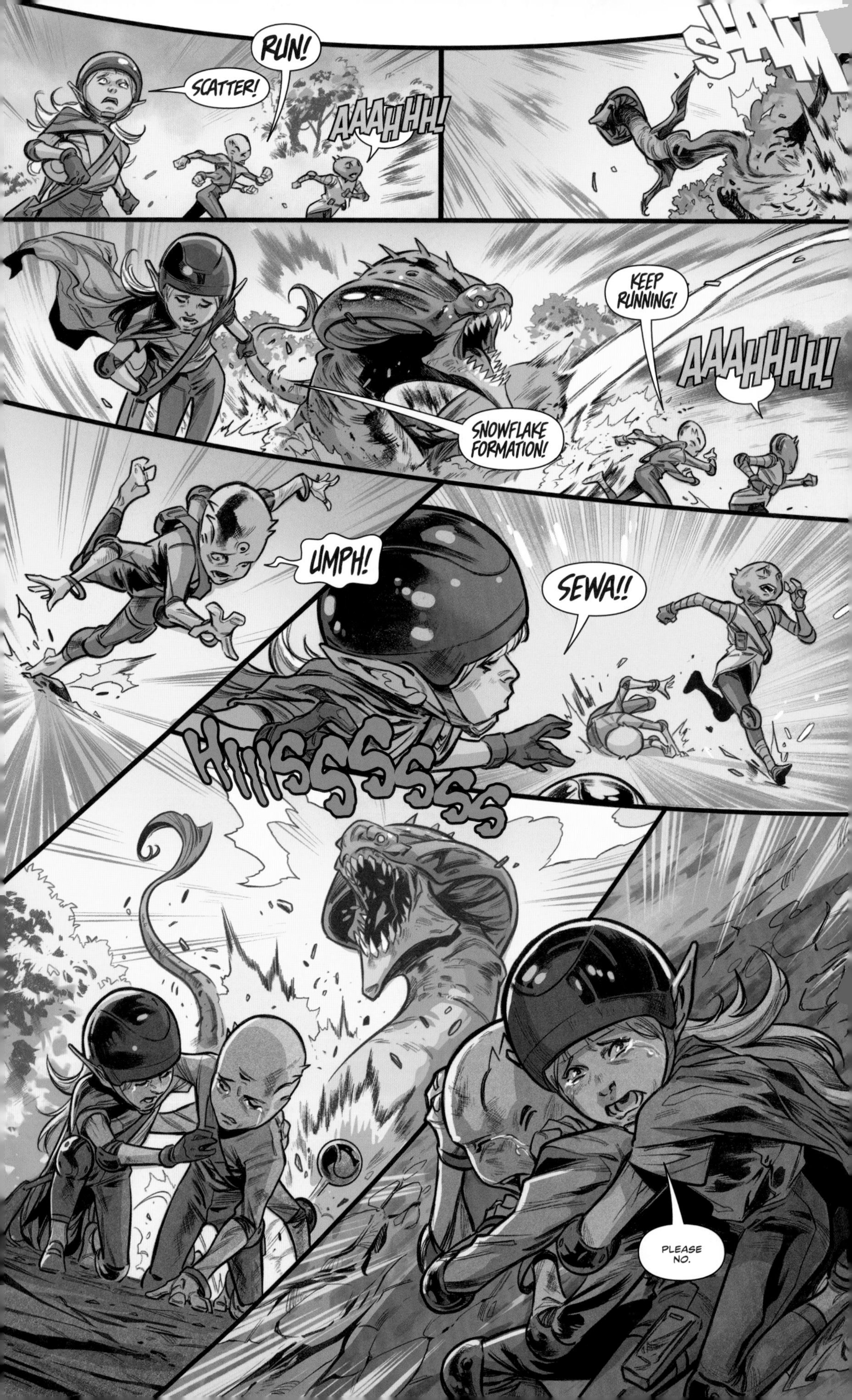
SCATTER!
RUN!
AAAHHH!
SHAM
KEEP RUNNING!
AAAHHHH!
SNOWFLAKE FORMATION!
UMPH!
SEWA!!
HIIISSSSSSS
PLEASE NO.

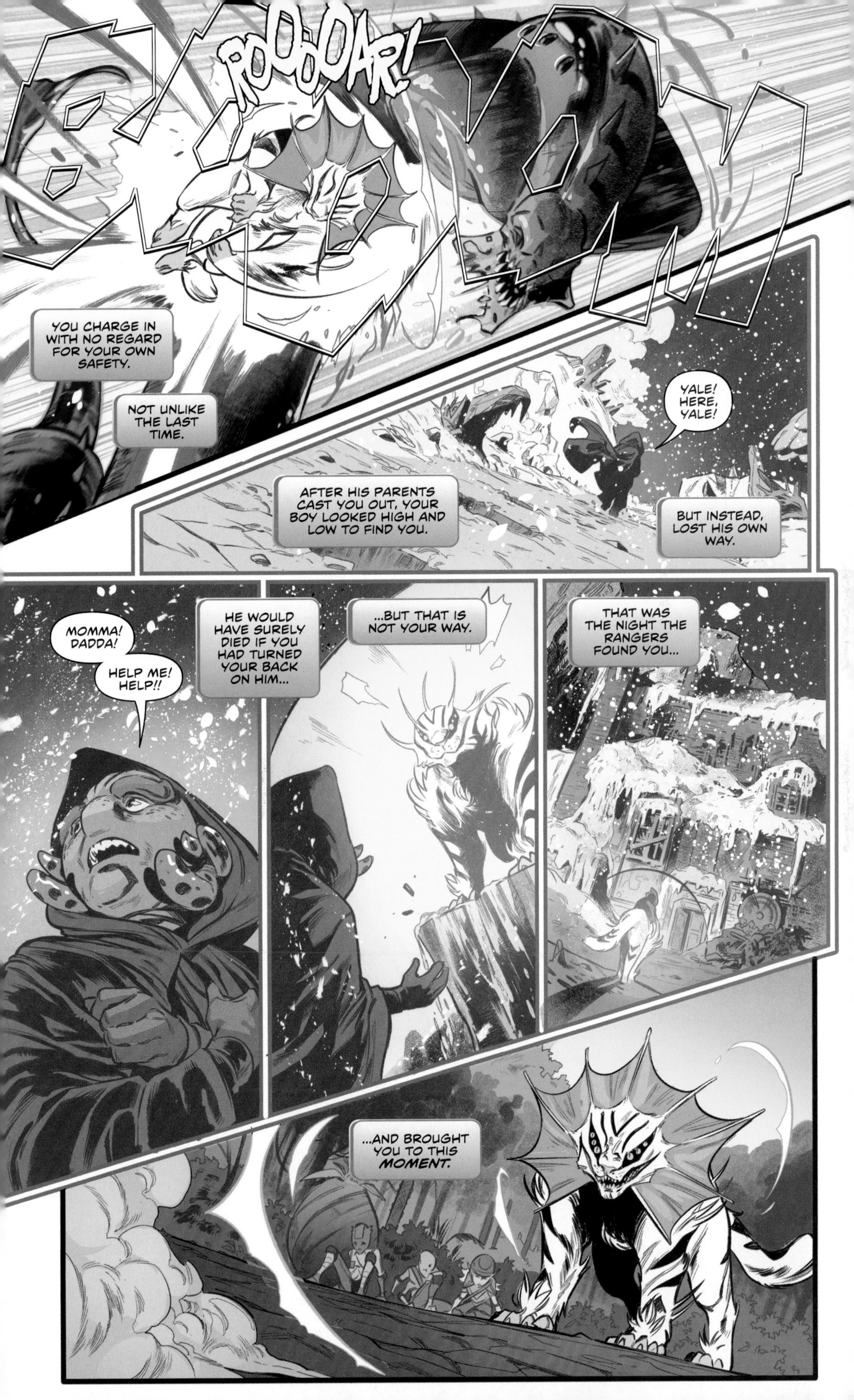
ROOOOAR!
YOU CHARGE IN WITH NO REGARD FOR YOUR OWN SAFETY.
NOT UNLIKE THE LAST TIME.
YALE! HERE, YALE!
AFTER HIS PARENTS CAST YOU OUT, YOUR BOY LOOKED HIGH AND LOW TO FIND YOU.
BUT INSTEAD, LOST HIS OWN WAY.
MOMMA! DADDA!
HELP ME! HELP!!
HE WOULD HAVE SURELY DIED IF YOU HAD TURNED YOUR BACK ON HIM...
...BUT THAT IS NOT YOUR WAY.
THAT WAS THE NIGHT THE RANGERS FOUND YOU...
...AND BROUGHT YOU TO THIS *MOMENT*.

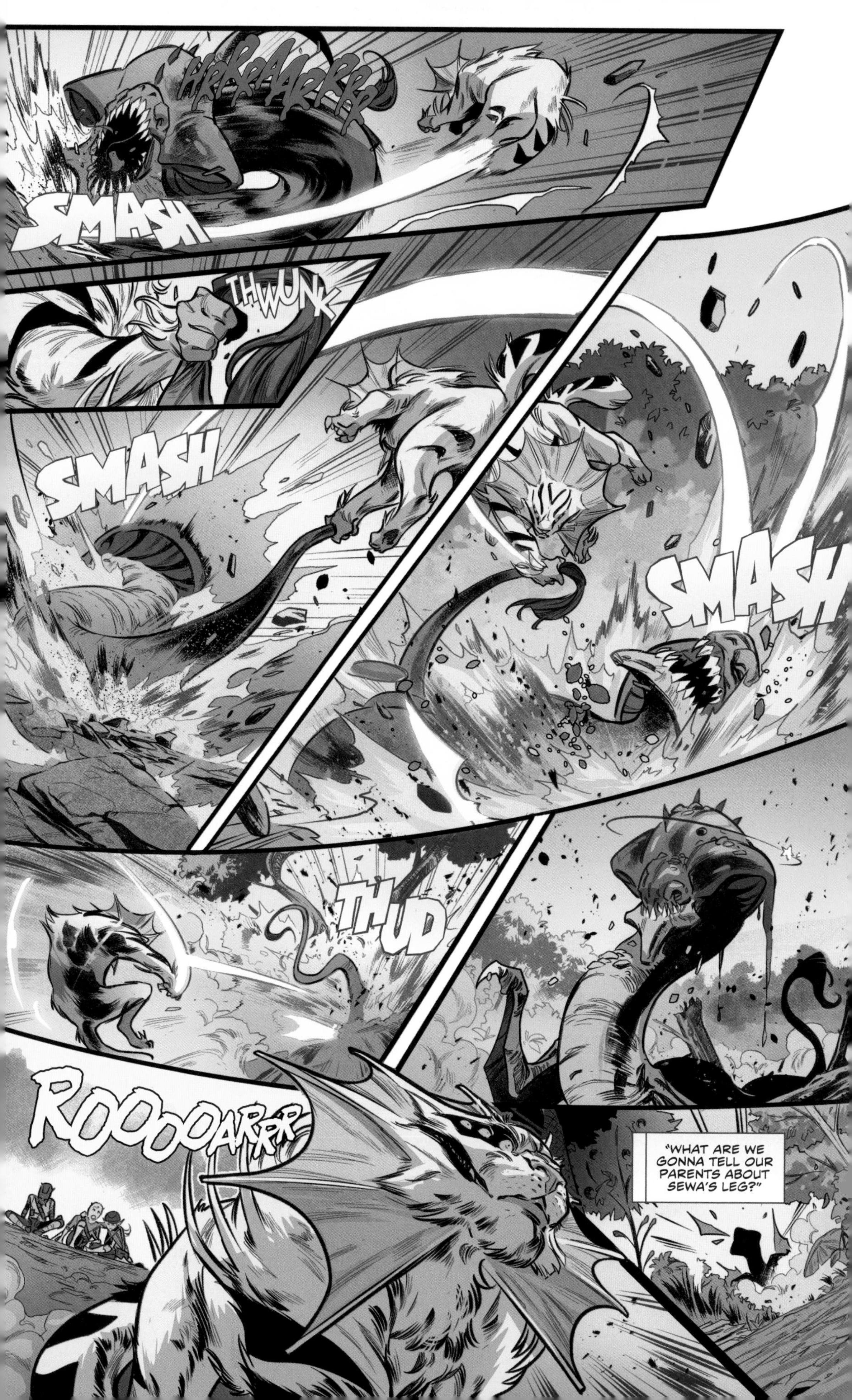
HRRRAARRRR
SMASH
THWUNK
SMASH
SMASH
THUD
ROOOOARRRR
"WHAT ARE WE GONNA TELL OUR PARENTS ABOUT SEWA'S LEG?"

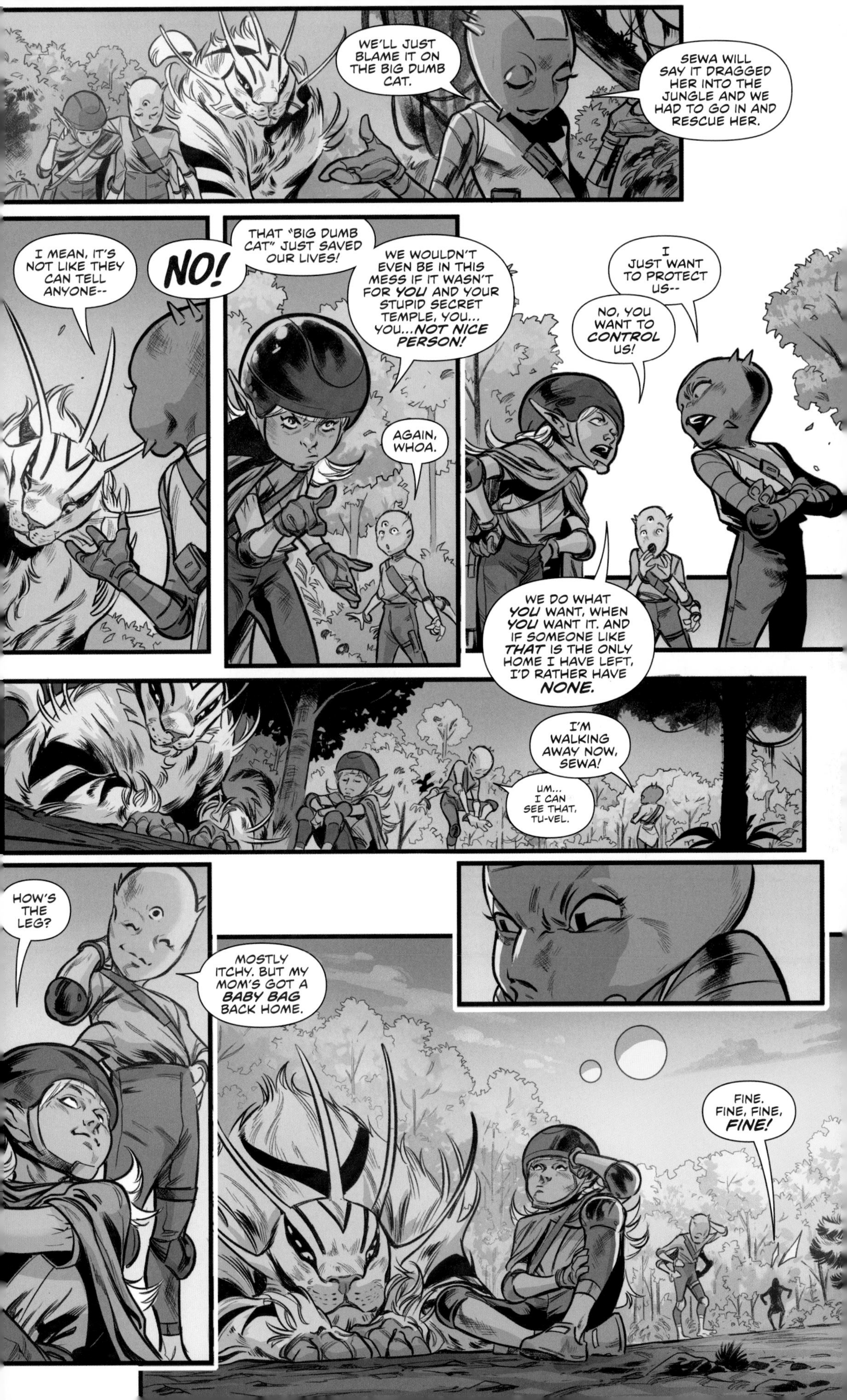
WE'LL JUST BLAME IT ON THE BIG DUMB CAT.
SEWA WILL SAY IT DRAGGED HER INTO THE JUNGLE AND WE HAD TO GO IN AND RESCUE HER.
I MEAN, IT'S NOT LIKE THEY CAN TELL ANYONE--
NO!
THAT "BIG DUMB CAT" JUST SAVED OUR LIVES!
WE WOULDN'T EVEN BE IN THIS MESS IF IT WASN'T FOR YOU AND YOUR STUPID SECRET TEMPLE, YOU... YOU...NOT NICE PERSON!
AGAIN, WHOA.
I JUST WANT TO PROTECT US--
NO, YOU WANT TO CONTROL US!
WE DO WHAT YOU WANT, WHEN YOU WANT IT. AND IF SOMEONE LIKE THAT IS THE ONLY HOME I HAVE LEFT, I'D RATHER HAVE NONE.
I'M WALKING AWAY NOW, SEWA!
UM... I CAN SEE THAT, TU-VEL.
HOW'S THE LEG?
MOSTLY ITCHY. BUT MY MOM'S GOT A BABY BAG BACK HOME.
FINE. FINE, FINE, FINE!

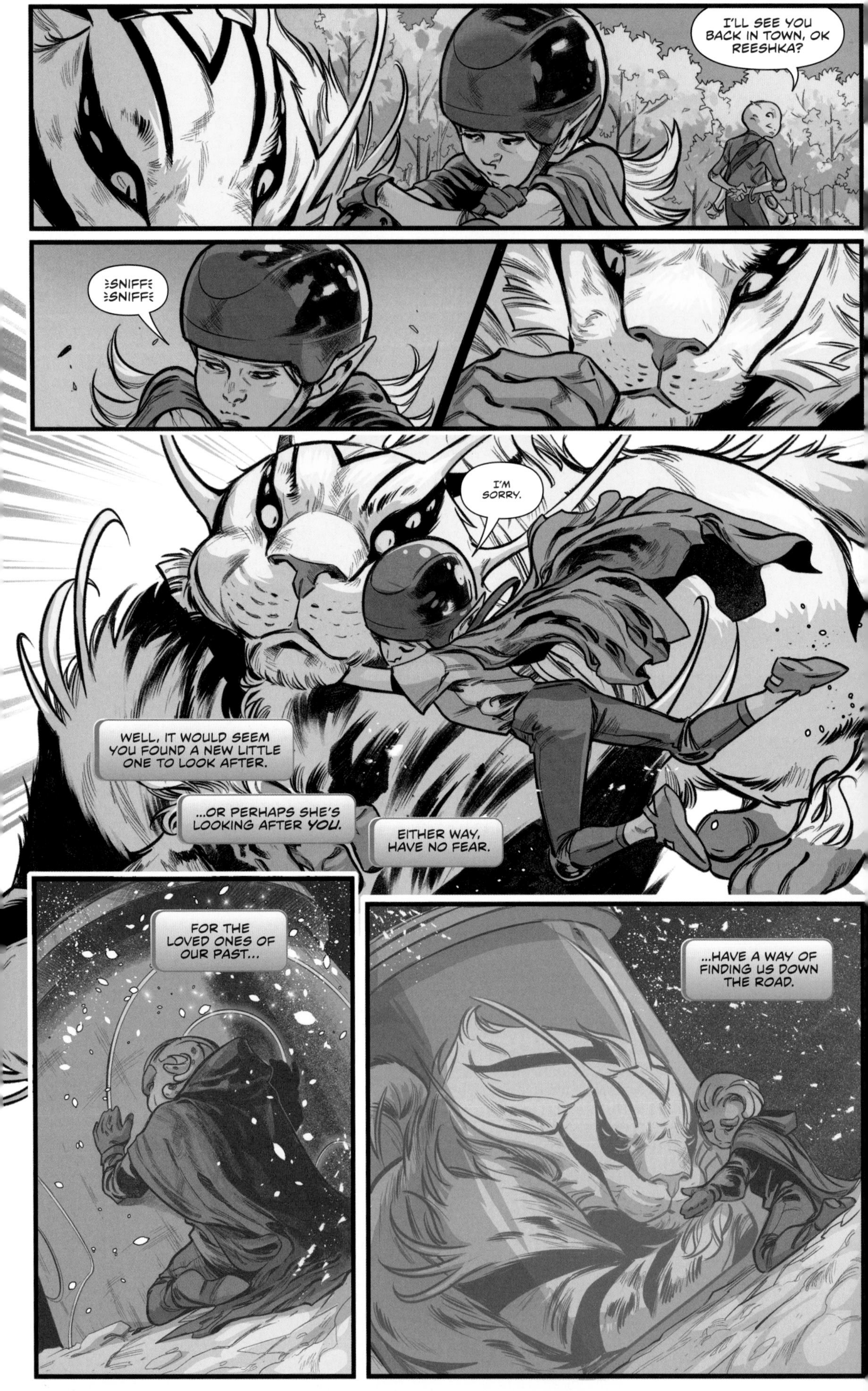
I'LL SEE YOU BACK IN TOWN, OK REESHKA?
SNIFF SNIFF
I'M SORRY.
WELL, IT WOULD SEEM YOU FOUND A NEW LITTLE ONE TO LOOK AFTER.
...OR PERHAPS SHE'S LOOKING AFTER YOU.
EITHER WAY, HAVE NO FEAR.
FOR THE LOVED ONES OF OUR PAST...
...HAVE A WAY OF FINDING US DOWN THE ROAD.

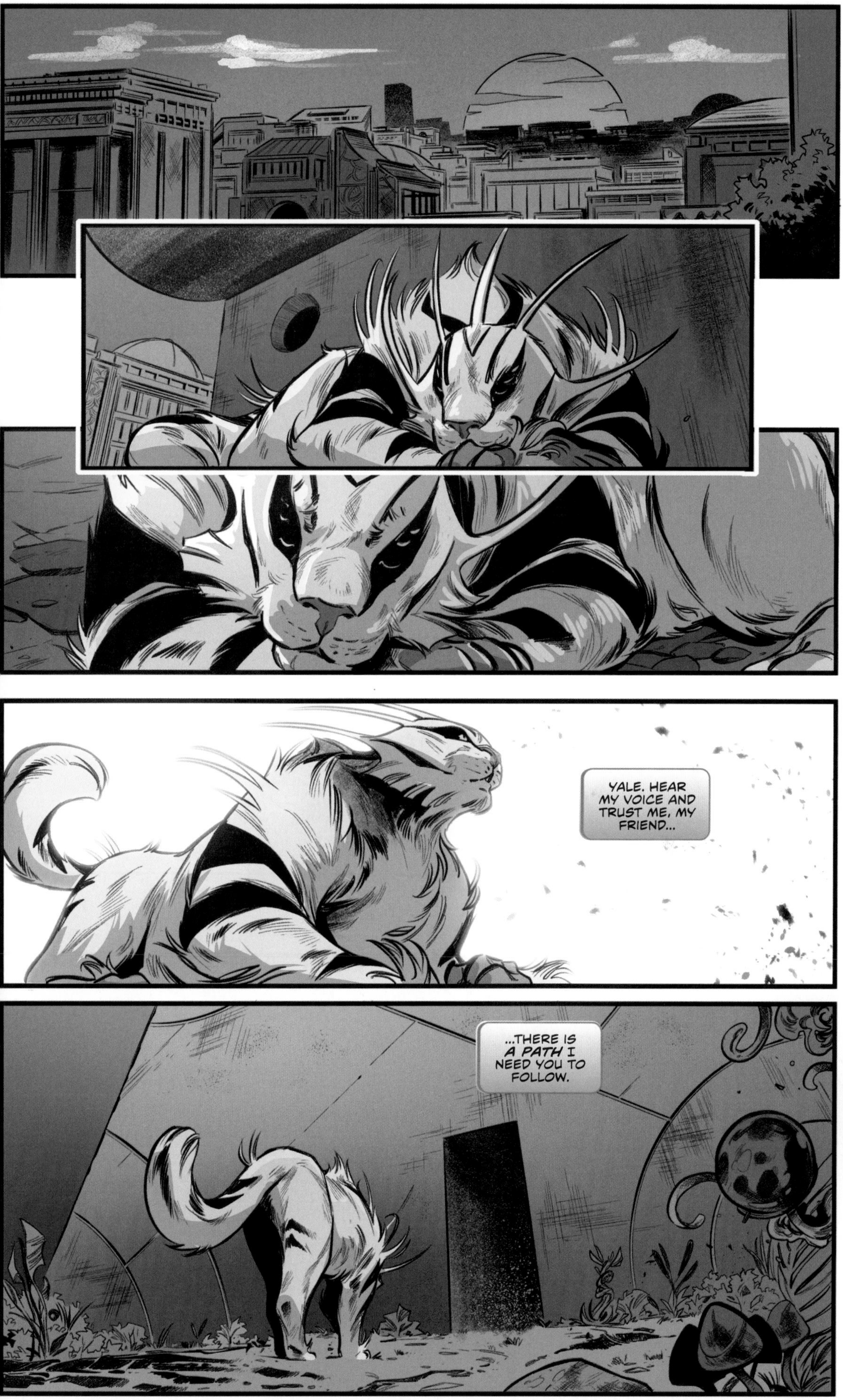
YALE. HEAR MY VOICE AND TRUST ME, MY FRIEND...
...THERE IS *A PATH* I NEED YOU TO FOLLOW.

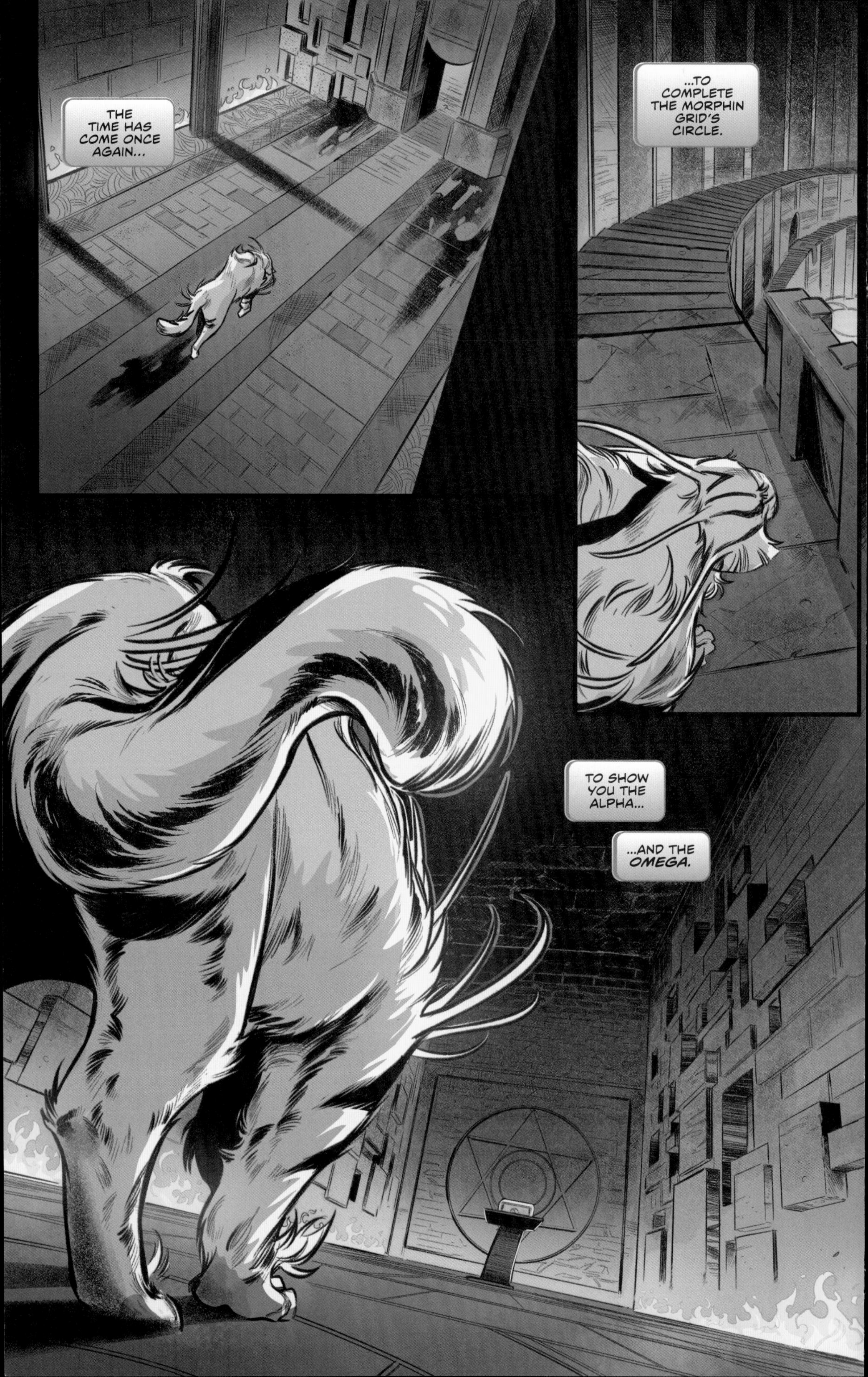
THE TIME HAS COME ONCE AGAIN...
...TO COMPLETE THE MORPHIN GRID'S CIRCLE.
TO SHOW YOU THE ALPHA...
...AND THE OMEGA.

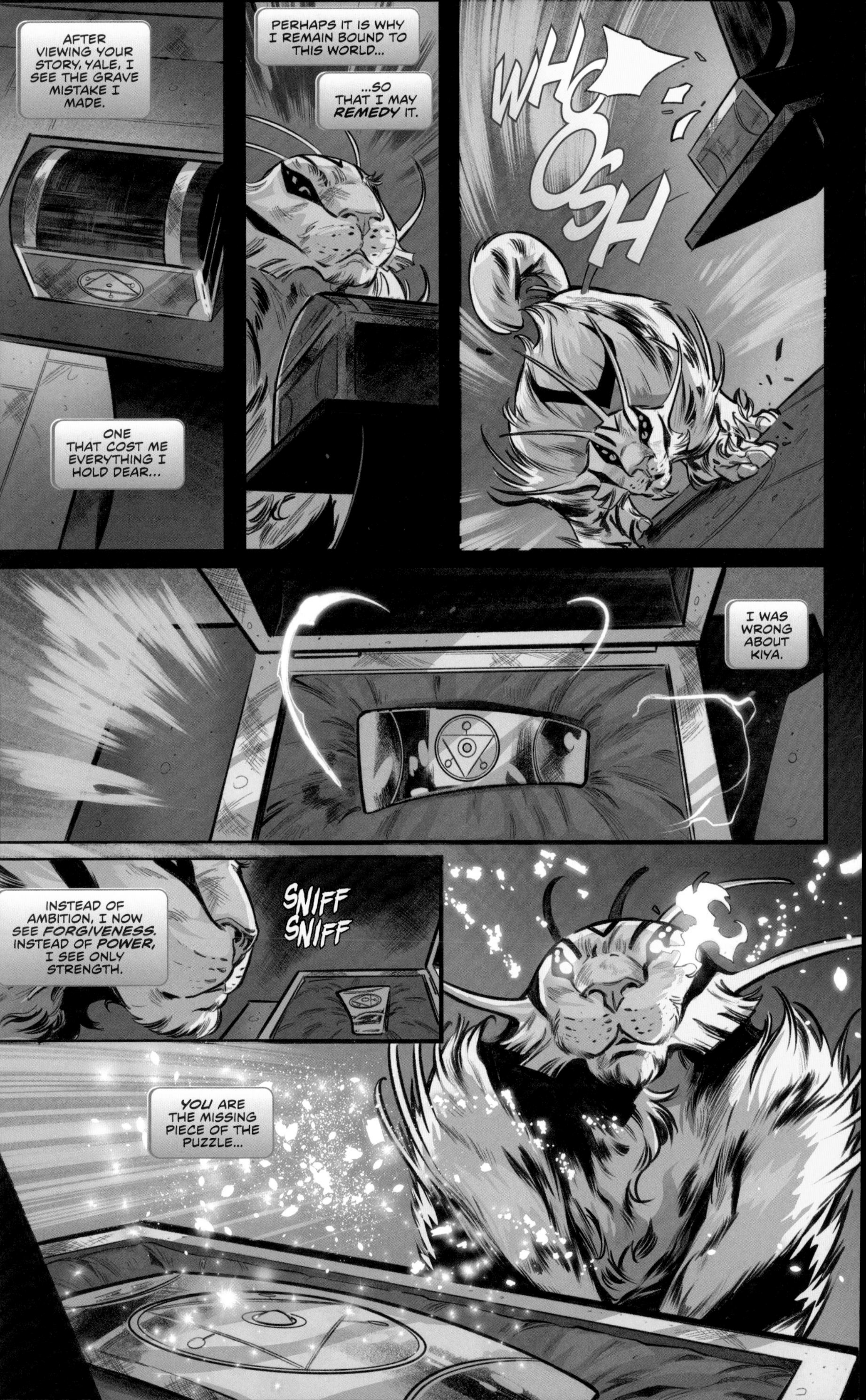
AFTER VIEWING YOUR STORY, YALE, I SEE THE GRAVE MISTAKE I MADE.
ONE THAT COST ME EVERYTHING I HOLD DEAR...
PERHAPS IT IS WHY I REMAIN BOUND TO THIS WORLD...
...SO THAT I MAY *REMEDY* IT.
WHOOSH
I WAS WRONG ABOUT KIYA.
INSTEAD OF AMBITION, I NOW SEE *FORGIVENESS*. INSTEAD OF *POWER*, I SEE ONLY STRENGTH.
SNIFF SNIFF
YOU ARE THE MISSING PIECE OF THE PUZZLE...

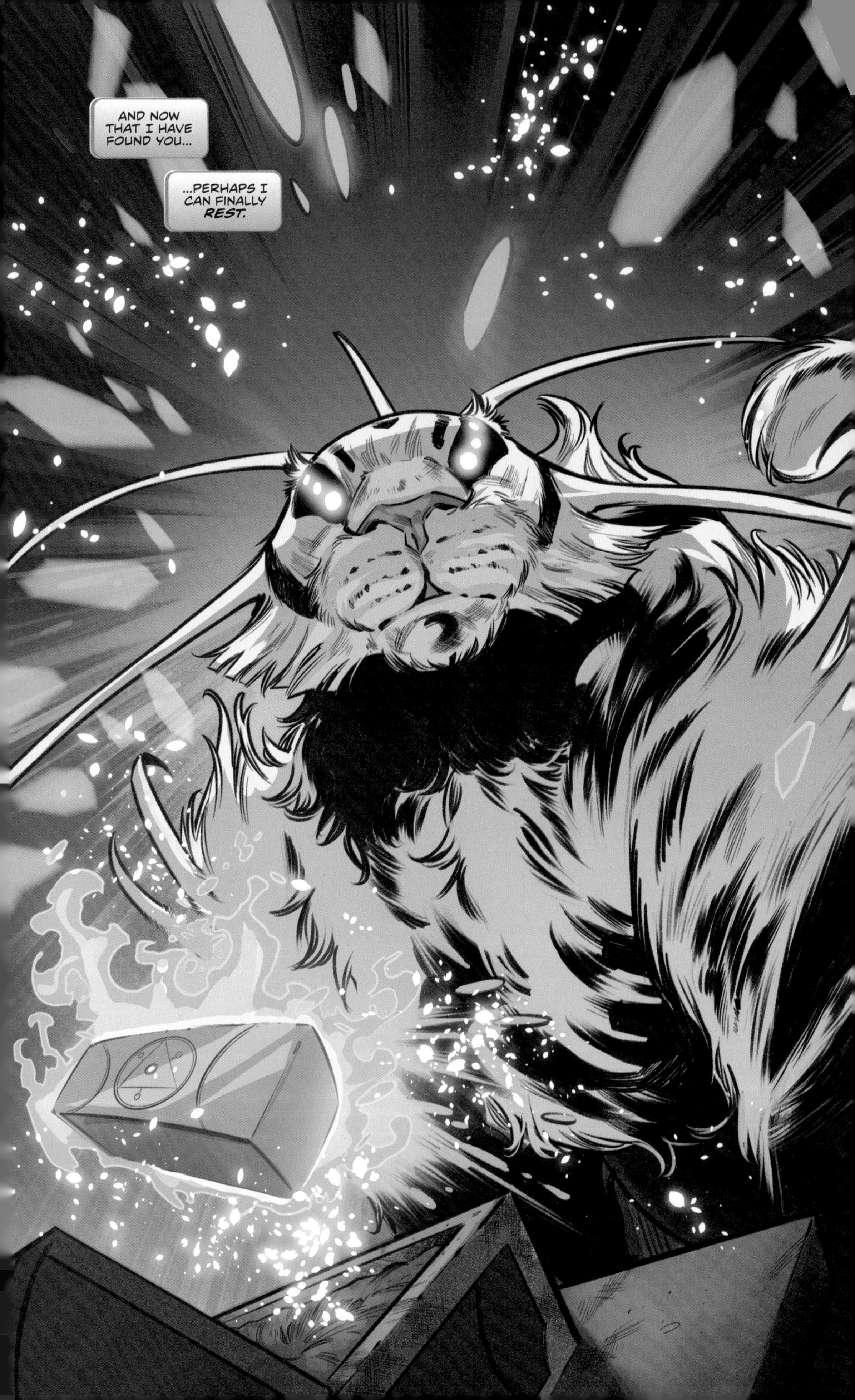
AND NOW THAT I HAVE FOUND YOU...
...PERHAPS I CAN FINALLY *REST.*

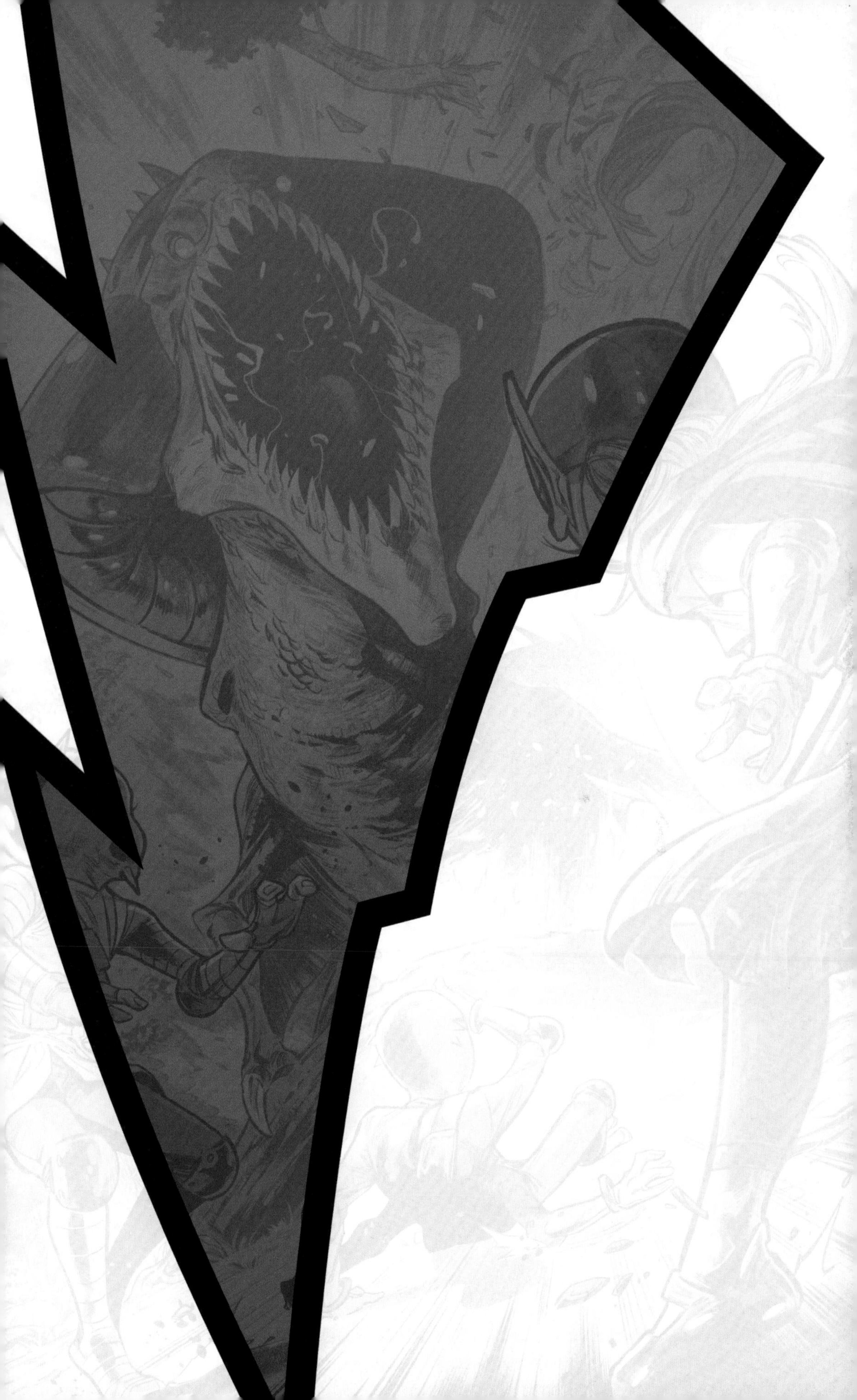

CHAPTER ELEVEN

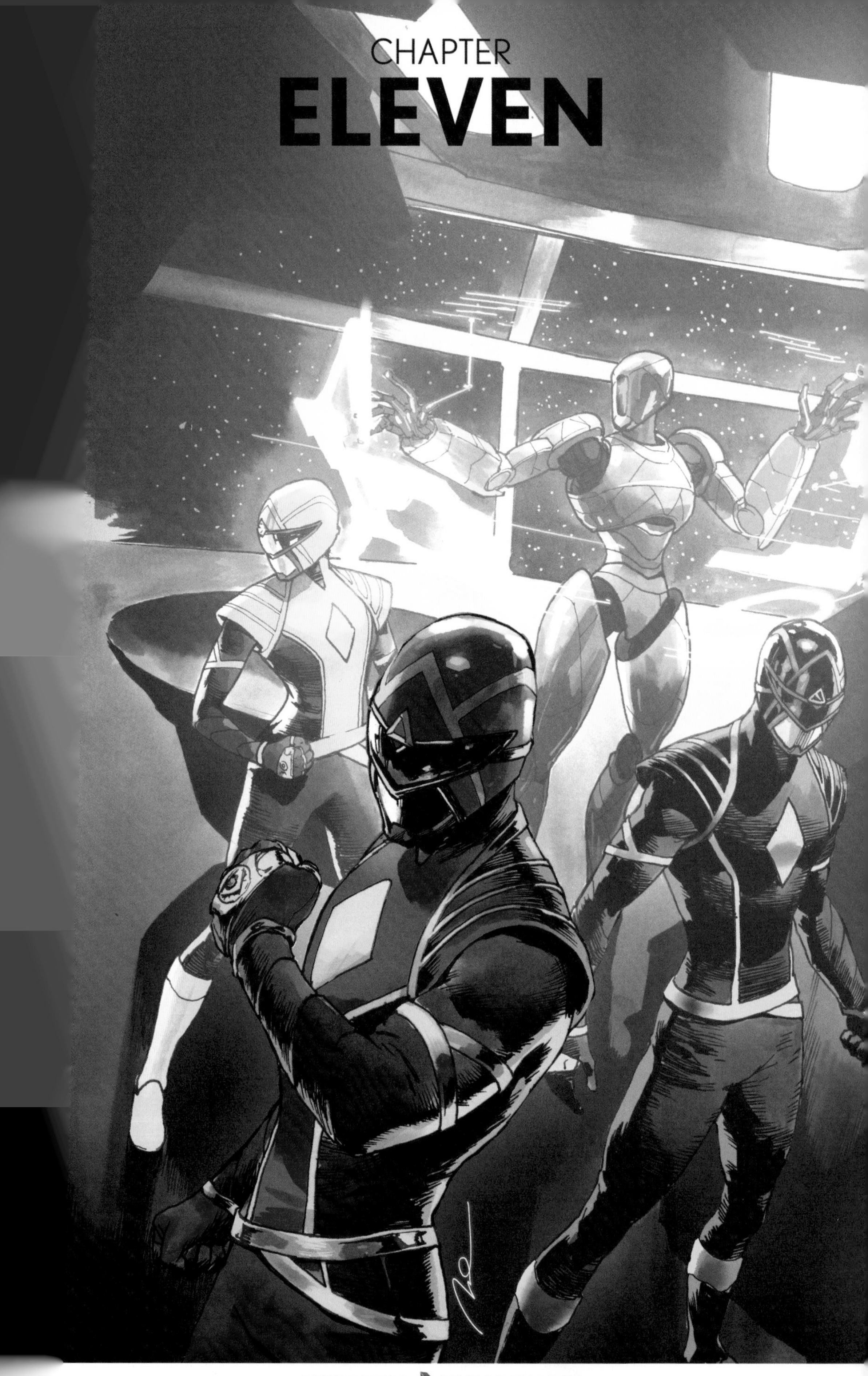

GERALD PAREL | ISSUE ELEVEN COVER

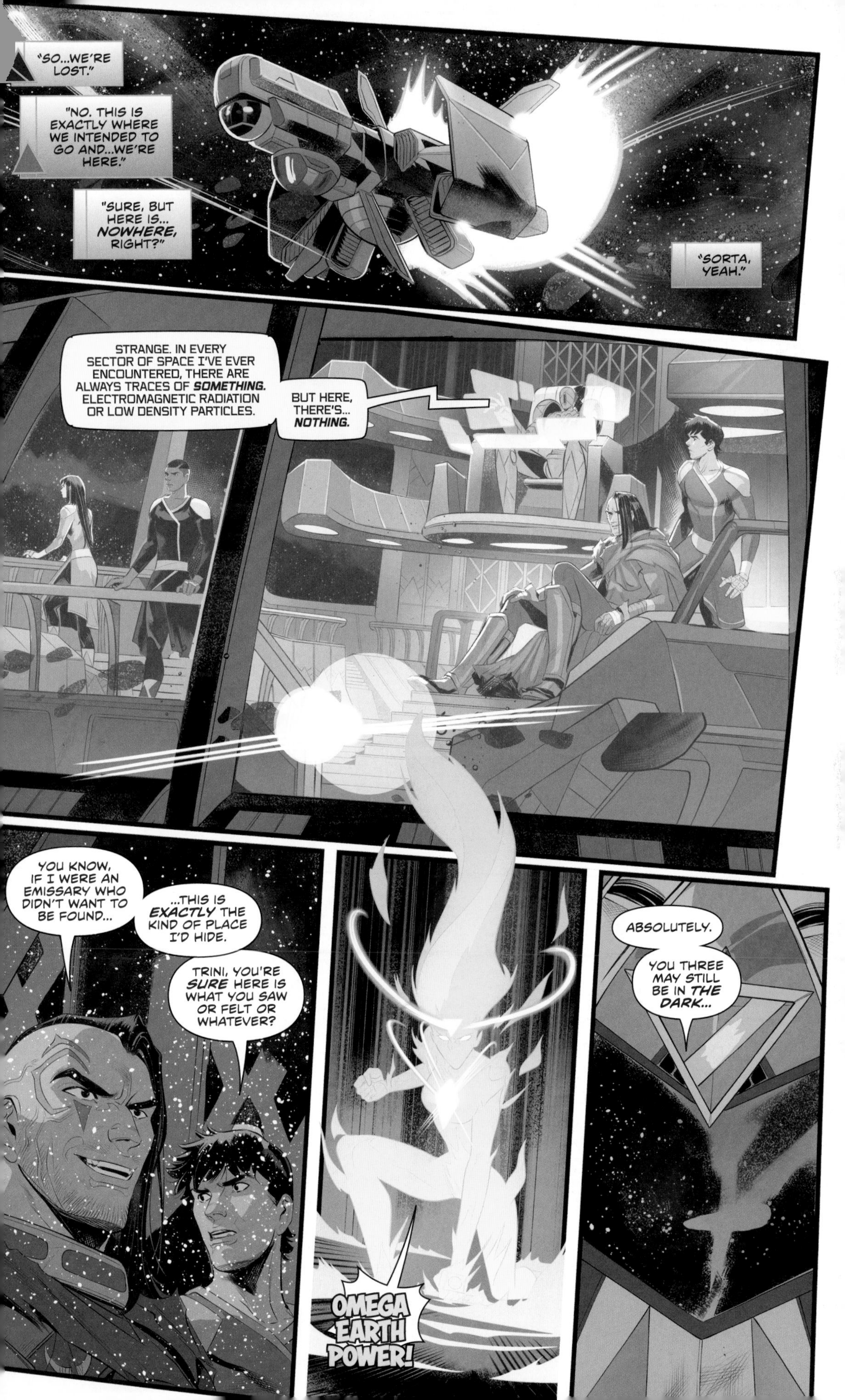
"SO...WE'RE LOST."
"NO. THIS IS EXACTLY WHERE WE INTENDED TO GO AND...WE'RE HERE."
"SURE, BUT HERE IS... NOWHERE, RIGHT?"
"SORTA, YEAH."
STRANGE. IN EVERY SECTOR OF SPACE I'VE EVER ENCOUNTERED, THERE ARE ALWAYS TRACES OF SOMETHING. ELECTROMAGNETIC RADIATION OR LOW DENSITY PARTICLES.
BUT HERE, THERE'S... NOTHING.
YOU KNOW, IF I WERE AN EMISSARY WHO DIDN'T WANT TO BE FOUND...
...THIS IS EXACTLY THE KIND OF PLACE I'D HIDE.
TRINI, YOU'RE SURE HERE IS WHAT YOU SAW OR FELT OR WHATEVER?
OMEGA EARTH POWER!
ABSOLUTELY.
YOU THREE MAY STILL BE IN THE DARK...

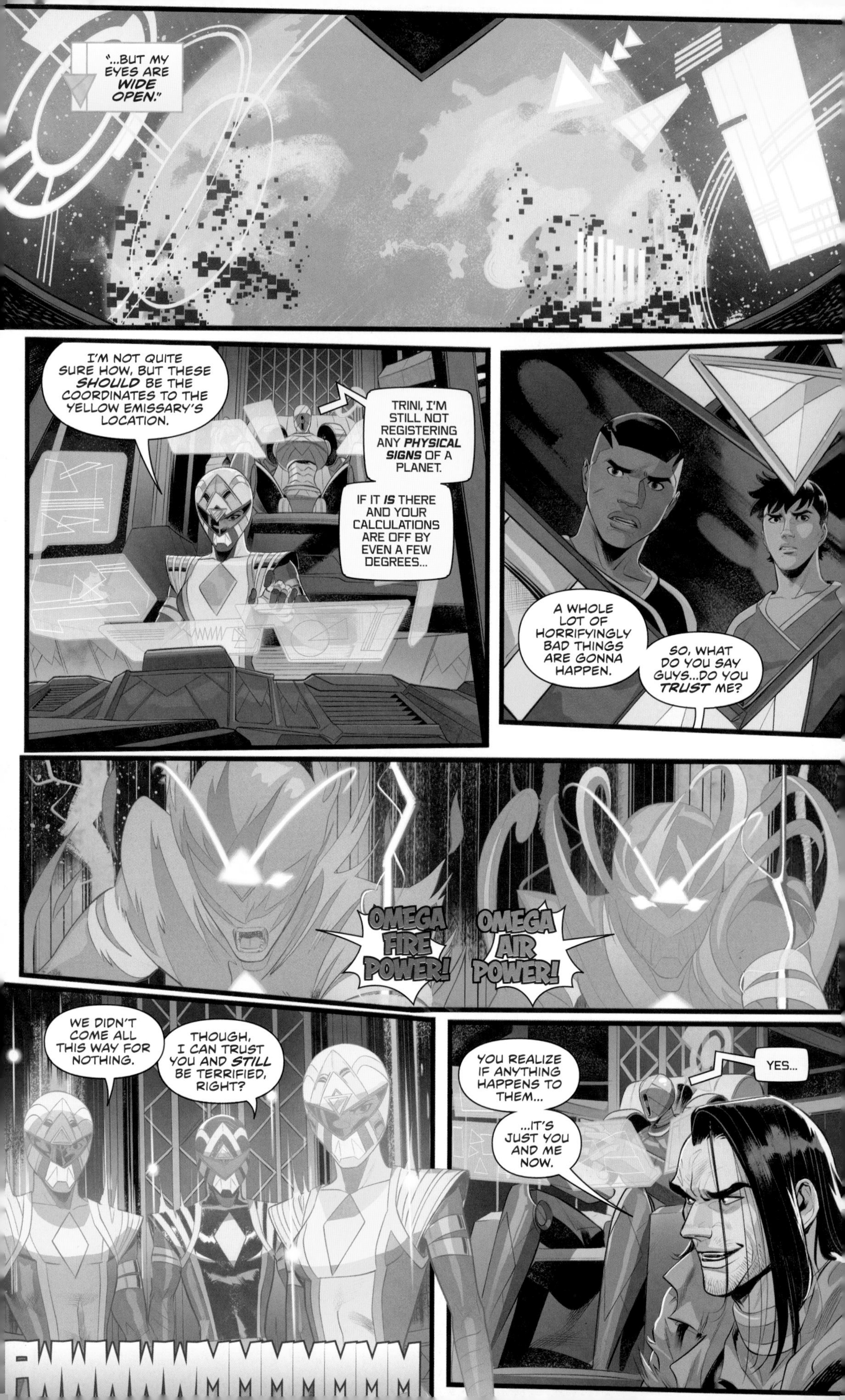
"...BUT MY EYES ARE WIDE OPEN."
I'M NOT QUITE SURE HOW, BUT THESE SHOULD BE THE COORDINATES TO THE YELLOW EMISSARY'S LOCATION.
TRINI, I'M STILL NOT REGISTERING ANY PHYSICAL SIGNS OF A PLANET.
IF IT IS THERE AND YOUR CALCULATIONS ARE OFF BY EVEN A FEW DEGREES...
A WHOLE LOT OF HORRIFYINGLY BAD THINGS ARE GONNA HAPPEN.
SO, WHAT DO YOU SAY GUYS...DO YOU TRUST ME?
OMEGA FIRE POWER!
OMEGA AIR POWER!
WE DIDN'T COME ALL THIS WAY FOR NOTHING.
THOUGH, I CAN TRUST YOU AND STILL BE TERRIFIED, RIGHT?
AAAAAAAMMMMMMMMMM
YOU REALIZE IF ANYTHING HAPPENS TO THEM...
YES...
...IT'S JUST YOU AND ME NOW.

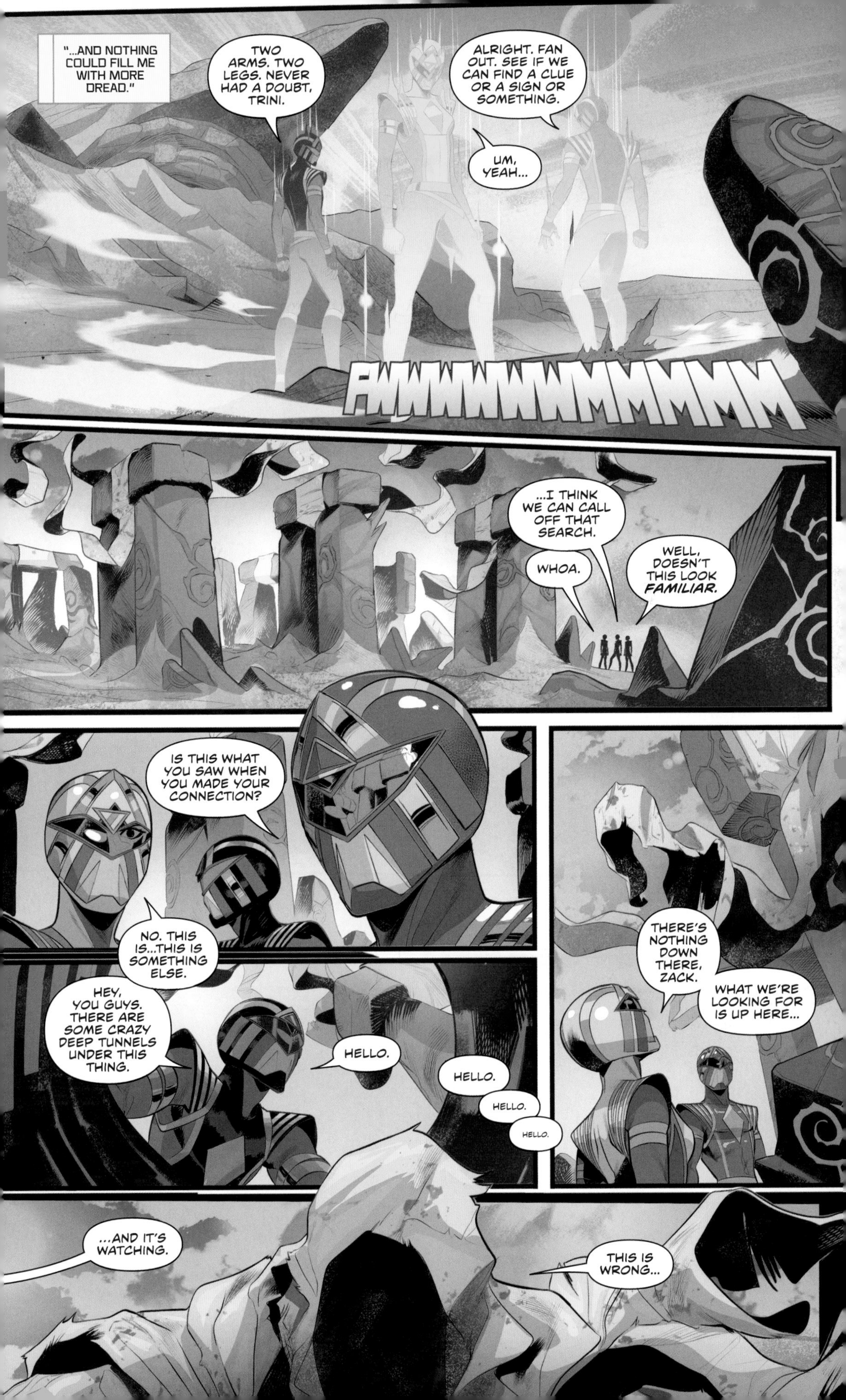
"...AND NOTHING COULD FILL ME WITH MORE DREAD."
TWO ARMS. TWO LEGS. NEVER HAD A DOUBT, TRINI.
ALRIGHT. FAN OUT. SEE IF WE CAN FIND A CLUE OR A SIGN OR SOMETHING.
UM, YEAH...
FWWWWWWWMMMMMM
...I THINK WE CAN CALL OFF THAT SEARCH.
WHOA.
WELL, DOESN'T THIS LOOK FAMILIAR.
IS THIS WHAT YOU SAW WHEN YOU MADE YOUR CONNECTION?
NO. THIS IS...THIS IS SOMETHING ELSE.
HEY, YOU GUYS. THERE ARE SOME CRAZY DEEP TUNNELS UNDER THIS THING.
HELLO.
HELLO.
HELLO.
HELLO.
THERE'S NOTHING DOWN THERE, ZACK.
WHAT WE'RE LOOKING FOR IS UP HERE...
...AND IT'S WATCHING.
THIS IS WRONG...

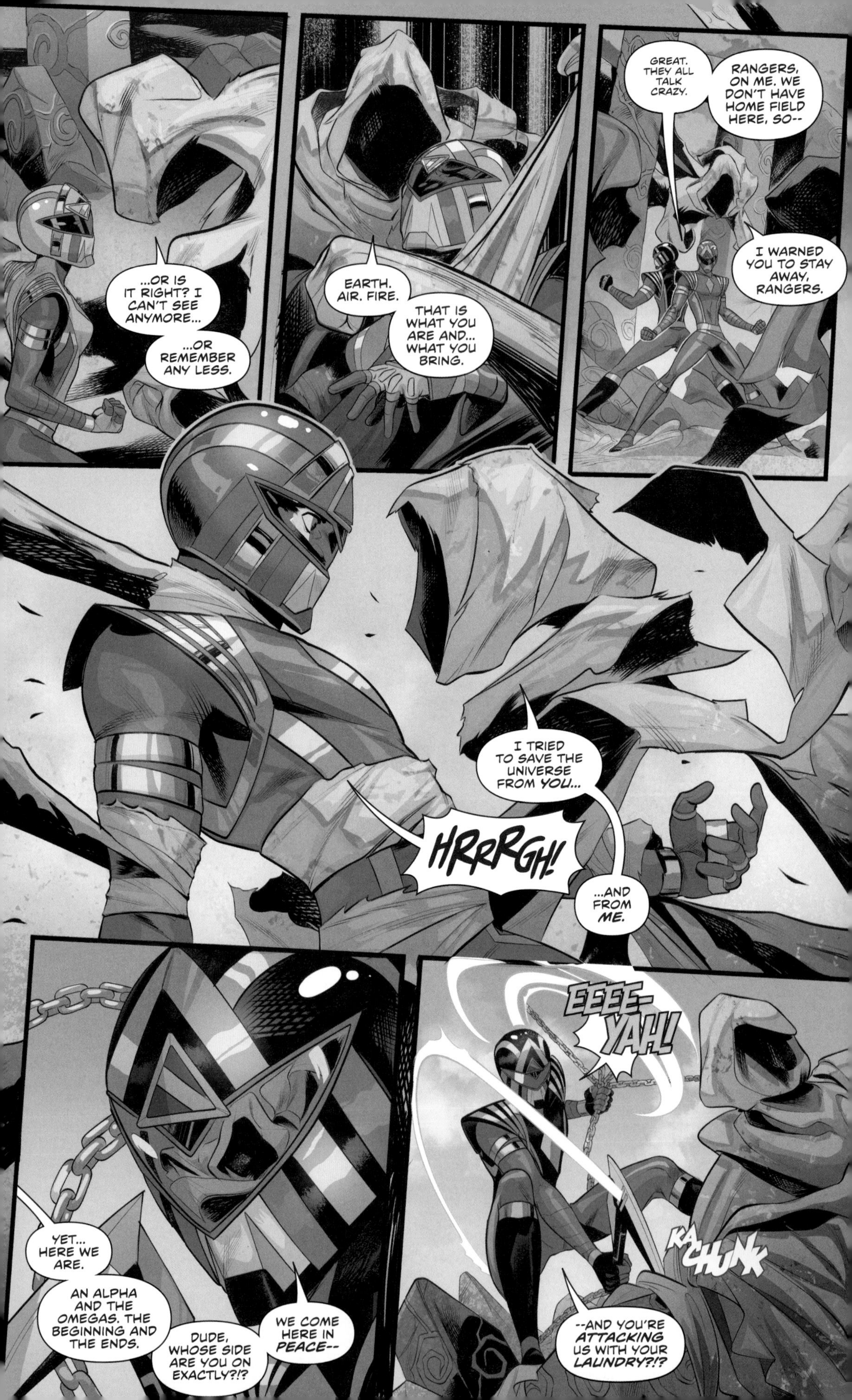
...OR IS IT RIGHT? I CAN'T SEE ANYMORE...
...OR REMEMBER ANY LESS.
EARTH. AIR. FIRE.
THAT IS WHAT YOU ARE AND... WHAT YOU BRING.
GREAT. THEY ALL TALK CRAZY.
RANGERS, ON ME. WE DON'T HAVE HOME FIELD HERE, SO--
I WARNED YOU TO STAY AWAY, RANGERS.
I TRIED TO SAVE THE UNIVERSE FROM *YOU*...
HRRRGH!
...AND FROM *ME*.
YET... HERE WE ARE.
AN ALPHA AND THE OMEGAS. THE BEGINNING AND THE ENDS.
DUDE, WHOSE SIDE ARE YOU ON EXACTLY?!?
WE COME HERE IN *PEACE*--
EEEE-YAH!
KA-CHUNK
--AND YOU'RE *ATTACKING* US WITH YOUR *LAUNDRY*?!?

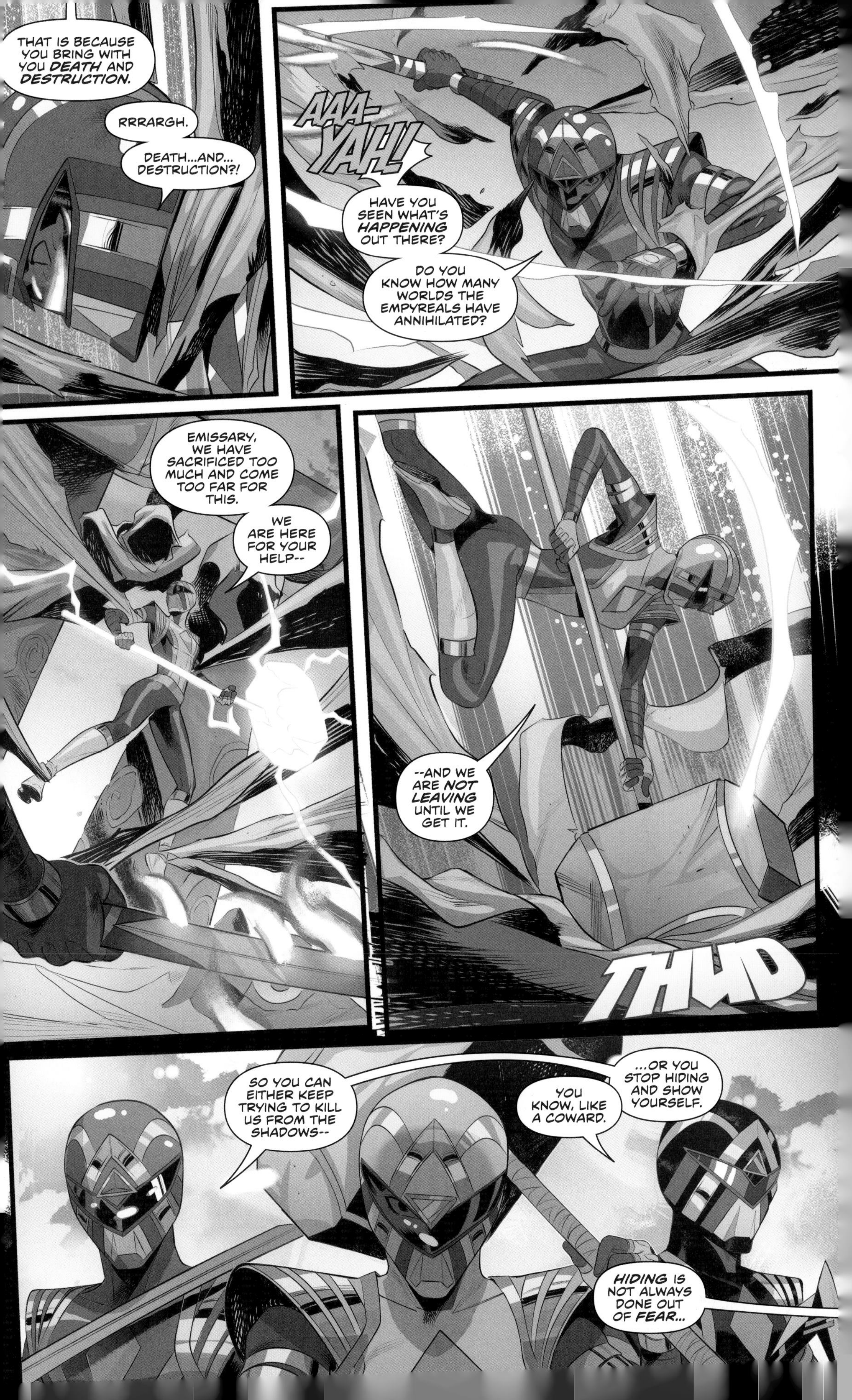
THAT IS BECAUSE YOU BRING WITH YOU DEATH AND DESTRUCTION.
RRRARGH.
DEATH...AND... DESTRUCTION?!
AAA-YAH!
HAVE YOU SEEN WHAT'S HAPPENING OUT THERE?
DO YOU KNOW HOW MANY WORLDS THE EMPYREALS HAVE ANNIHILATED?
EMISSARY, WE HAVE SACRIFICED TOO MUCH AND COME TOO FAR FOR THIS.
WE ARE HERE FOR YOUR HELP--
--AND WE ARE NOT LEAVING UNTIL WE GET IT.
THUD
SO YOU CAN EITHER KEEP TRYING TO KILL US FROM THE SHADOWS--
...OR YOU STOP HIDING AND SHOW YOURSELF.
YOU KNOW, LIKE A COWARD.
HIDING IS NOT ALWAYS DONE OUT OF FEAR...

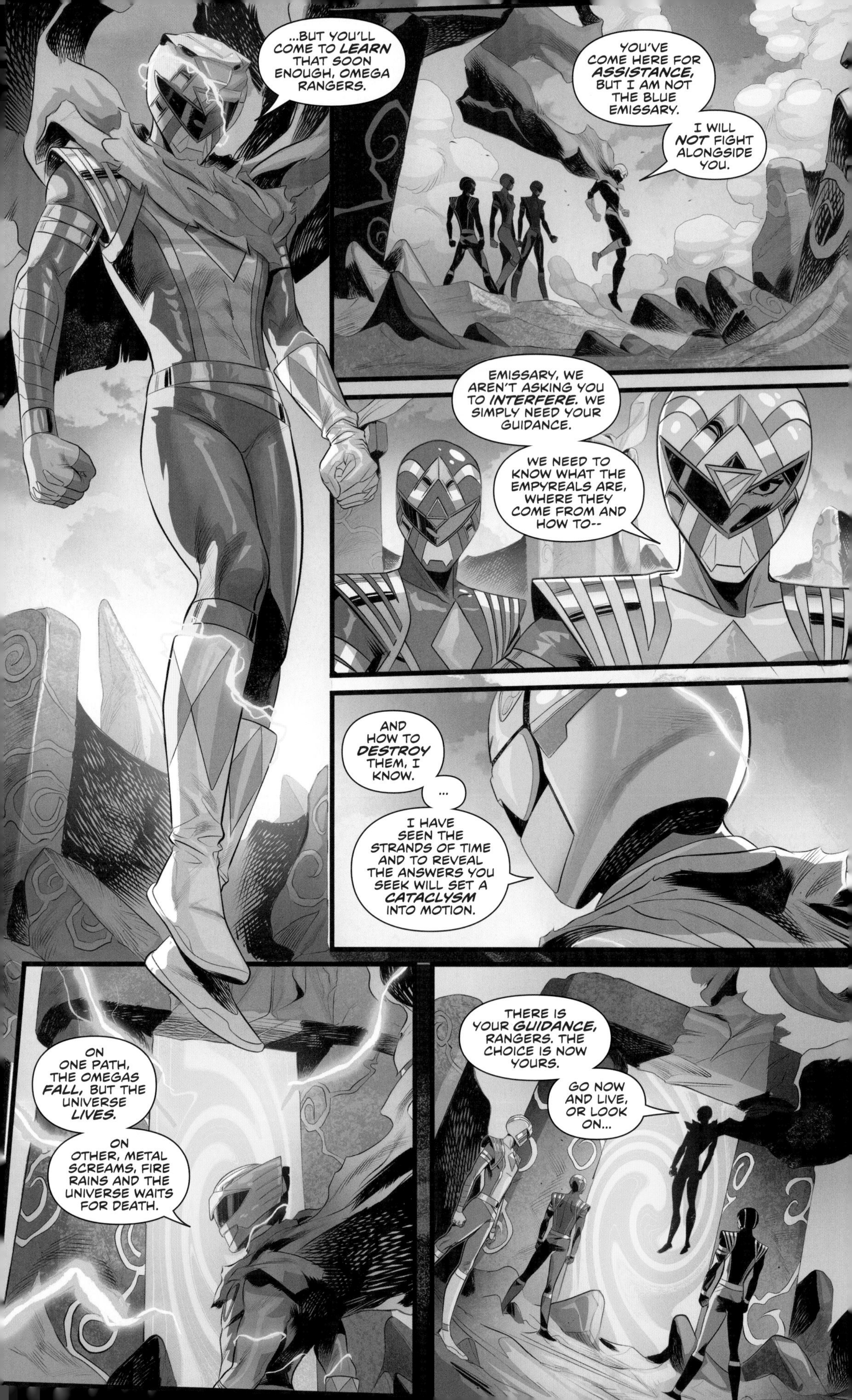
...BUT YOU'LL COME TO LEARN THAT SOON ENOUGH, OMEGA RANGERS.
YOU'VE COME HERE FOR ASSISTANCE, BUT I AM NOT THE BLUE EMISSARY.
I WILL NOT FIGHT ALONGSIDE YOU.
EMISSARY, WE AREN'T ASKING YOU TO INTERFERE. WE SIMPLY NEED YOUR GUIDANCE.
WE NEED TO KNOW WHAT THE EMPYREALS ARE, WHERE THEY COME FROM AND HOW TO--
AND HOW TO DESTROY THEM, I KNOW.
...
I HAVE SEEN THE STRANDS OF TIME AND TO REVEAL THE ANSWERS YOU SEEK WILL SET A CATACLYSM INTO MOTION.
ON ONE PATH, THE OMEGAS FALL, BUT THE UNIVERSE LIVES.
ON OTHER, METAL SCREAMS, FIRE RAINS AND THE UNIVERSE WAITS FOR DEATH.
THERE IS YOUR GUIDANCE, RANGERS. THE CHOICE IS NOW YOURS.
GO NOW AND LIVE, OR LOOK ON...

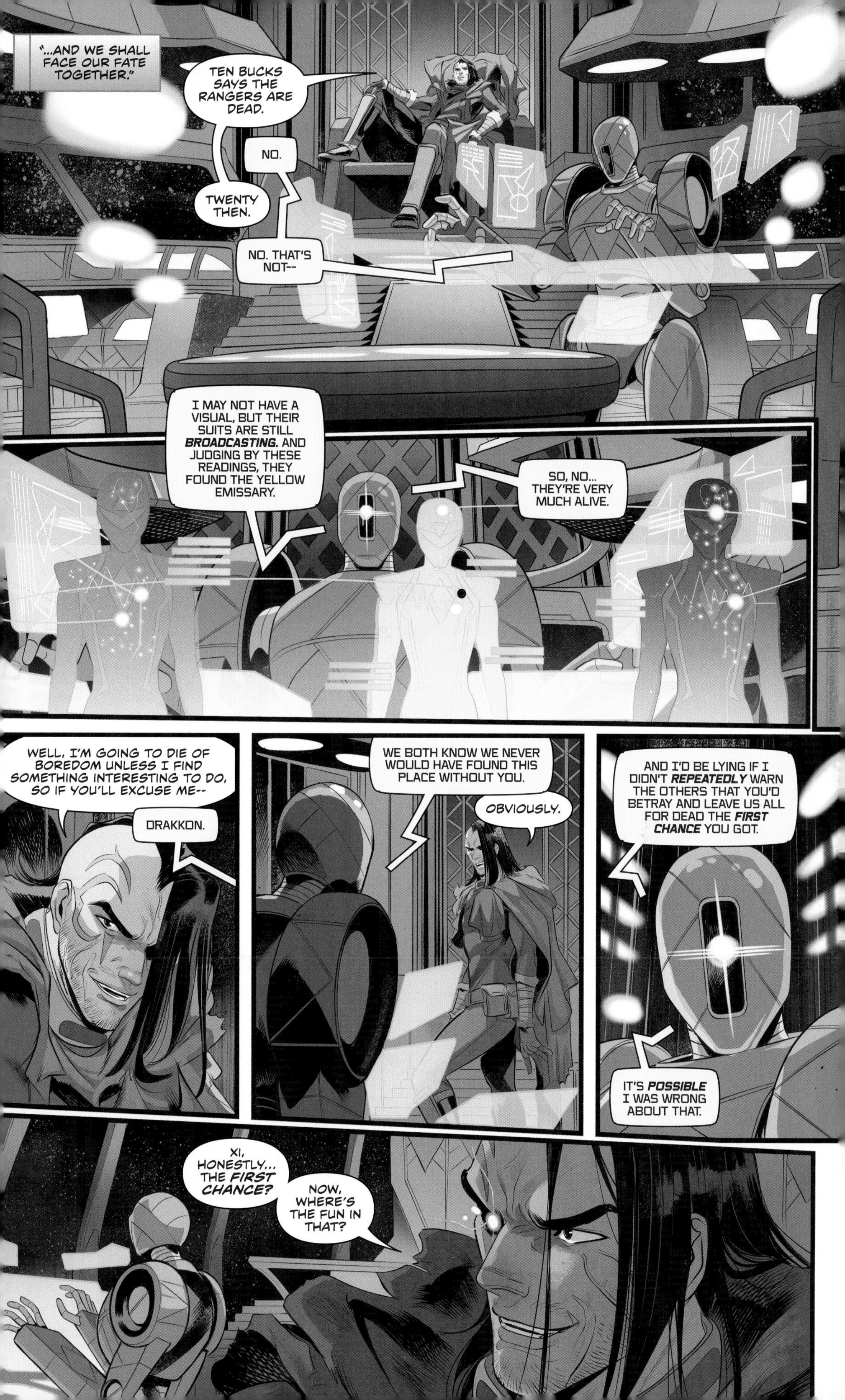
"...AND WE SHALL FACE OUR FATE TOGETHER."
TEN BUCKS SAYS THE RANGERS ARE DEAD.
NO.
TWENTY THEN.
NO. THAT'S NOT--
I MAY NOT HAVE A VISUAL, BUT THEIR SUITS ARE STILL BROADCASTING. AND JUDGING BY THESE READINGS, THEY FOUND THE YELLOW EMISSARY.
SO, NO... THEY'RE VERY MUCH ALIVE.
WELL, I'M GOING TO DIE OF BOREDOM UNLESS I FIND SOMETHING INTERESTING TO DO, SO IF YOU'LL EXCUSE ME--
DRAKKON.
WE BOTH KNOW WE NEVER WOULD HAVE FOUND THIS PLACE WITHOUT YOU.
OBVIOUSLY.
AND I'D BE LYING IF I DIDN'T REPEATEDLY WARN THE OTHERS THAT YOU'D BETRAY AND LEAVE US ALL FOR DEAD THE FIRST CHANCE YOU GOT.
IT'S POSSIBLE I WAS WRONG ABOUT THAT.
XI, HONESTLY... THE FIRST CHANCE?
NOW, WHERE'S THE FUN IN THAT?

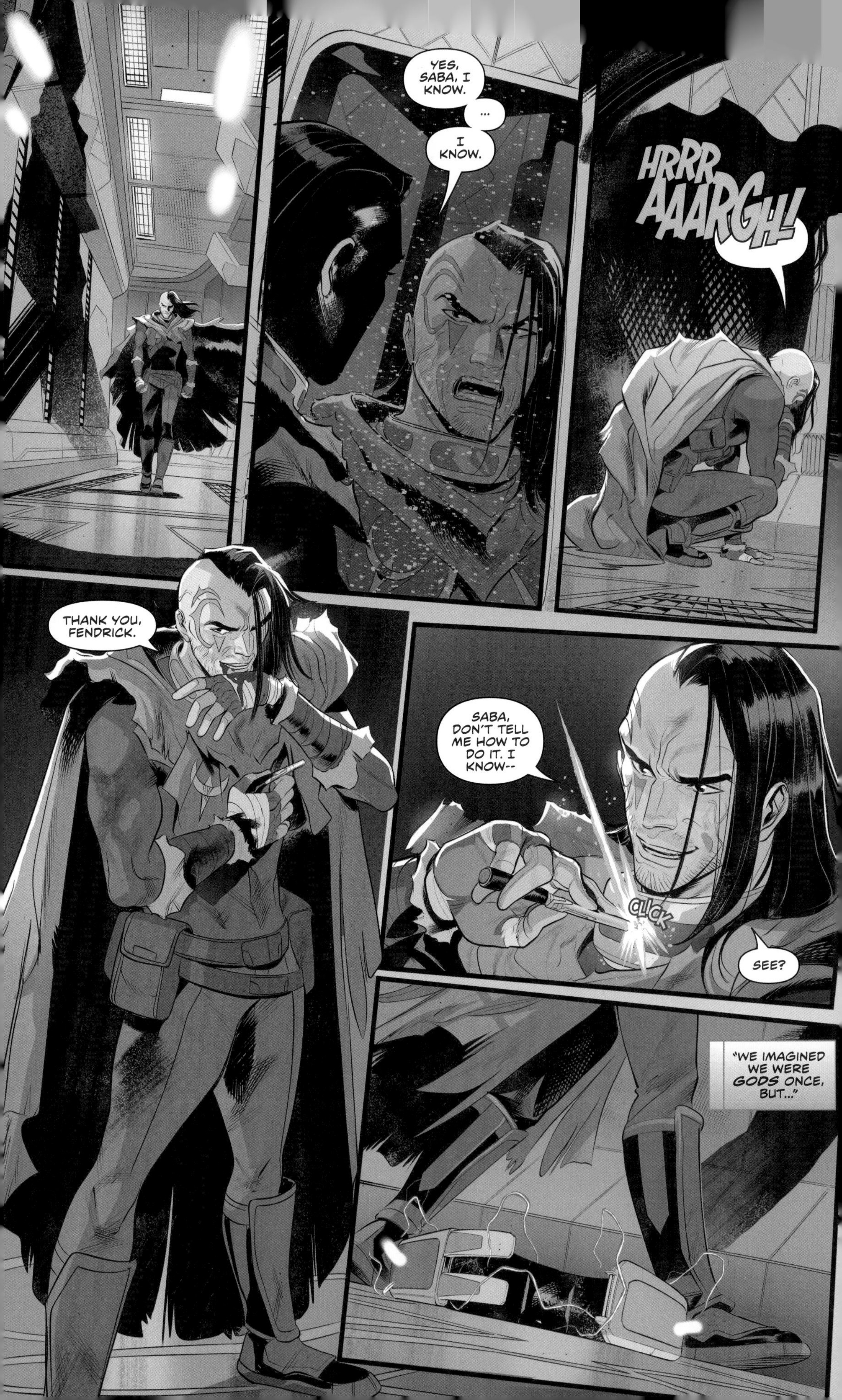
YES, SABA, I KNOW.
...
I KNOW.
HRRR AAARGH!
THANK YOU, FENDRICK.
SABA, DON'T TELL ME HOW TO DO IT. I KNOW--
CLICK
SEE?
"WE IMAGINED WE WERE GODS ONCE, BUT..."

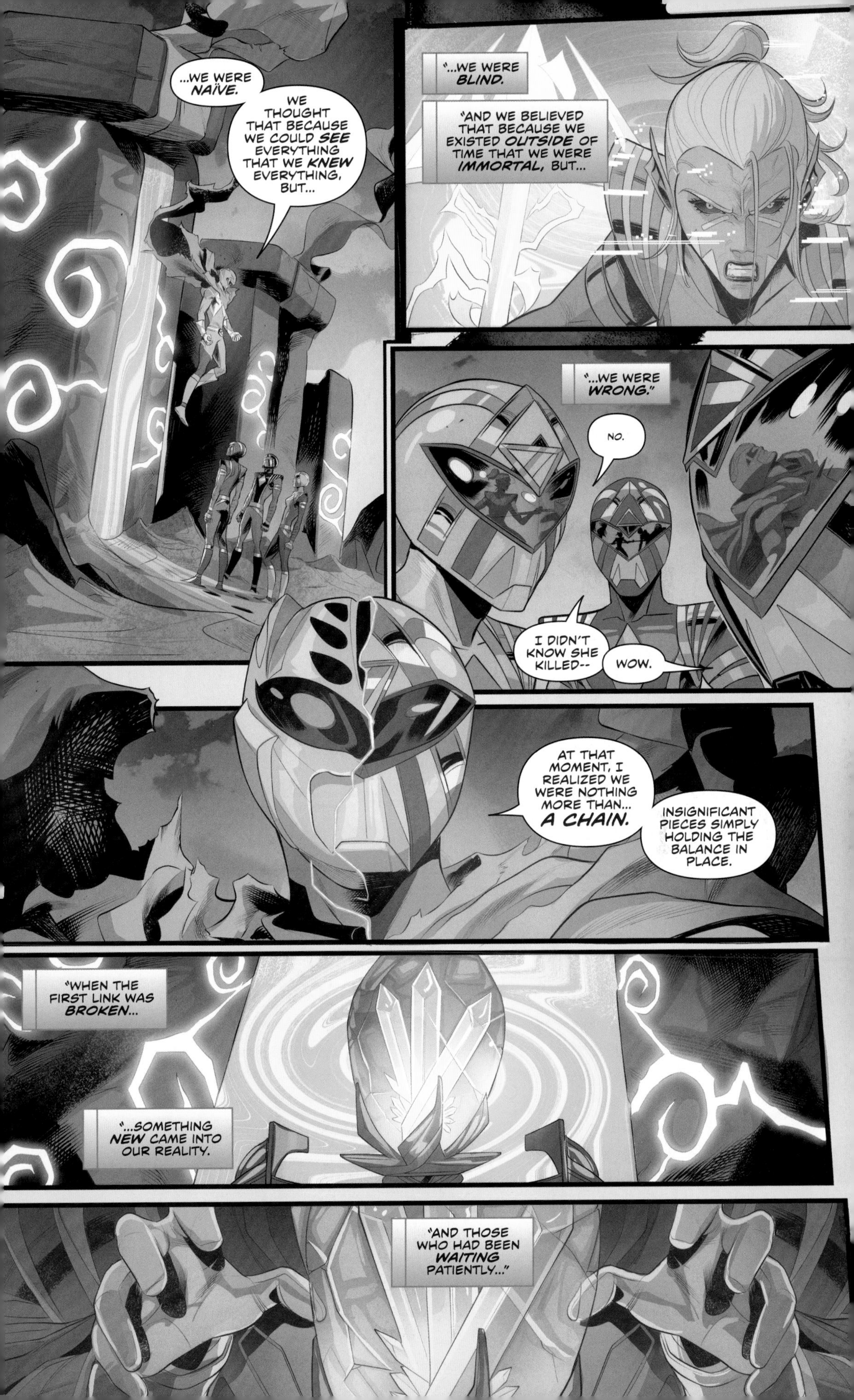
...WE WERE NAÏVE.
WE THOUGHT THAT BECAUSE WE COULD SEE EVERYTHING THAT WE KNEW EVERYTHING, BUT...
"...WE WERE BLIND.
"AND WE BELIEVED THAT BECAUSE WE EXISTED OUTSIDE OF TIME THAT WE WERE IMMORTAL, BUT...
"...WE WERE WRONG."
NO.
I DIDN'T KNOW SHE KILLED--
WOW.
AT THAT MOMENT, I REALIZED WE WERE NOTHING MORE THAN... A CHAIN.
INSIGNIFICANT PIECES SIMPLY HOLDING THE BALANCE IN PLACE.
"WHEN THE FIRST LINK WAS BROKEN...
"...SOMETHING NEW CAME INTO OUR REALITY.
"AND THOSE WHO HAD BEEN WAITING PATIENTLY..."

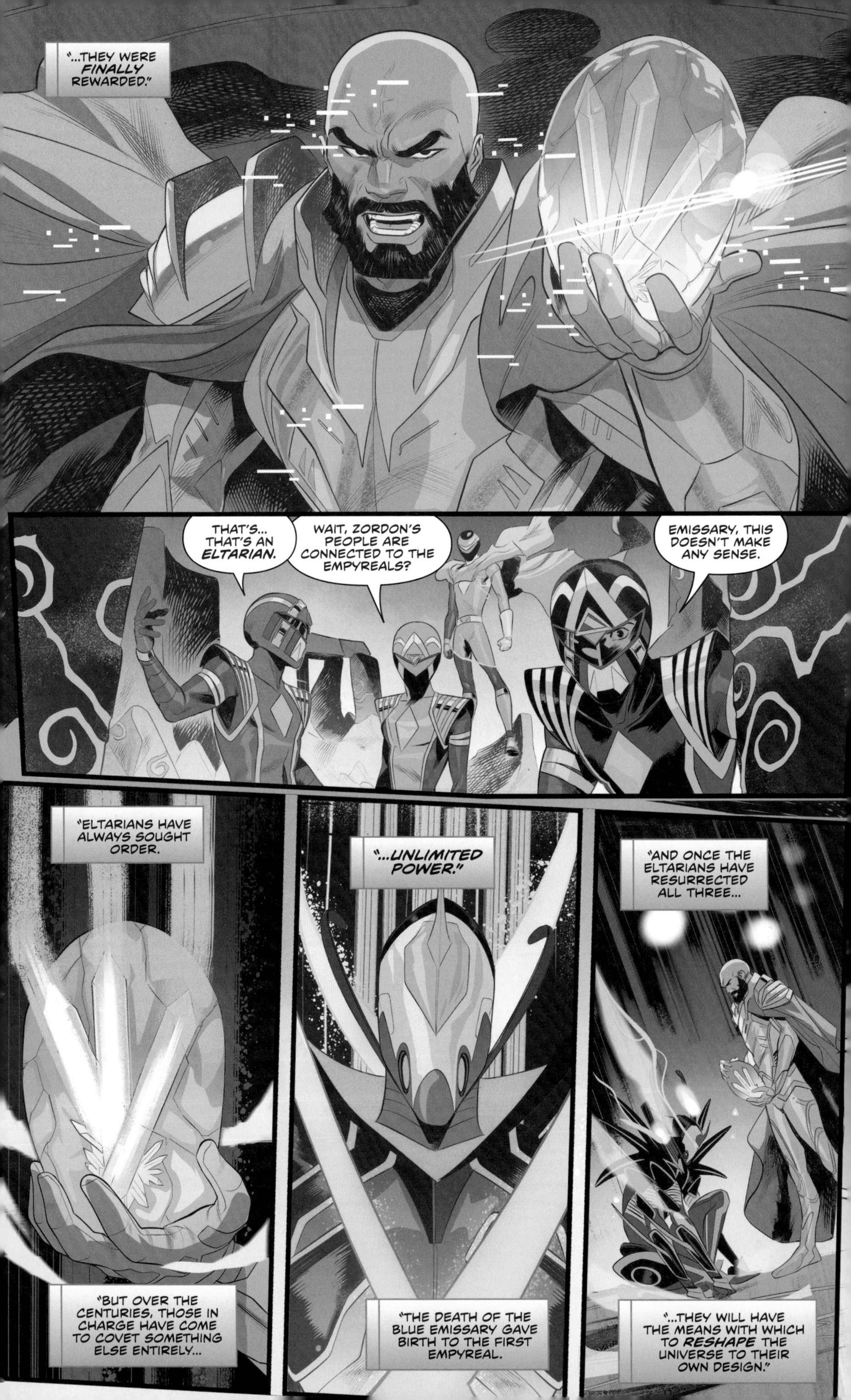
"...THEY WERE *FINALLY* REWARDED."
THAT'S... THAT'S AN *ELTARIAN.*
WAIT, ZORDON'S PEOPLE ARE CONNECTED TO THE EMPYREALS?
EMISSARY, THIS DOESN'T MAKE ANY SENSE.
"ELTARIANS HAVE ALWAYS SOUGHT ORDER.
"BUT OVER THE CENTURIES, THOSE IN CHARGE HAVE COME TO COVET SOMETHING ELSE ENTIRELY...
"...*UNLIMITED POWER.*"
"THE DEATH OF THE BLUE EMISSARY GAVE BIRTH TO THE FIRST EMPYREAL.
"AND ONCE THE ELTARIANS HAVE RESURRECTED ALL THREE...
"...THEY WILL HAVE THE MEANS WITH WHICH TO *RESHAPE* THE UNIVERSE TO THEIR OWN DESIGN."

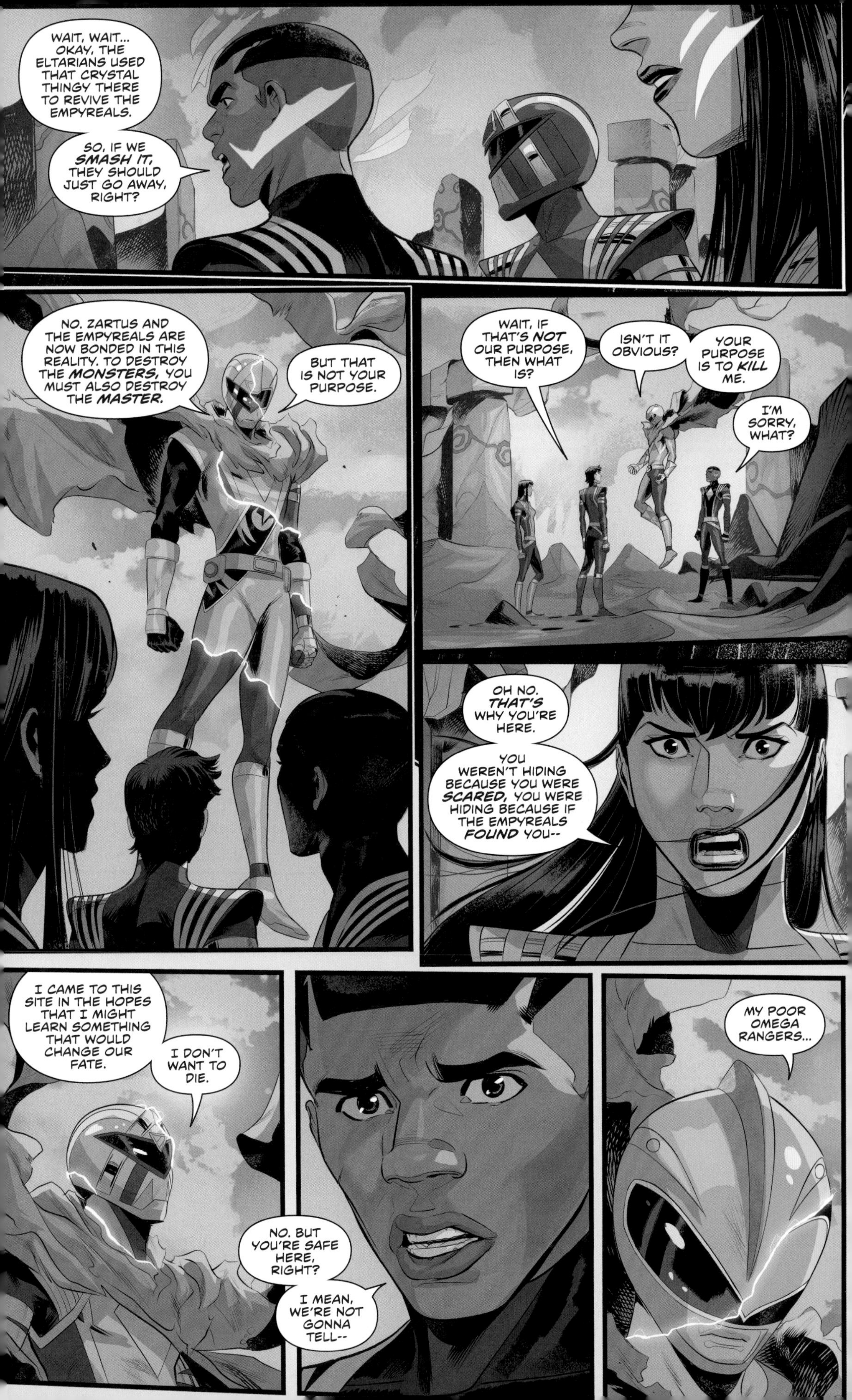
WAIT, WAIT... OKAY, THE ELTARIANS USED THAT CRYSTAL THINGY THERE TO REVIVE THE EMPYREALS.
SO, IF WE SMASH IT, THEY SHOULD JUST GO AWAY, RIGHT?
NO. ZARTUS AND THE EMPYREALS ARE NOW BONDED IN THIS REALITY. TO DESTROY THE MONSTERS, YOU MUST ALSO DESTROY THE MASTER.
BUT THAT IS NOT YOUR PURPOSE.
WAIT, IF THAT'S NOT OUR PURPOSE, THEN WHAT IS?
ISN'T IT OBVIOUS?
YOUR PURPOSE IS TO KILL ME.
I'M SORRY, WHAT?
OH NO. THAT'S WHY YOU'RE HERE.
YOU WEREN'T HIDING BECAUSE YOU WERE SCARED, YOU WERE HIDING BECAUSE IF THE EMPYREALS FOUND YOU--
I CAME TO THIS SITE IN THE HOPES THAT I MIGHT LEARN SOMETHING THAT WOULD CHANGE OUR FATE.
I DON'T WANT TO DIE.
NO. BUT YOU'RE SAFE HERE, RIGHT?
I MEAN, WE'RE NOT GONNA TELL--
MY POOR OMEGA RANGERS...

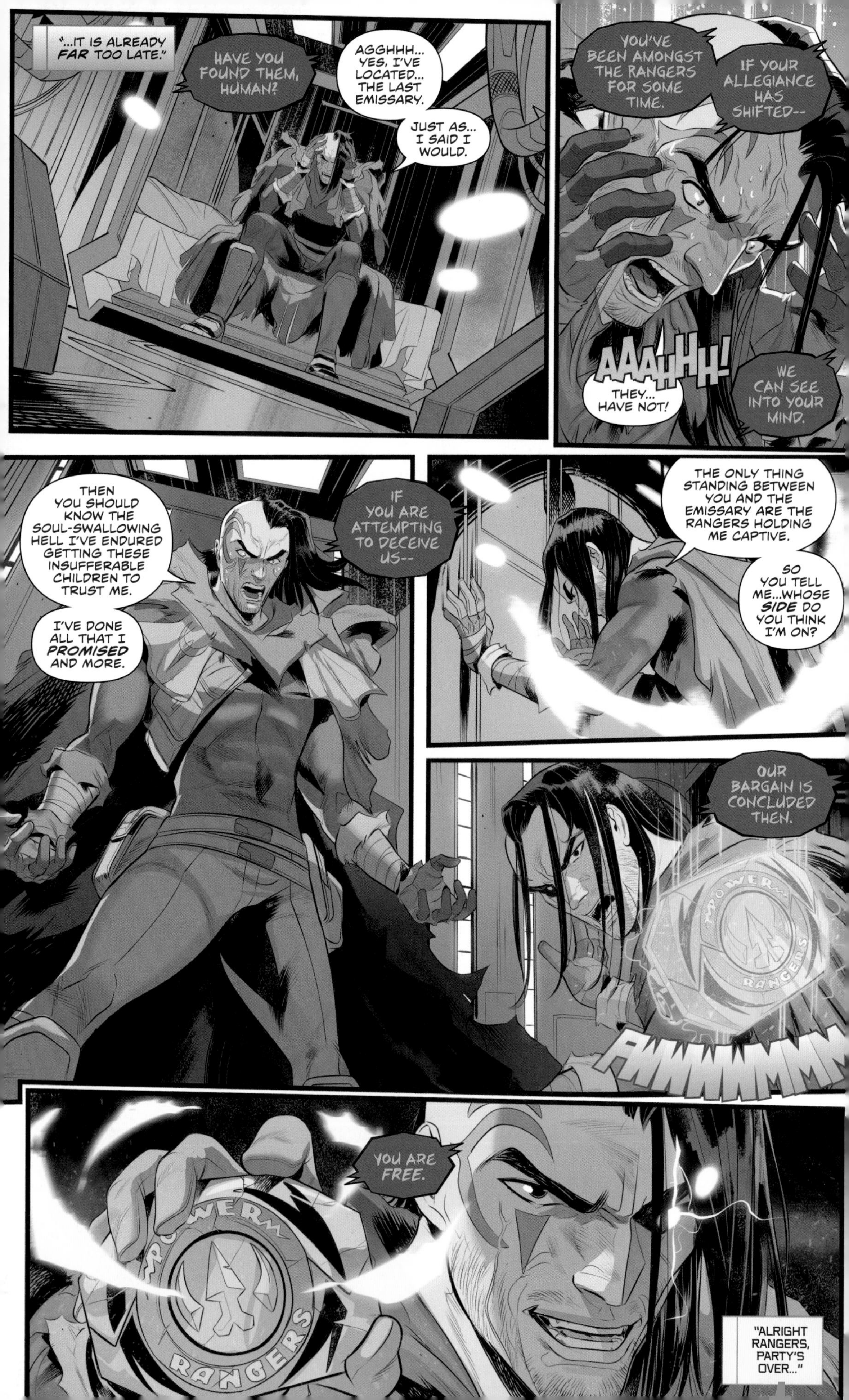
"...IT IS ALREADY FAR TOO LATE."
HAVE YOU FOUND THEM, HUMAN?
AGGHHH... YES, I'VE LOCATED... THE LAST EMISSARY.
JUST AS... I SAID I WOULD.
YOU'VE BEEN AMONGST THE RANGERS FOR SOME TIME.
IF YOUR ALLEGIANCE HAS SHIFTED--
AAAHHH!
THEY... HAVE NOT!
WE CAN SEE INTO YOUR MIND.
THEN YOU SHOULD KNOW THE SOUL-SWALLOWING HELL I'VE ENDURED GETTING THESE INSUFFERABLE CHILDREN TO TRUST ME.
IF YOU ARE ATTEMPTING TO DECEIVE US--
I'VE DONE ALL THAT I PROMISED AND MORE.
THE ONLY THING STANDING BETWEEN YOU AND THE EMISSARY ARE THE RANGERS HOLDING ME CAPTIVE.
SO YOU TELL ME...WHOSE SIDE DO YOU THINK I'M ON?
OUR BARGAIN IS CONCLUDED THEN.
YOU ARE FREE.
"ALRIGHT RANGERS, PARTY'S OVER..."

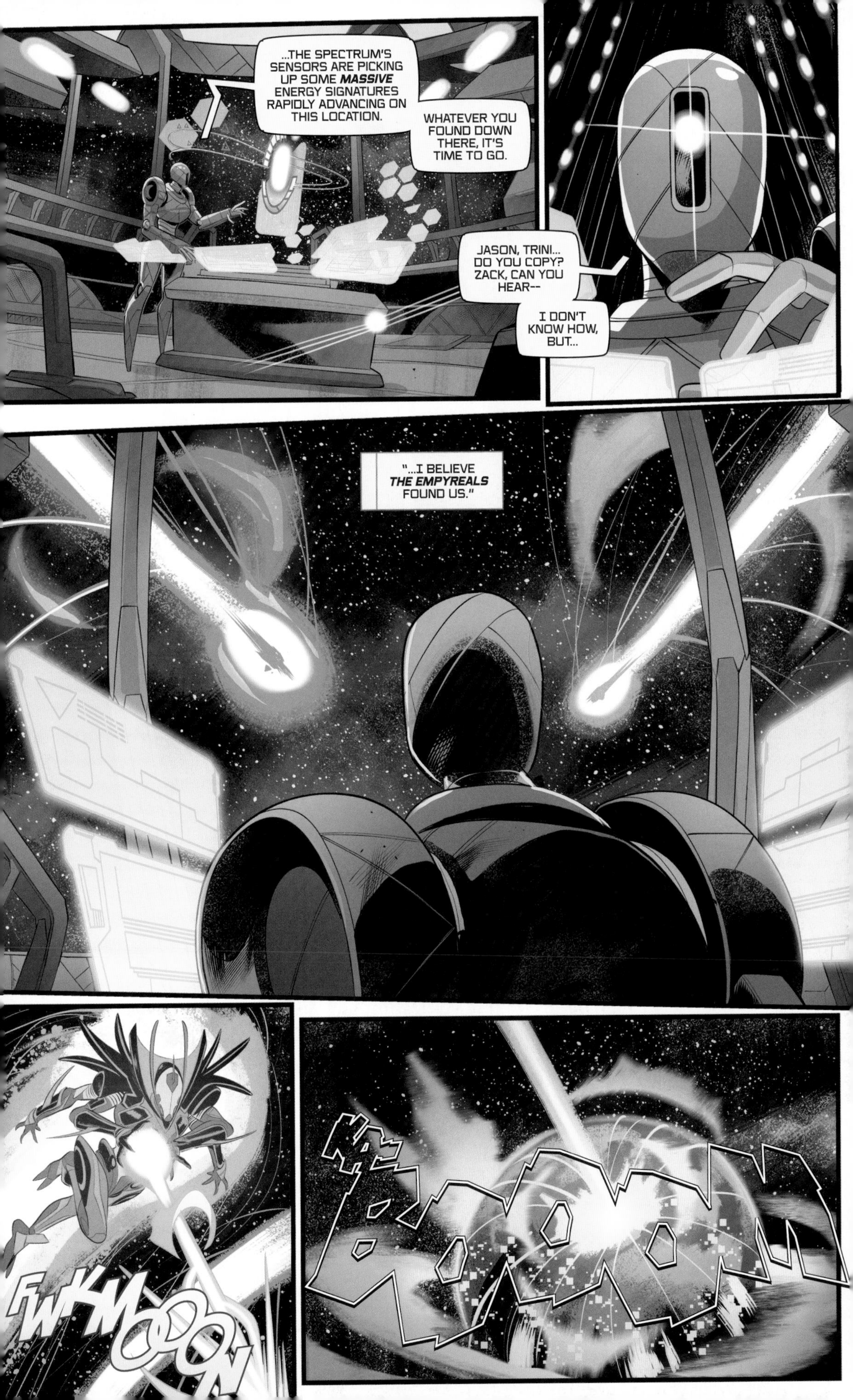
...THE SPECTRUM'S SENSORS ARE PICKING UP SOME MASSIVE ENERGY SIGNATURES RAPIDLY ADVANCING ON THIS LOCATION.
WHATEVER YOU FOUND DOWN THERE, IT'S TIME TO GO.
JASON, TRINI... DO YOU COPY? ZACK, CAN YOU HEAR--
I DON'T KNOW HOW, BUT...
"...I BELIEVE THE EMPYREALS FOUND US."
FWKMOOON
KA-BOOOM

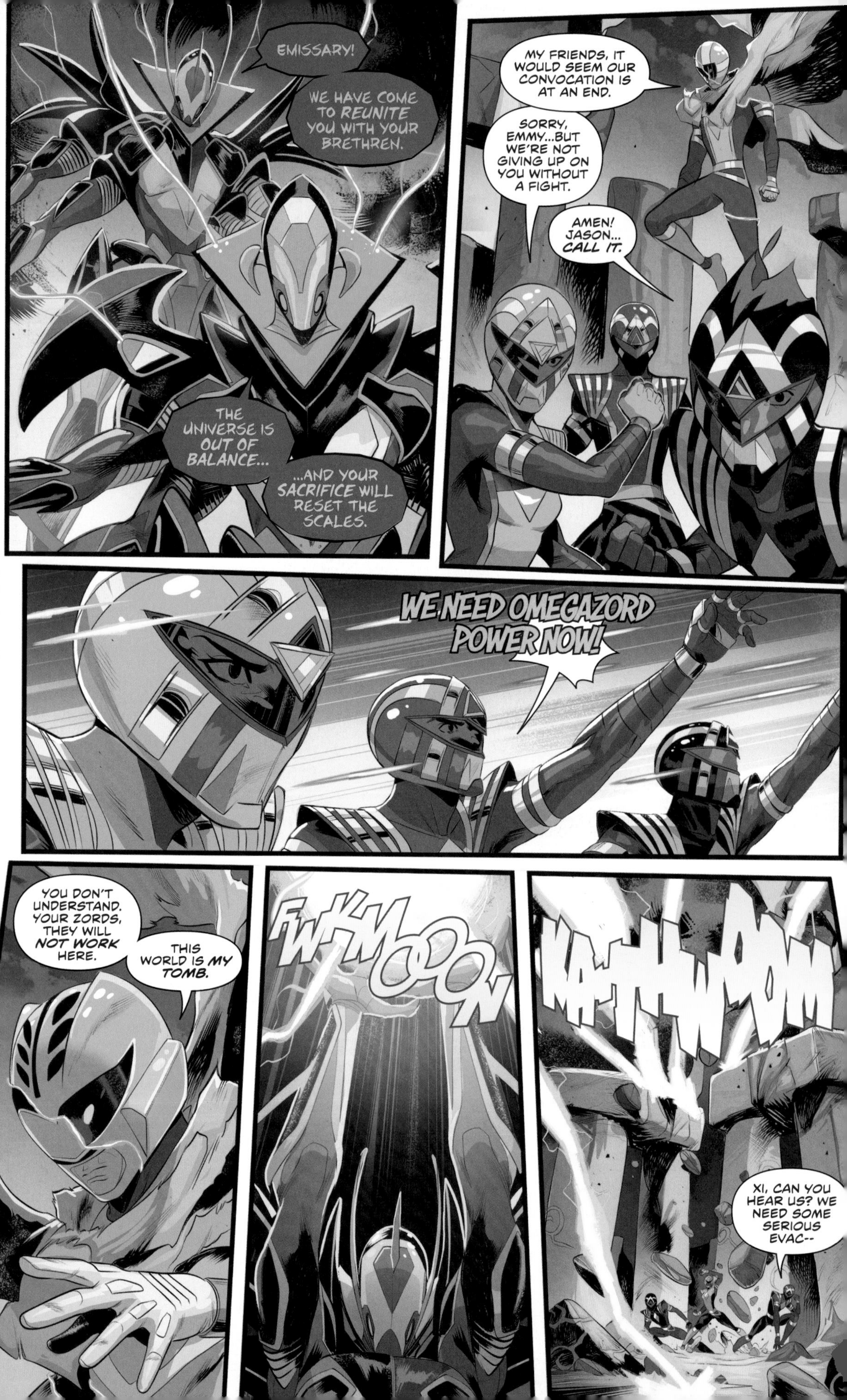
EMISSARY!
WE HAVE COME TO *REUNITE* YOU WITH YOUR BRETHREN.
THE UNIVERSE IS *OUT OF BALANCE*...
...AND YOUR *SACRIFICE* WILL RESET THE SCALES.
MY FRIENDS, IT WOULD SEEM OUR CONVOCATION IS AT AN END.
SORRY, EMMY...BUT WE'RE NOT GIVING UP ON YOU WITHOUT A FIGHT.
AMEN! JASON... ***CALL IT.***
WE NEED OMEGAZORD POWER NOW!
YOU DON'T UNDERSTAND. YOUR ZORDS, THEY WILL ***NOT WORK*** HERE.
THIS WORLD IS ***MY TOMB.***
FWKMOOOON
KA-THWOOM
XI, CAN YOU HEAR US? WE NEED SOME SERIOUS EVAC--

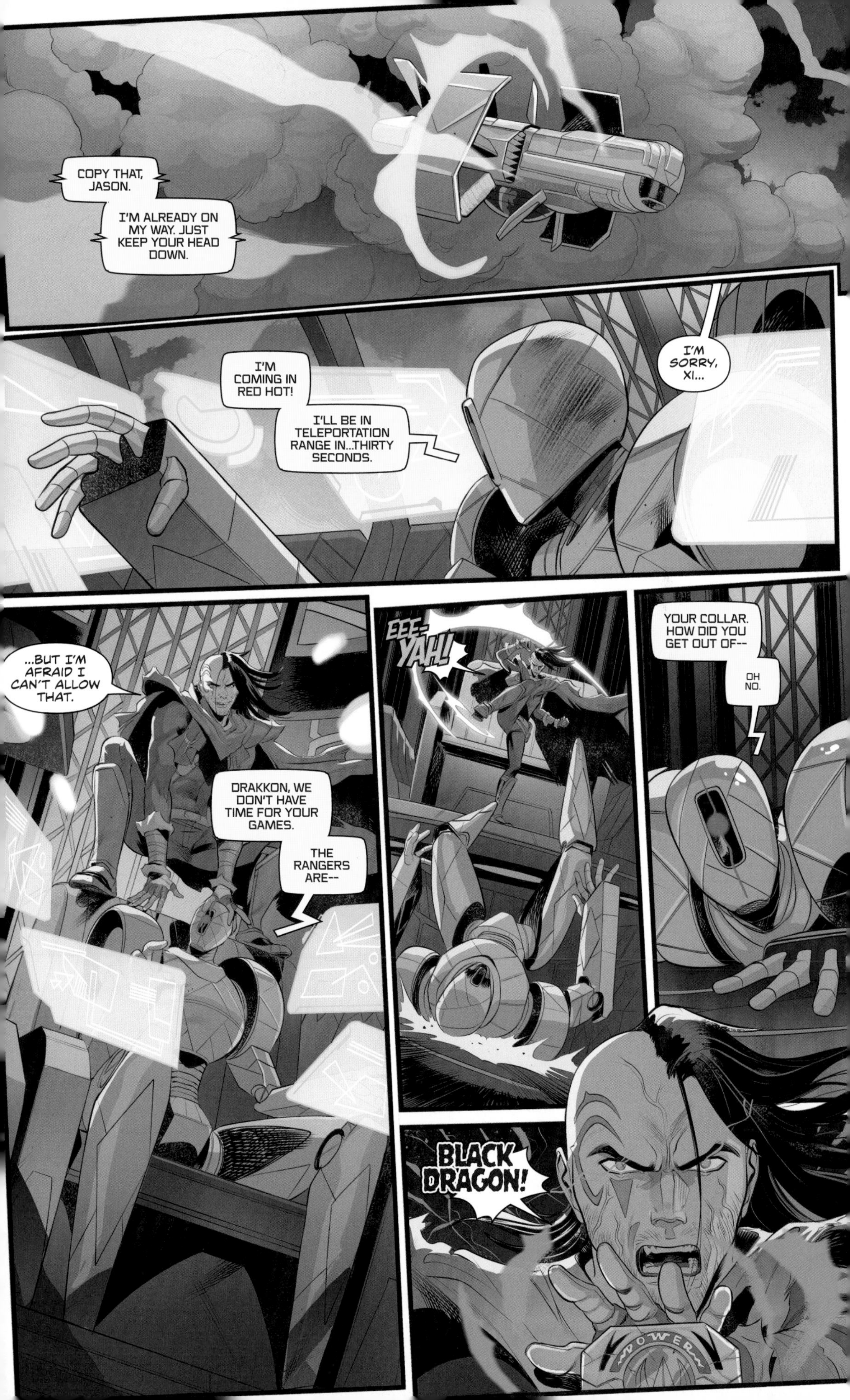
COPY THAT, JASON.
I'M ALREADY ON MY WAY. JUST KEEP YOUR HEAD DOWN.
I'M COMING IN RED HOT!
I'LL BE IN TELEPORTATION RANGE IN...THIRTY SECONDS.
I'M SORRY, XI...
...BUT I'M AFRAID I CAN'T ALLOW THAT.
DRAKKON, WE DON'T HAVE TIME FOR YOUR GAMES.
THE RANGERS ARE--
EEE-YAH!
YOUR COLLAR. HOW DID YOU GET OUT OF--
OH NO.
BLACK DRAGON!

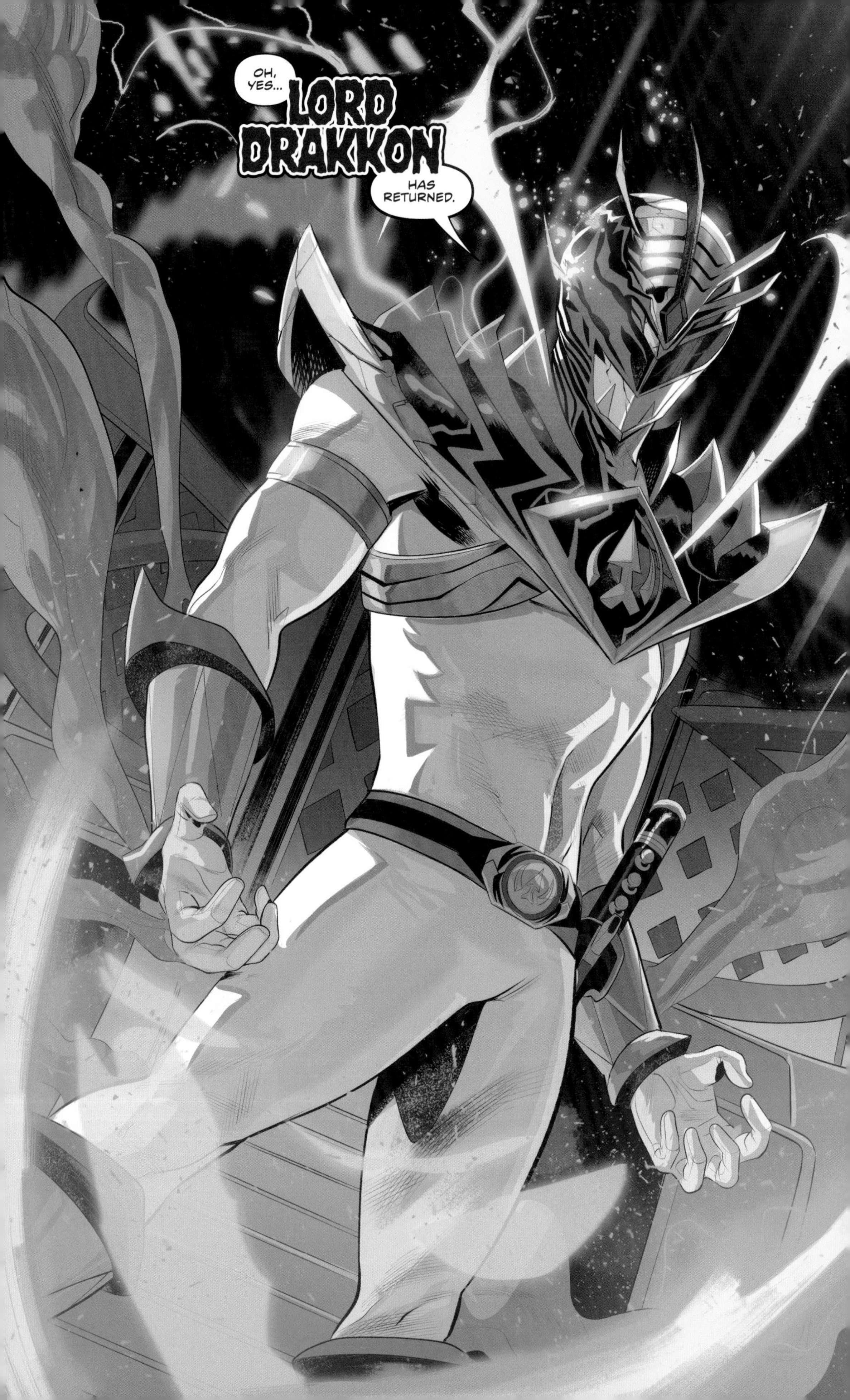
OH, YES...
LORD DRAKKON
HAS RETURNED.

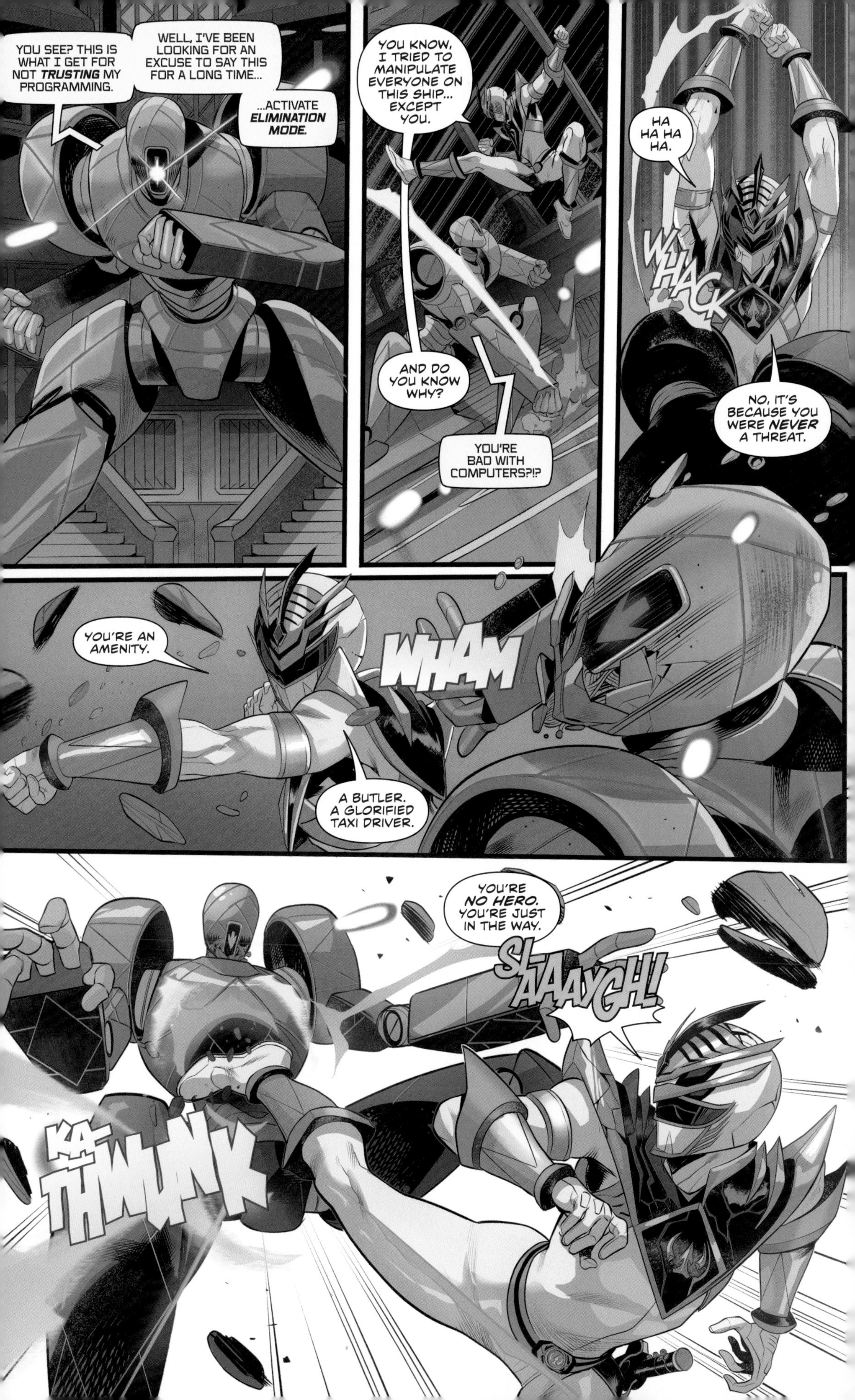
YOU SEE? THIS IS WHAT I GET FOR NOT TRUSTING MY PROGRAMMING.
WELL, I'VE BEEN LOOKING FOR AN EXCUSE TO SAY THIS FOR A LONG TIME...
...ACTIVATE ELIMINATION MODE.
YOU KNOW, I TRIED TO MANIPULATE EVERYONE ON THIS SHIP... EXCEPT YOU.
AND DO YOU KNOW WHY?
YOU'RE BAD WITH COMPUTERS?!?
HA HA HA HA.
WHACK
NO, IT'S BECAUSE YOU WERE NEVER A THREAT.
YOU'RE AN AMENITY.
WHAM
A BUTLER. A GLORIFIED TAXI DRIVER.
YOU'RE NO HERO. YOU'RE JUST IN THE WAY.
SLAAAYGH!
KA-THWUNK

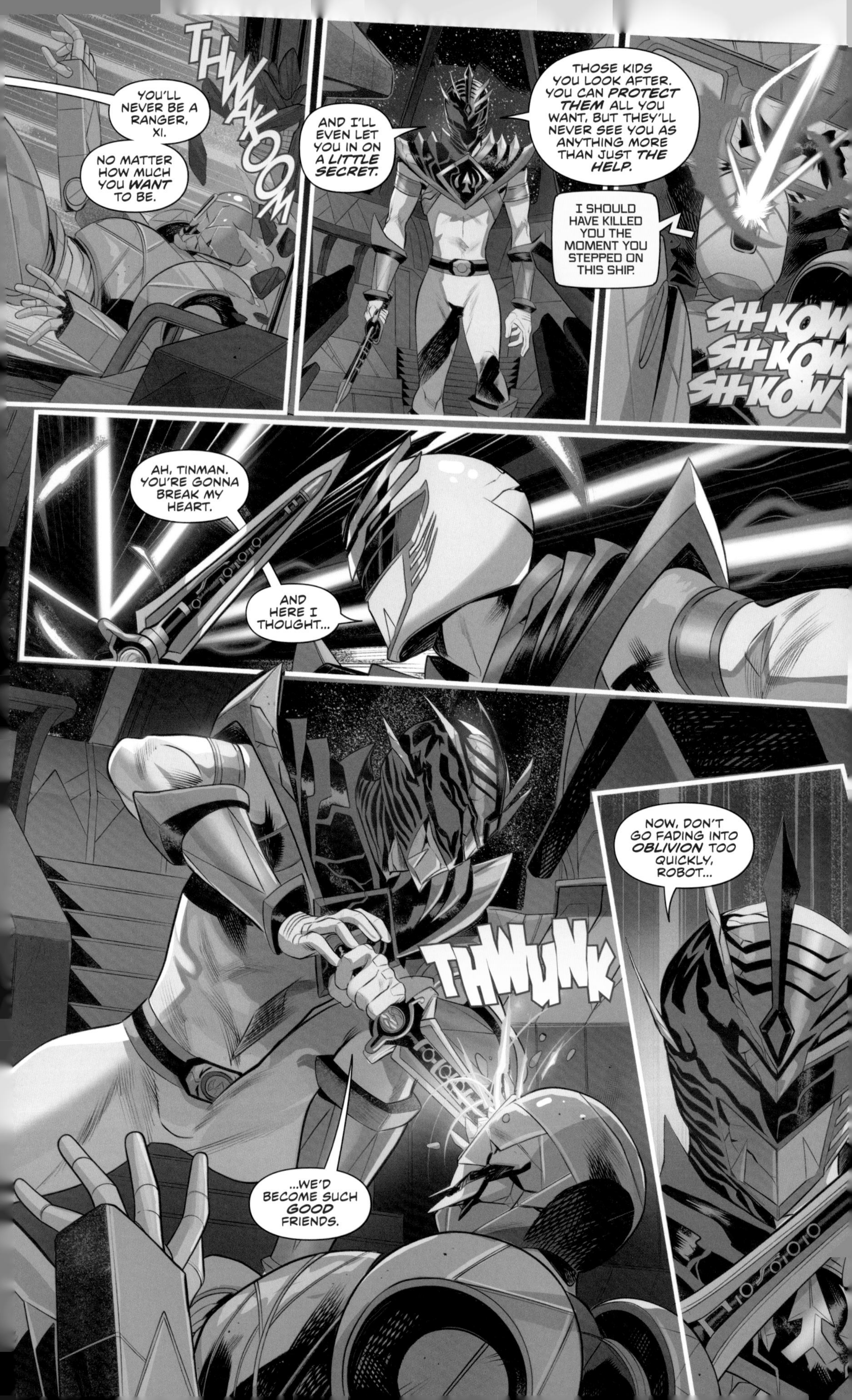
THWAKOOM
YOU'LL NEVER BE A RANGER, XI.
NO MATTER HOW MUCH YOU WANT TO BE.
AND I'LL EVEN LET YOU IN ON A LITTLE SECRET.
THOSE KIDS YOU LOOK AFTER. YOU CAN PROTECT THEM ALL YOU WANT, BUT THEY'LL NEVER SEE YOU AS ANYTHING MORE THAN JUST THE HELP.
I SHOULD HAVE KILLED YOU THE MOMENT YOU STEPPED ON THIS SHIP.
SH-KOW SH-KOW SH-KOW
AH, TINMAN. YOU'RE GONNA BREAK MY HEART.
AND HERE I THOUGHT...
...WE'D BECOME SUCH GOOD FRIENDS.
THWUNK
NOW, DON'T GO FADING INTO OBLIVION TOO QUICKLY, ROBOT...

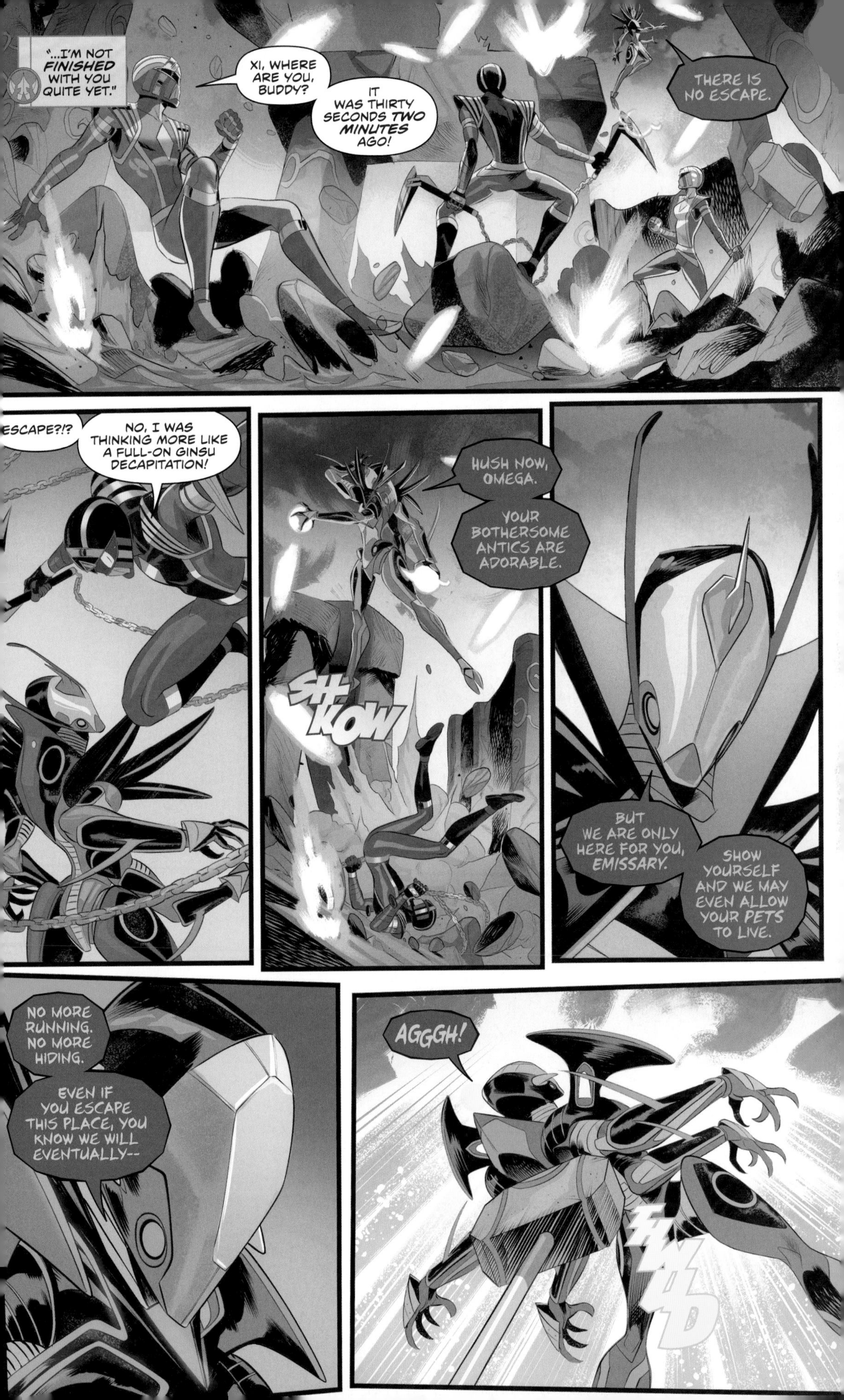
"...I'M NOT FINISHED WITH YOU QUITE YET."
XI, WHERE ARE YOU, BUDDY?
IT WAS THIRTY SECONDS TWO MINUTES AGO!
THERE IS NO ESCAPE.
ESCAPE?!?
NO, I WAS THINKING MORE LIKE A FULL-ON GINSU DECAPITATION!
HUSH NOW, OMEGA.
YOUR BOTHERSOME ANTICS ARE ADORABLE.
SH-KOW
BUT WE ARE ONLY HERE FOR YOU, EMISSARY.
SHOW YOURSELF AND WE MAY EVEN ALLOW YOUR PETS TO LIVE.
NO MORE RUNNING. NO MORE HIDING.
EVEN IF YOU ESCAPE THIS PLACE, YOU KNOW WE WILL EVENTUALLY--
AGGGH!
THWAD

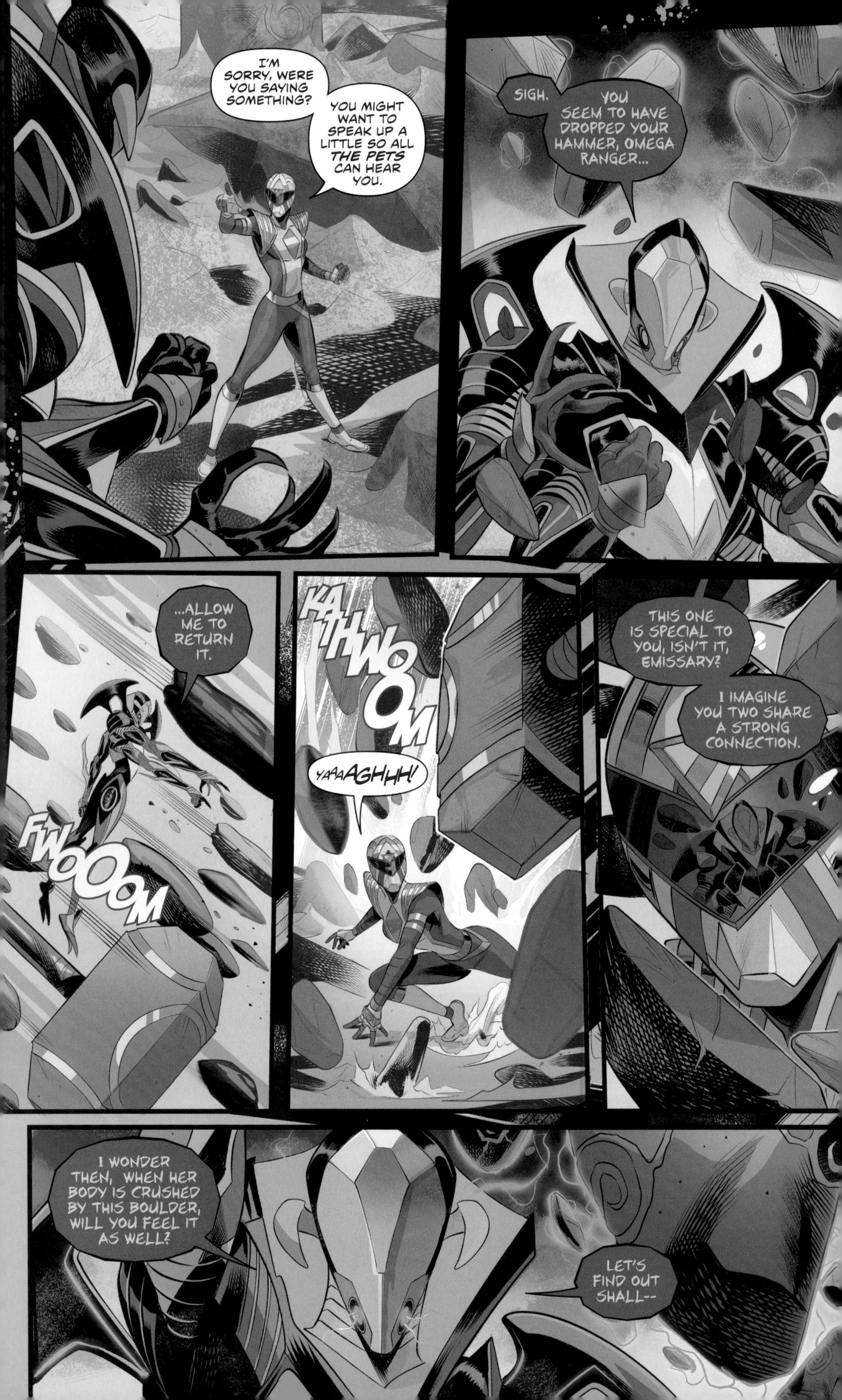

I'M SORRY, WERE YOU SAYING SOMETHING?
YOU MIGHT WANT TO SPEAK UP A LITTLE SO ALL THE PETS CAN HEAR YOU.
SIGH.
YOU SEEM TO HAVE DROPPED YOUR HAMMER, OMEGA RANGER...
...ALLOW ME TO RETURN IT.
FWOOOM
KATHWOOM
YAAAAGHHH!
THIS ONE IS SPECIAL TO YOU, ISN'T IT, EMISSARY?
I IMAGINE YOU TWO SHARE A STRONG CONNECTION.
I WONDER THEN, WHEN HER BODY IS CRUSHED BY THIS BOULDER, WILL YOU FEEL IT AS WELL?
LET'S FIND OUT SHALL--

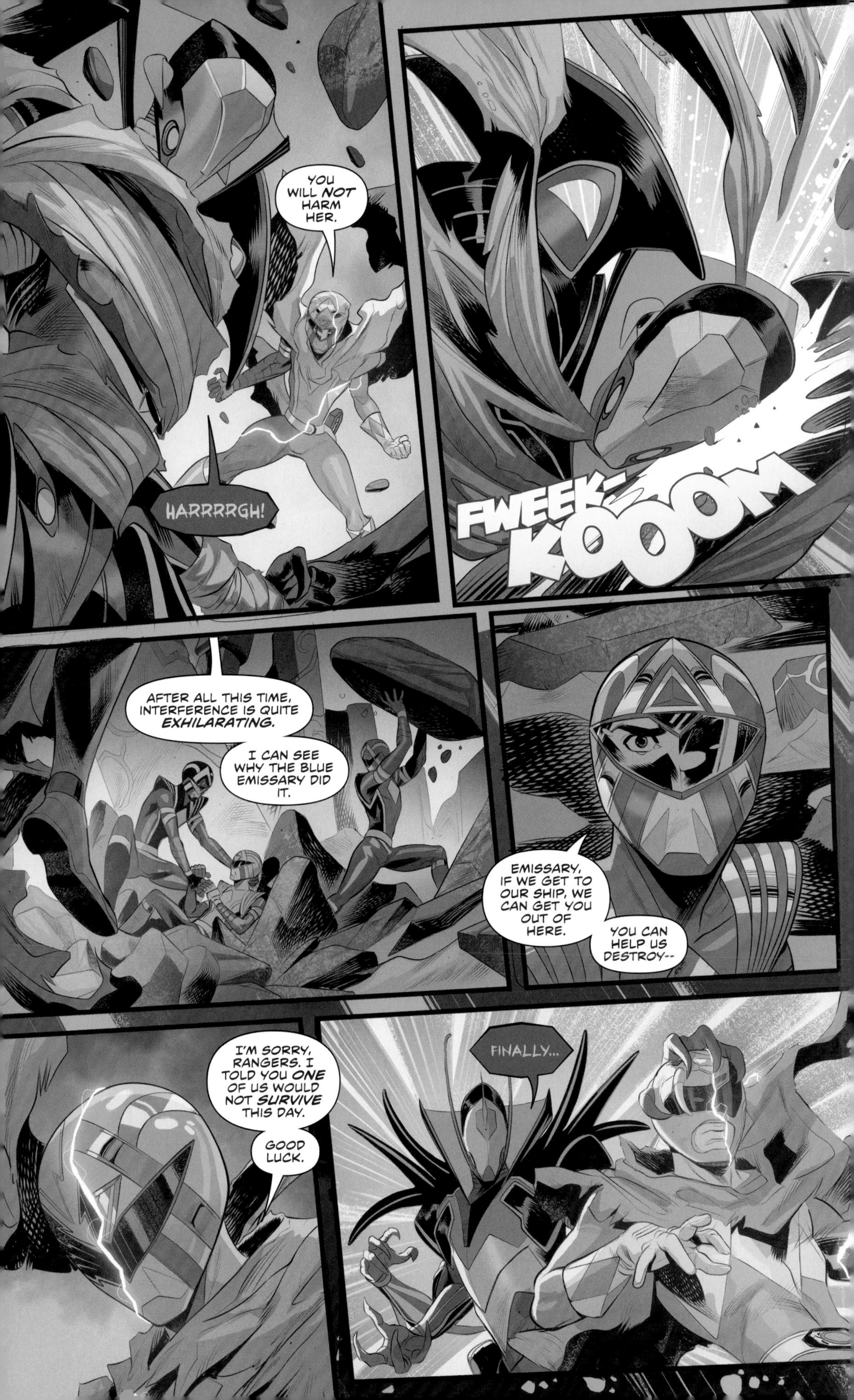
YOU WILL NOT HARM HER.
HARRRRGH!
FWEEK-KOOOM
AFTER ALL THIS TIME, INTERFERENCE IS QUITE EXHILARATING.
I CAN SEE WHY THE BLUE EMISSARY DID IT.
EMISSARY, IF WE GET TO OUR SHIP, WE CAN GET YOU OUT OF HERE.
YOU CAN HELP US DESTROY--
I'M SORRY, RANGERS. I TOLD YOU ONE OF US WOULD NOT SURVIVE THIS DAY.
GOOD LUCK.
FINALLY...

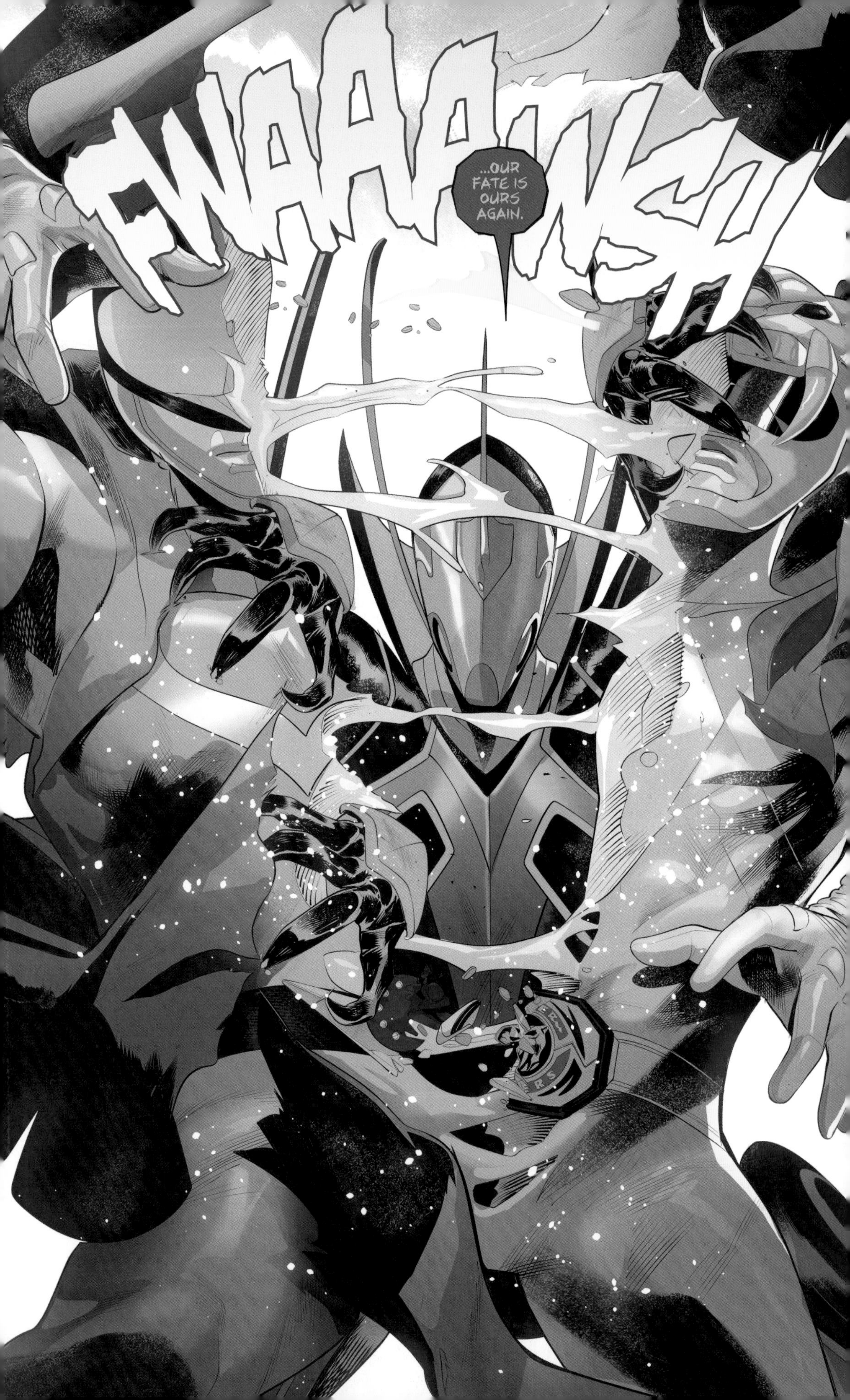
TWAAANG
...OUR FATE IS OURS AGAIN.

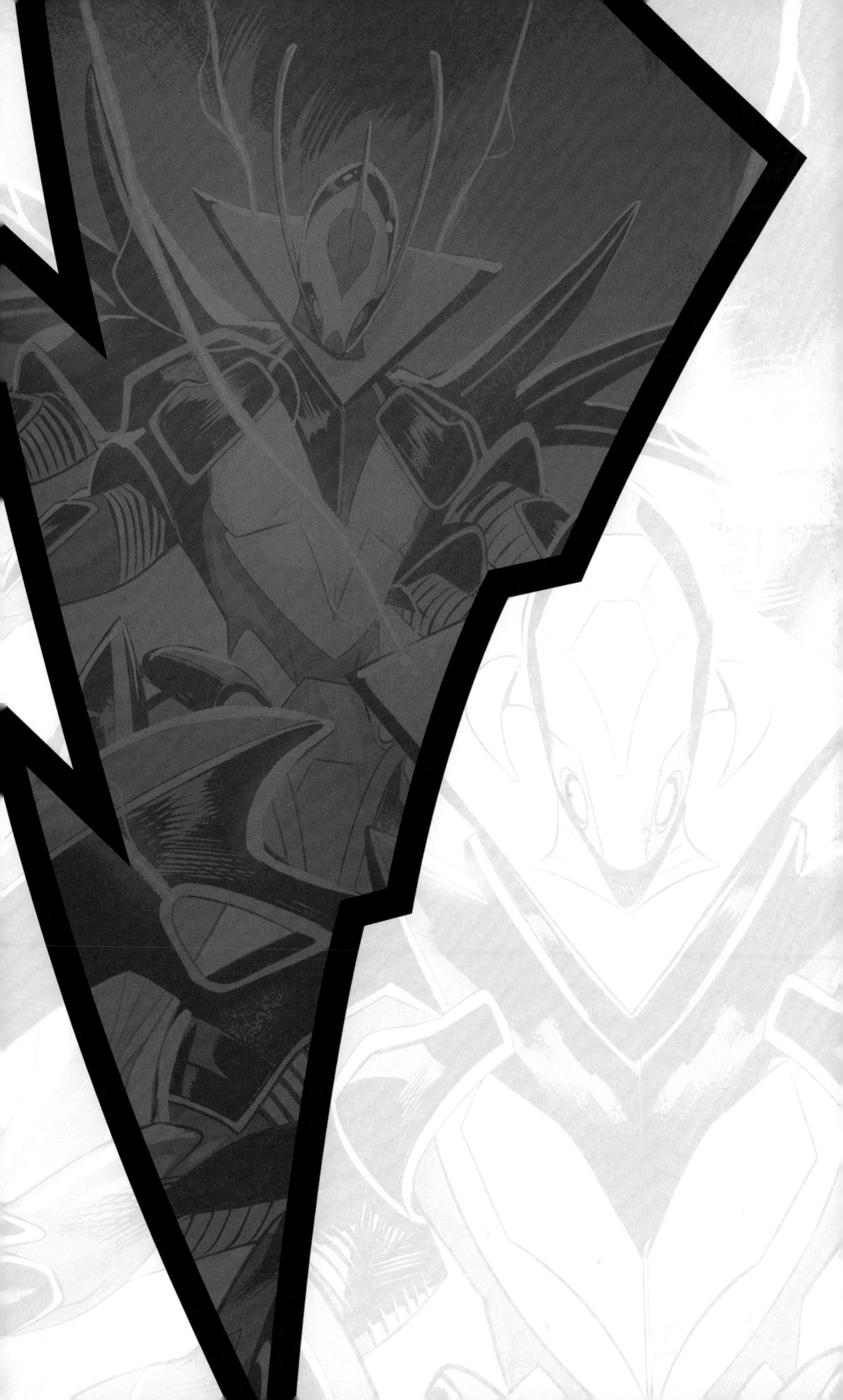

CHAPTER TWELVE

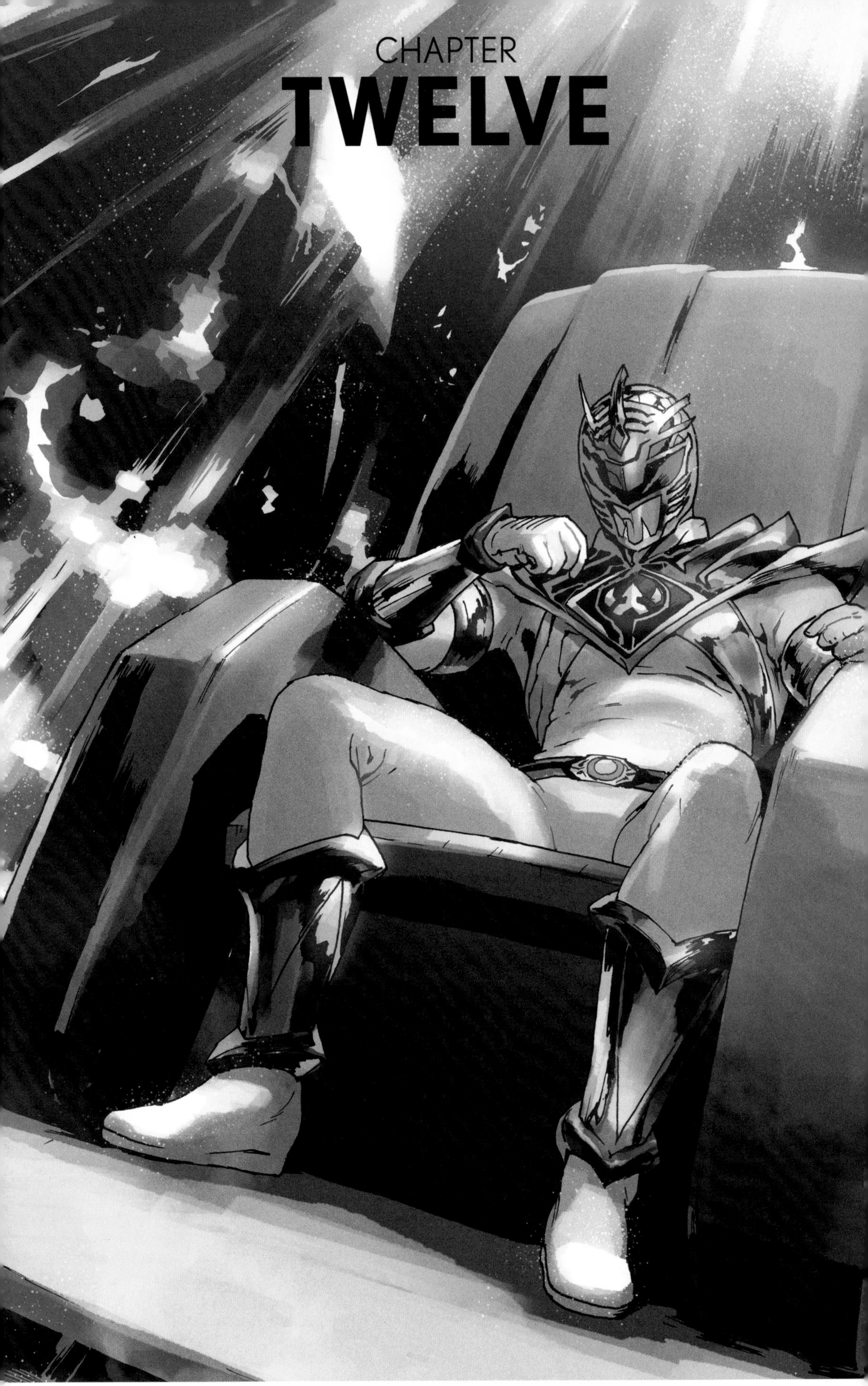

GERALD PAREL ISSUE TWELVE COVER

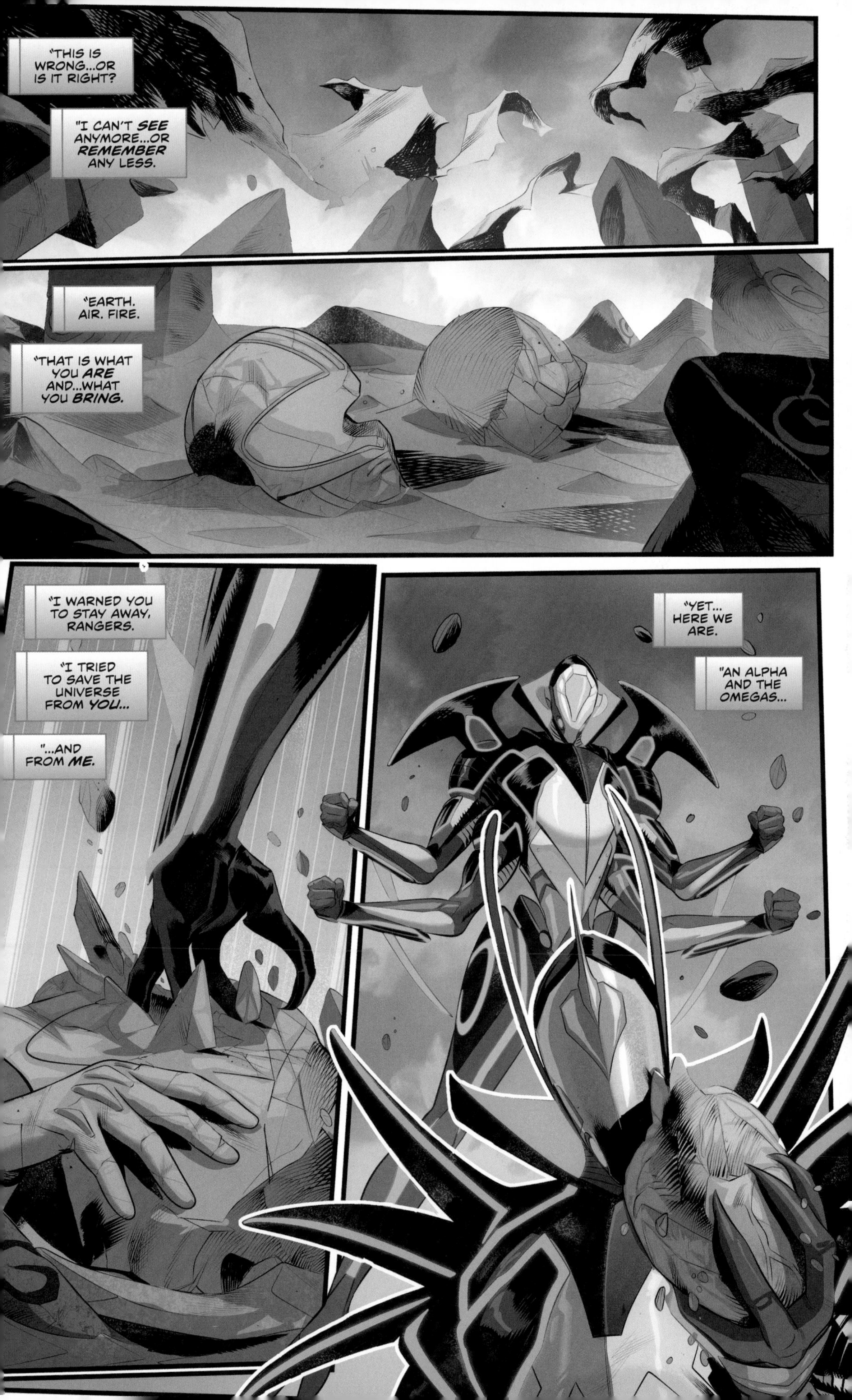
"THIS IS WRONG...OR IS IT RIGHT?
"I CAN'T SEE ANYMORE...OR REMEMBER ANY LESS.
"EARTH. AIR. FIRE.
"THAT IS WHAT YOU ARE AND...WHAT YOU BRING.
"I WARNED YOU TO STAY AWAY, RANGERS.
"I TRIED TO SAVE THE UNIVERSE FROM YOU...
"...AND FROM ME.
"YET... HERE WE ARE.
"AN ALPHA AND THE OMEGAS...

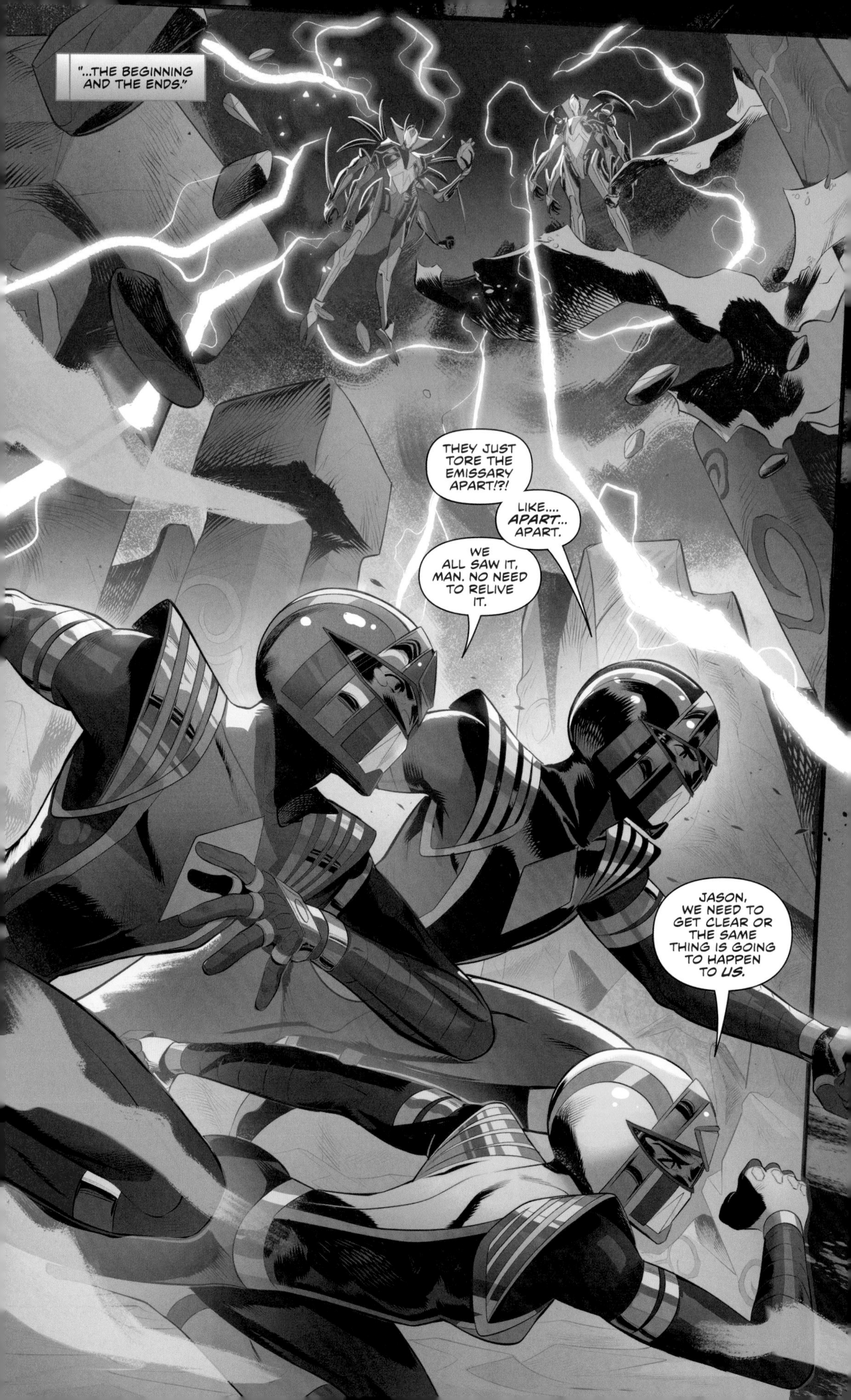
"...THE BEGINNING AND THE ENDS."
THEY JUST TORE THE EMISSARY APART!?!
LIKE.... *APART*... APART.
WE ALL SAW IT, MAN. NO NEED TO RELIVE IT.
JASON, WE NEED TO GET CLEAR OR THE SAME THING IS GOING TO HAPPEN TO *US*.

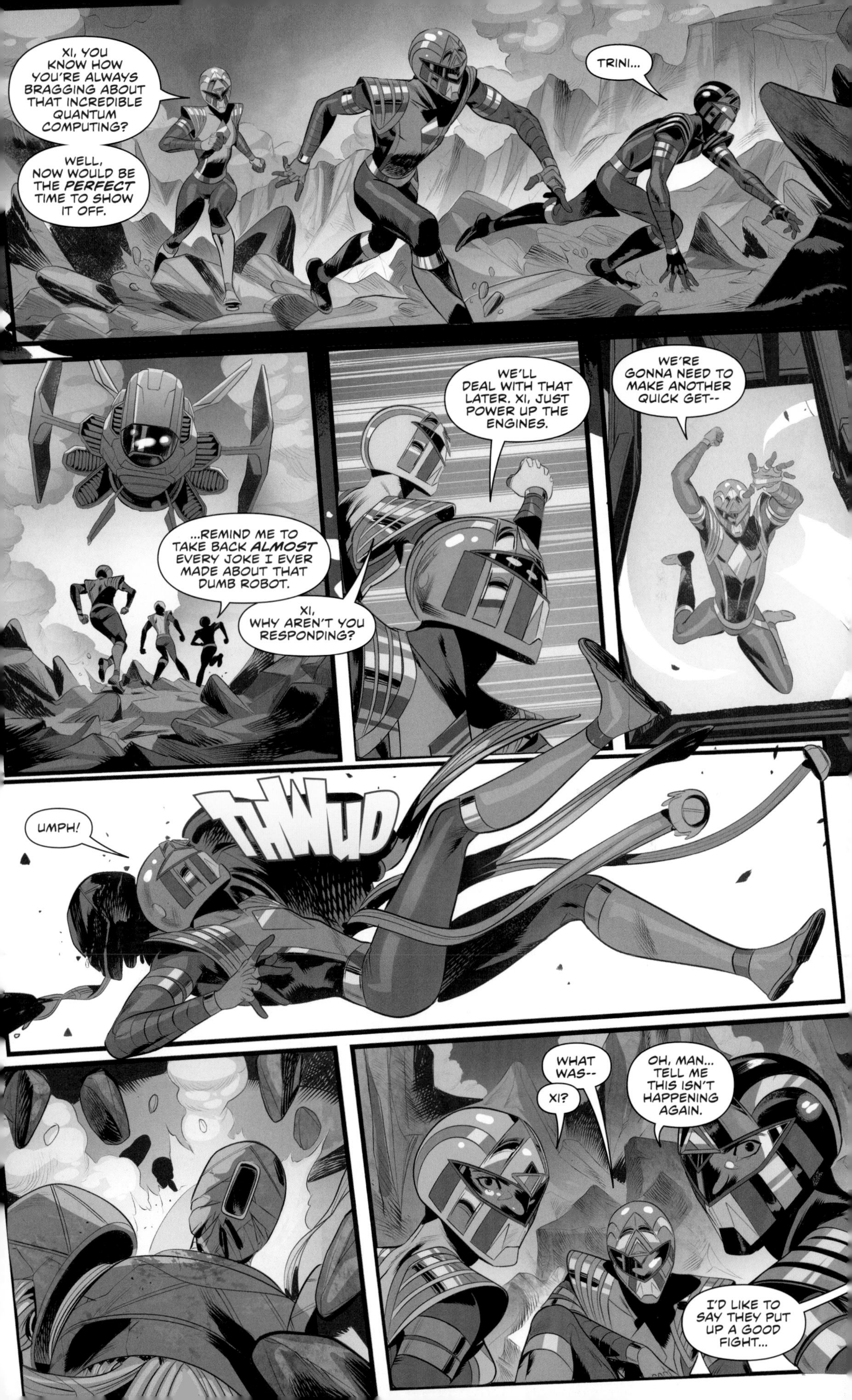
XI, YOU KNOW HOW YOU'RE ALWAYS BRAGGING ABOUT THAT INCREDIBLE QUANTUM COMPUTING?
WELL, NOW WOULD BE THE *PERFECT* TIME TO SHOW IT OFF.
TRINI...
...REMIND ME TO TAKE BACK **ALMOST** EVERY JOKE I EVER MADE ABOUT THAT DUMB ROBOT.
XI, WHY AREN'T YOU RESPONDING?
WE'LL DEAL WITH THAT LATER. XI, JUST POWER UP THE ENGINES.
WE'RE GONNA NEED TO MAKE ANOTHER QUICK GET--
UMPH!
THWUD
WHAT WAS--
XI?
OH, MAN... TELL ME THIS ISN'T HAPPENING AGAIN.
I'D LIKE TO SAY THEY PUT UP A GOOD FIGHT...

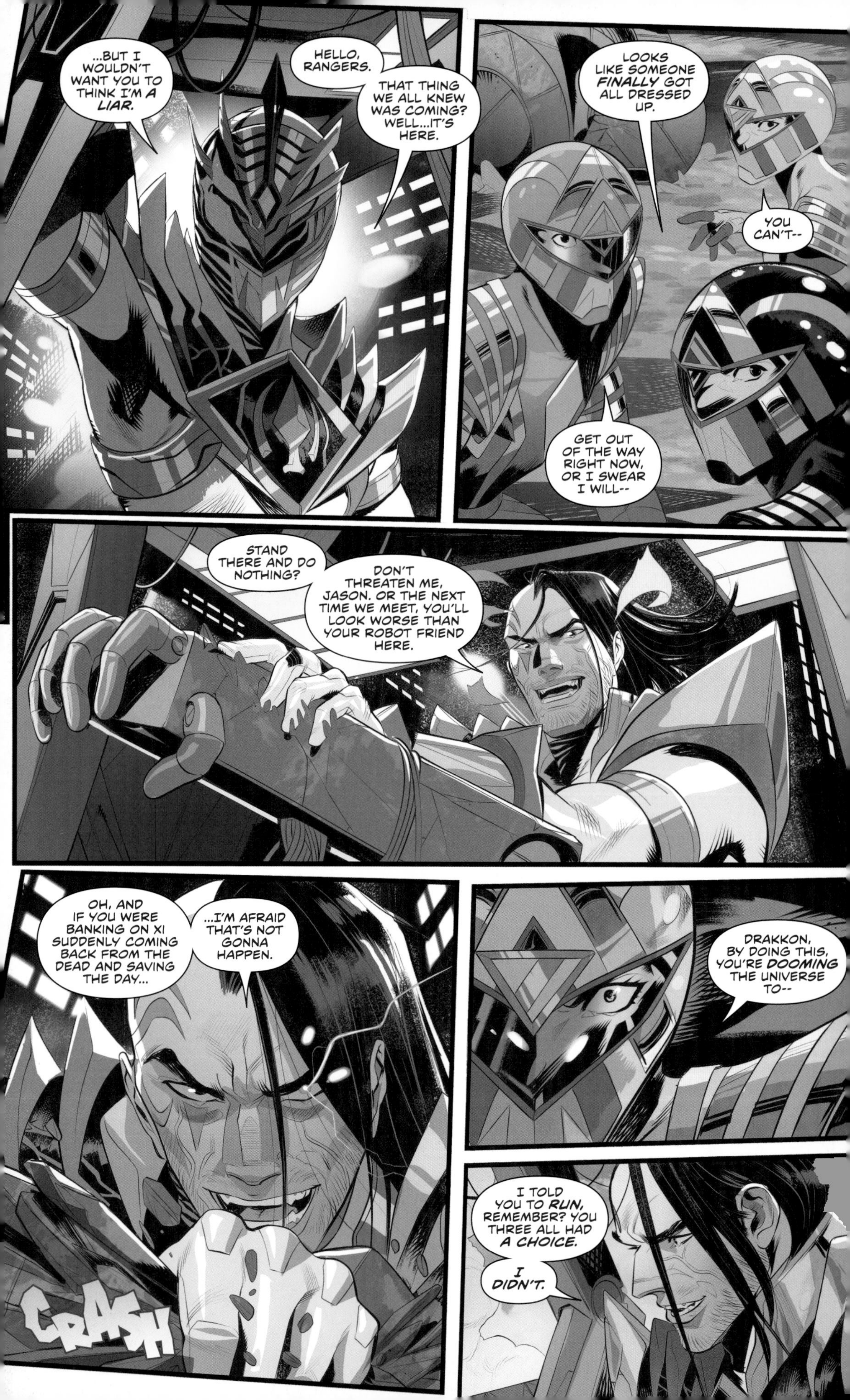
...BUT I WOULDN'T WANT YOU TO THINK I'M A *LIAR.*
HELLO, RANGERS.
THAT THING WE ALL KNEW WAS COMING? WELL...IT'S HERE.
LOOKS LIKE SOMEONE *FINALLY* GOT ALL DRESSED UP.
YOU CAN'T--
GET OUT OF THE WAY RIGHT NOW, OR I SWEAR I WILL--
STAND THERE AND DO NOTHING?
DON'T THREATEN ME, JASON. OR THE NEXT TIME WE MEET, YOU'LL LOOK WORSE THAN YOUR ROBOT FRIEND HERE.
OH, AND IF YOU WERE BANKING ON XI SUDDENLY COMING BACK FROM THE DEAD AND SAVING THE DAY...
...I'M AFRAID THAT'S NOT GONNA HAPPEN.
CRASH
DRAKKON, BY DOING THIS, YOU'RE *DOOMING* THE UNIVERSE TO--
I TOLD YOU TO *RUN*, REMEMBER? YOU THREE ALL HAD *A CHOICE.*
I DIDN'T.

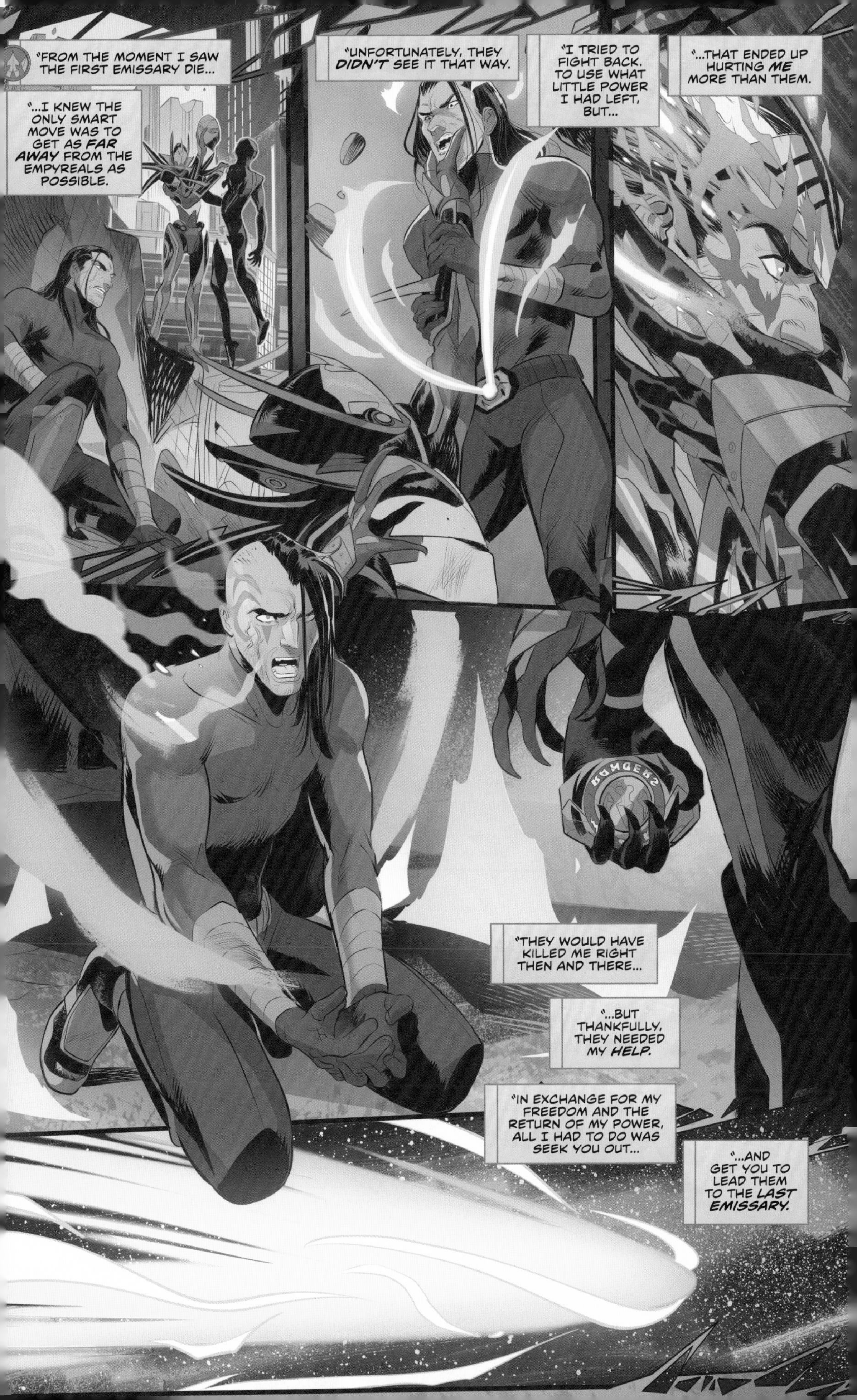
"FROM THE MOMENT I SAW THE FIRST EMISSARY DIE...
"...I KNEW THE ONLY SMART MOVE WAS TO GET AS *FAR AWAY* FROM THE EMPYREALS AS POSSIBLE.
"UNFORTUNATELY, THEY *DIDN'T* SEE IT THAT WAY.
"I TRIED TO FIGHT BACK. TO USE WHAT LITTLE POWER I HAD LEFT, BUT...
"...THAT ENDED UP HURTING *ME* MORE THAN THEM.
"THEY WOULD HAVE KILLED ME RIGHT THEN AND THERE...
"...BUT THANKFULLY, THEY NEEDED MY *HELP*.
"IN EXCHANGE FOR MY FREEDOM AND THE RETURN OF MY POWER, ALL I HAD TO DO WAS SEEK YOU OUT...
"...AND GET YOU TO LEAD THEM TO THE *LAST EMISSARY*.

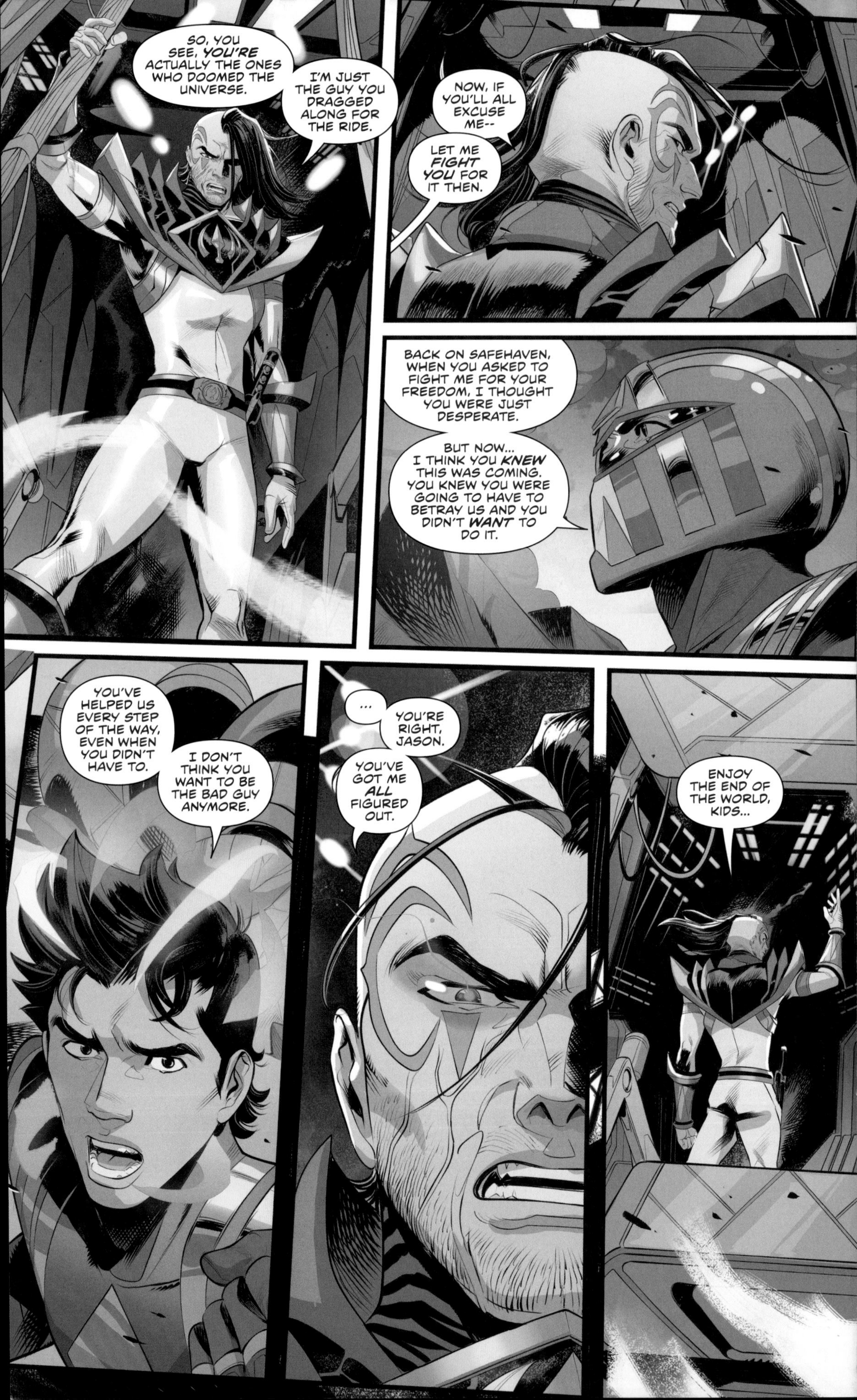
SO, YOU SEE, YOU'RE ACTUALLY THE ONES WHO DOOMED THE UNIVERSE.
I'M JUST THE GUY YOU DRAGGED ALONG FOR THE RIDE.
NOW, IF YOU'LL ALL EXCUSE ME--
LET ME FIGHT YOU FOR IT THEN.
BACK ON SAFEHAVEN, WHEN YOU ASKED TO FIGHT ME FOR YOUR FREEDOM, I THOUGHT YOU WERE JUST DESPERATE.
BUT NOW... I THINK YOU KNEW THIS WAS COMING. YOU KNEW YOU WERE GOING TO HAVE TO BETRAY US AND YOU DIDN'T WANT TO DO IT.
YOU'VE HELPED US EVERY STEP OF THE WAY, EVEN WHEN YOU DIDN'T HAVE TO.
I DON'T THINK YOU WANT TO BE THE BAD GUY ANYMORE.
...
YOU'RE RIGHT, JASON.
YOU'VE GOT ME ALL FIGURED OUT.
ENJOY THE END OF THE WORLD, KIDS...

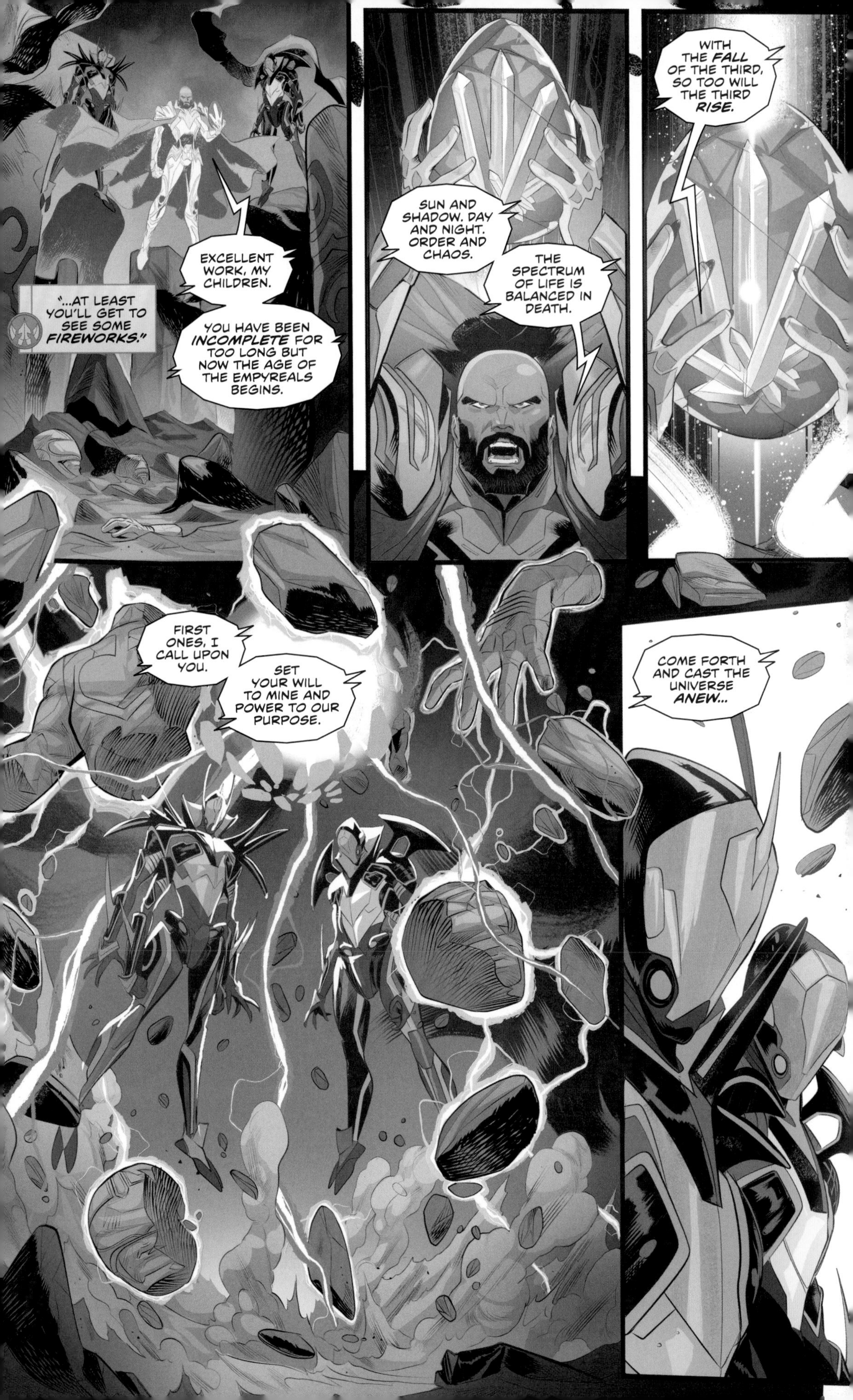
EXCELLENT WORK, MY CHILDREN.
"...AT LEAST YOU'LL GET TO SEE SOME FIREWORKS."
YOU HAVE BEEN INCOMPLETE FOR TOO LONG BUT NOW THE AGE OF THE EMPYREALS BEGINS.
SUN AND SHADOW. DAY AND NIGHT. ORDER AND CHAOS.
THE SPECTRUM OF LIFE IS BALANCED IN DEATH.
WITH THE FALL OF THE THIRD, SO TOO WILL THE THIRD RISE.
FIRST ONES, I CALL UPON YOU.
SET YOUR WILL TO MINE AND POWER TO OUR PURPOSE.
COME FORTH AND CAST THE UNIVERSE ANEW...

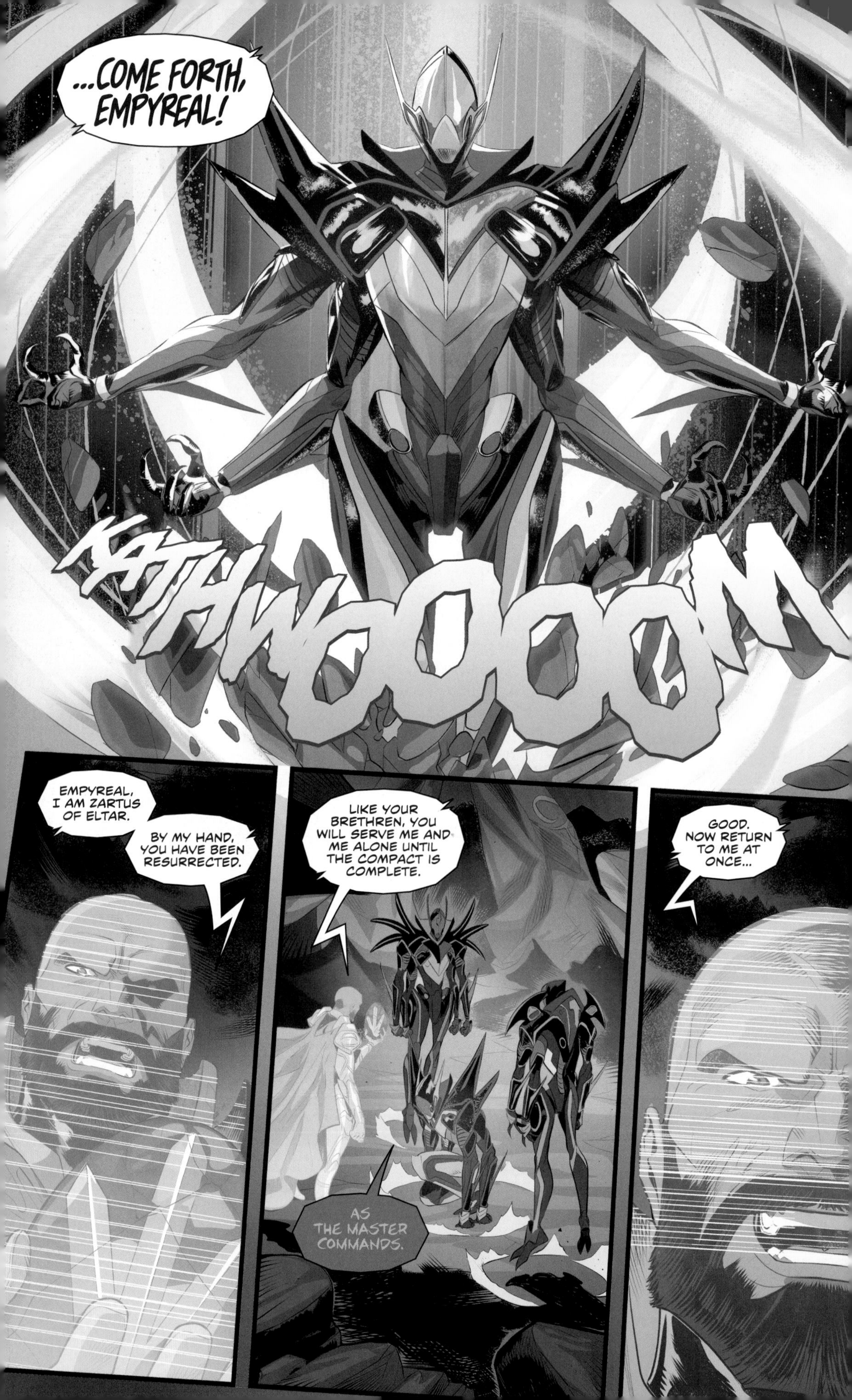
...COME FORTH, EMPYREAL!
KATHWOOOOOM
EMPYREAL, I AM ZARTUS OF ELTAR.
BY MY HAND, YOU HAVE BEEN RESURRECTED.
LIKE YOUR BRETHREN, YOU WILL SERVE ME AND ME ALONE UNTIL THE COMPACT IS COMPLETE.
AS THE MASTER COMMANDS.
GOOD. NOW RETURN TO ME AT ONCE...

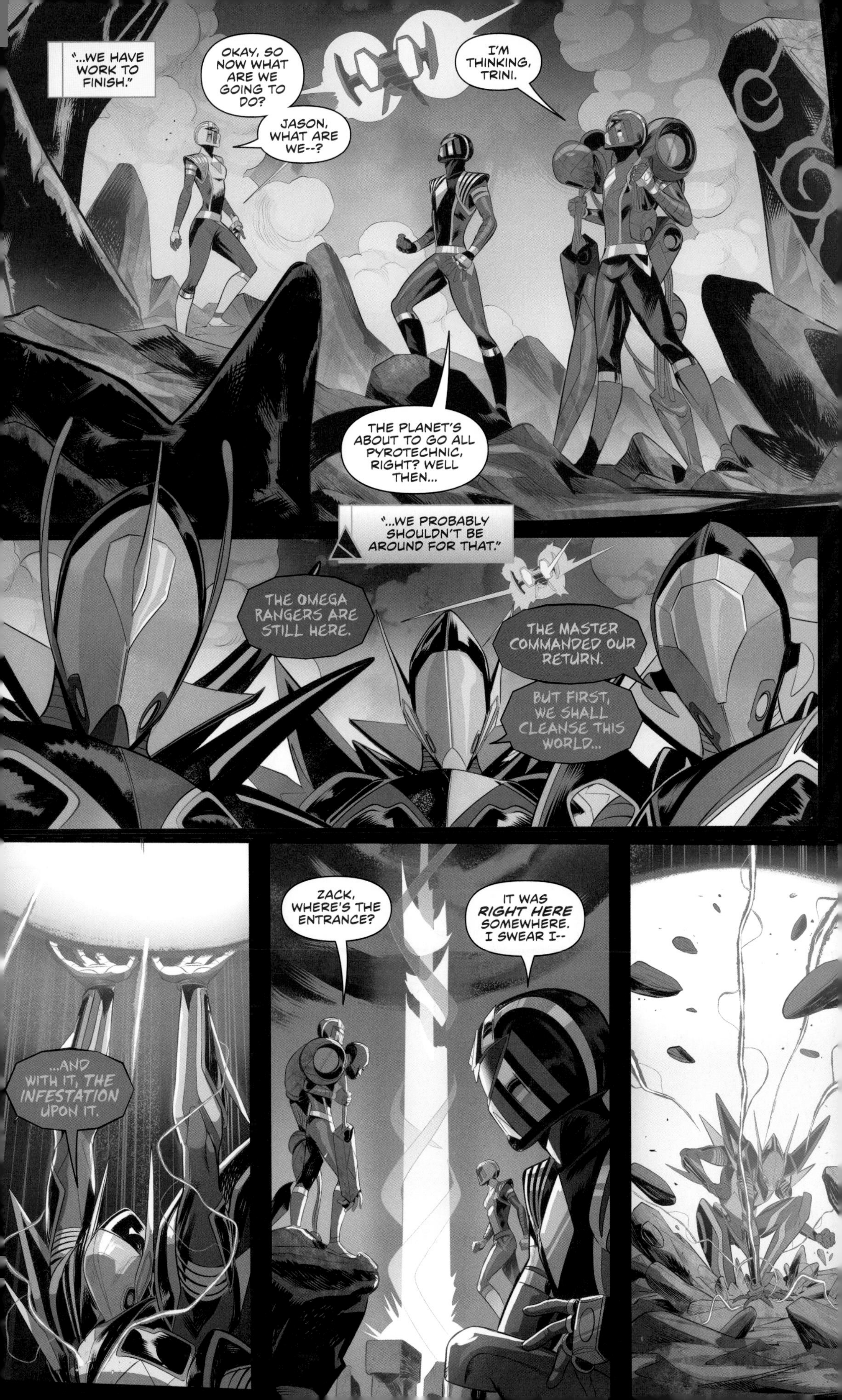
"...WE HAVE WORK TO FINISH."
OKAY, SO NOW WHAT ARE WE GOING TO DO?
JASON, WHAT ARE WE--?
I'M THINKING, TRINI.
THE PLANET'S ABOUT TO GO ALL PYROTECHNIC, RIGHT? WELL THEN...
"...WE PROBABLY SHOULDN'T BE AROUND FOR THAT."
THE OMEGA RANGERS ARE STILL HERE.
THE MASTER COMMANDED OUR RETURN.
BUT FIRST, WE SHALL CLEANSE THIS WORLD...
...AND WITH IT, THE INFESTATION UPON IT.
ZACK, WHERE'S THE ENTRANCE?
IT WAS RIGHT HERE SOMEWHERE. I SWEAR I--

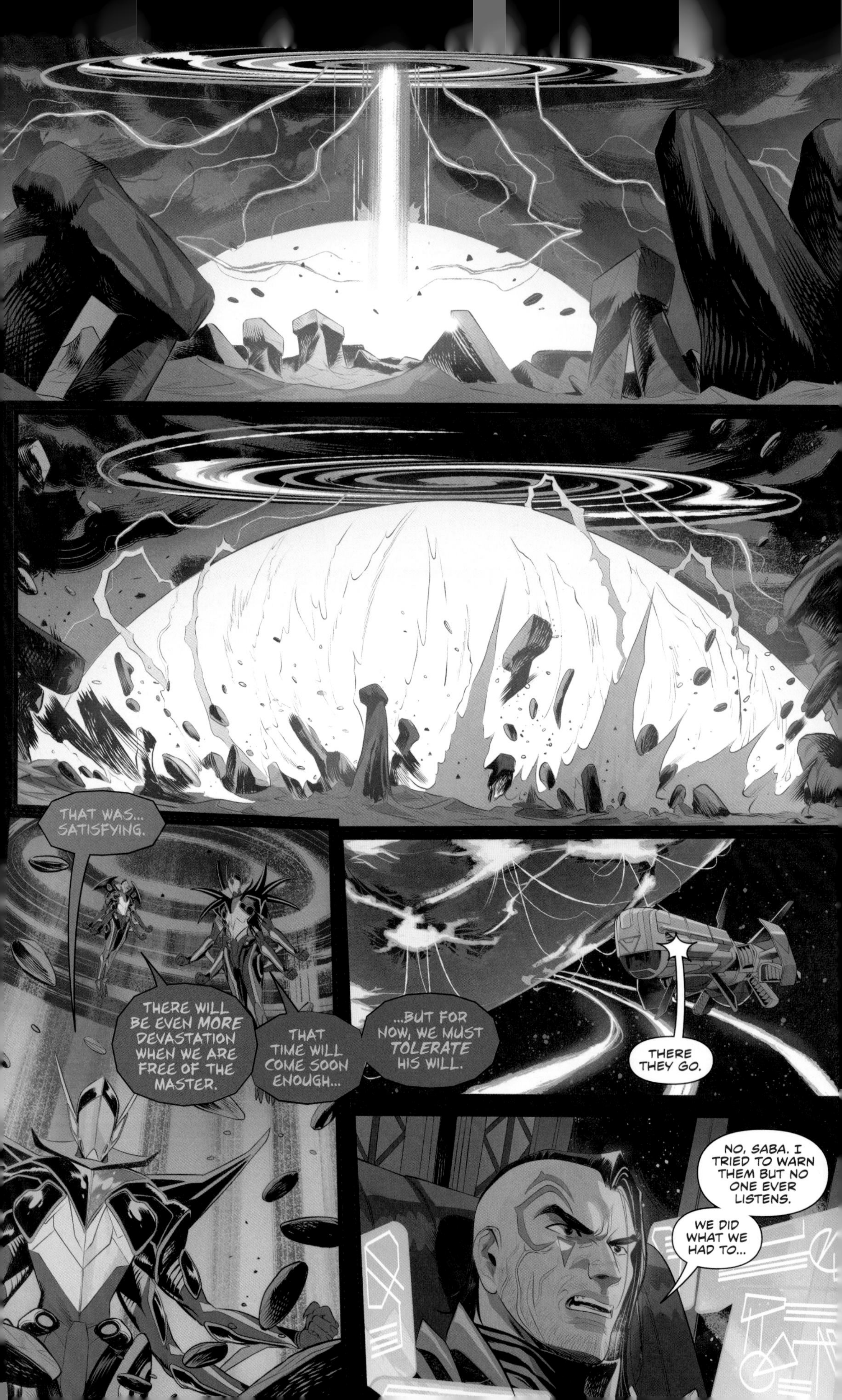
THAT WAS... SATISFYING.
THERE WILL BE EVEN MORE DEVASTATION WHEN WE ARE FREE OF THE MASTER.
THAT TIME WILL COME SOON ENOUGH...
...BUT FOR NOW, WE MUST TOLERATE HIS WILL.
THERE THEY GO.
NO, SABA. I TRIED TO WARN THEM BUT NO ONE EVER LISTENS.
WE DID WHAT WE HAD TO...

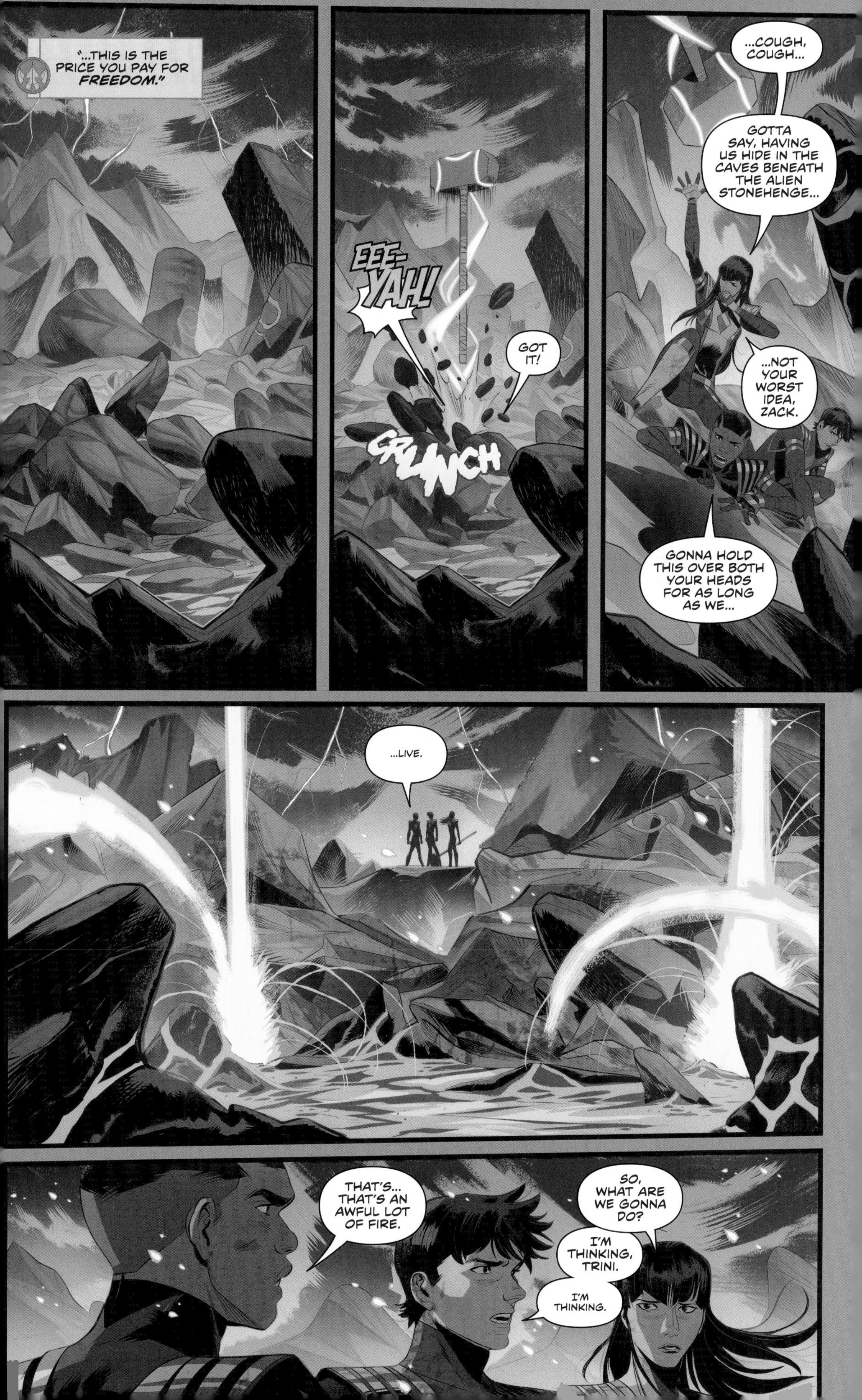
"...THIS IS THE PRICE YOU PAY FOR FREEDOM."
EEE-YAH!
GOT IT!
CRUNCH
...COUGH, COUGH...
GOTTA SAY, HAVING US HIDE IN THE CAVES BENEATH THE ALIEN STONEHENGE...
...NOT YOUR WORST IDEA, ZACK.
GONNA HOLD THIS OVER BOTH YOUR HEADS FOR AS LONG AS WE...
...LIVE.
THAT'S... THAT'S AN AWFUL LOT OF FIRE.
SO, WHAT ARE WE GONNA DO?
I'M THINKING, TRINI.
I'M THINKING.

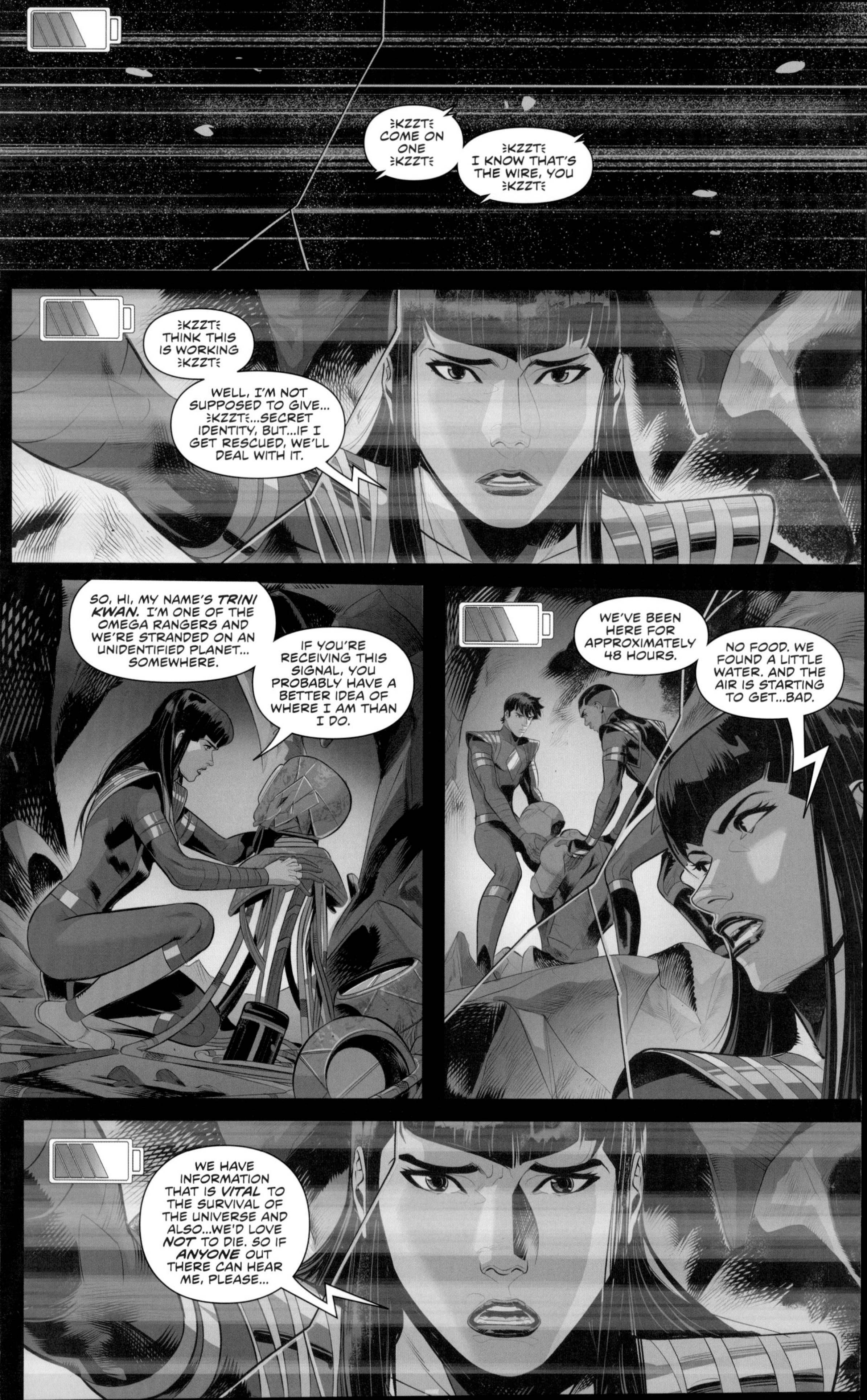
KZZT COME ON ONE KZZT
KZZT I KNOW THAT'S THE WIRE, YOU KZZT
KZZT THINK THIS IS WORKING KZZT
WELL, I'M NOT SUPPOSED TO GIVE... KZZT ...SECRET IDENTITY, BUT...IF I GET RESCUED, WE'LL DEAL WITH IT.
SO, HI, MY NAME'S *TRINI KWAN.* I'M ONE OF THE OMEGA RANGERS AND WE'RE STRANDED ON AN UNIDENTIFIED PLANET... SOMEWHERE.
IF YOU'RE RECEIVING THIS SIGNAL, YOU PROBABLY HAVE A BETTER IDEA OF WHERE I AM THAN I DO.
WE'VE BEEN HERE FOR APPROXIMATELY 48 HOURS.
NO FOOD. WE FOUND A LITTLE WATER. AND THE AIR IS STARTING TO GET...BAD.
WE HAVE INFORMATION THAT IS *VITAL* TO THE SURVIVAL OF THE UNIVERSE AND ALSO...WE'D LOVE *NOT* TO DIE. SO IF *ANYONE* OUT THERE CAN HEAR ME, PLEASE...

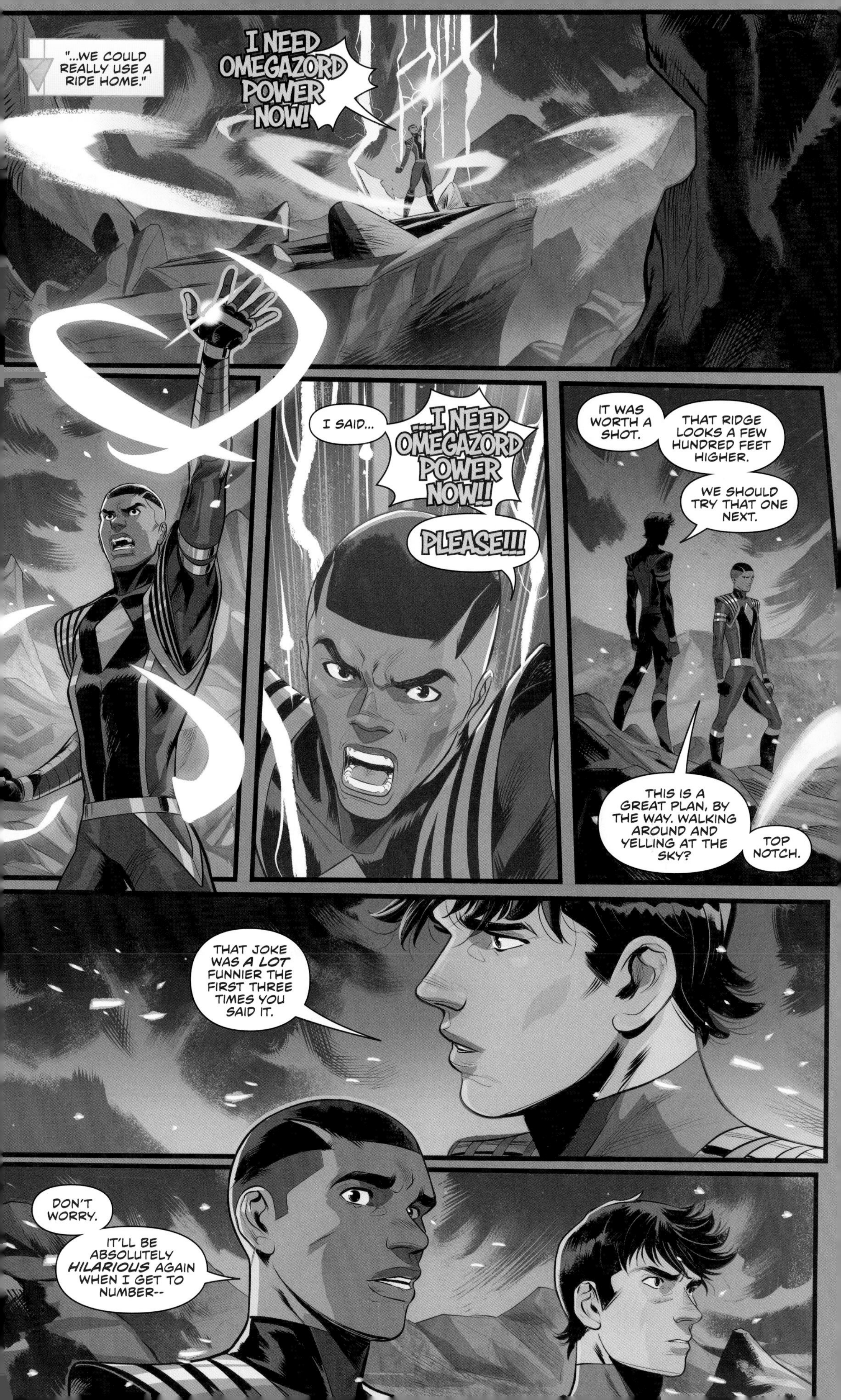
"...WE COULD REALLY USE A RIDE HOME."
I NEED OMEGAZORD POWER NOW!
I SAID...
...I NEED OMEGAZORD POWER NOW!!
PLEASE!!!
IT WAS WORTH A SHOT.
THAT RIDGE LOOKS A FEW HUNDRED FEET HIGHER.
WE SHOULD TRY THAT ONE NEXT.
THIS IS A GREAT PLAN, BY THE WAY. WALKING AROUND AND YELLING AT THE SKY?
TOP NOTCH.
THAT JOKE WAS A LOT FUNNIER THE FIRST THREE TIMES YOU SAID IT.
DON'T WORRY.
IT'LL BE ABSOLUTELY HILARIOUS AGAIN WHEN I GET TO NUMBER--

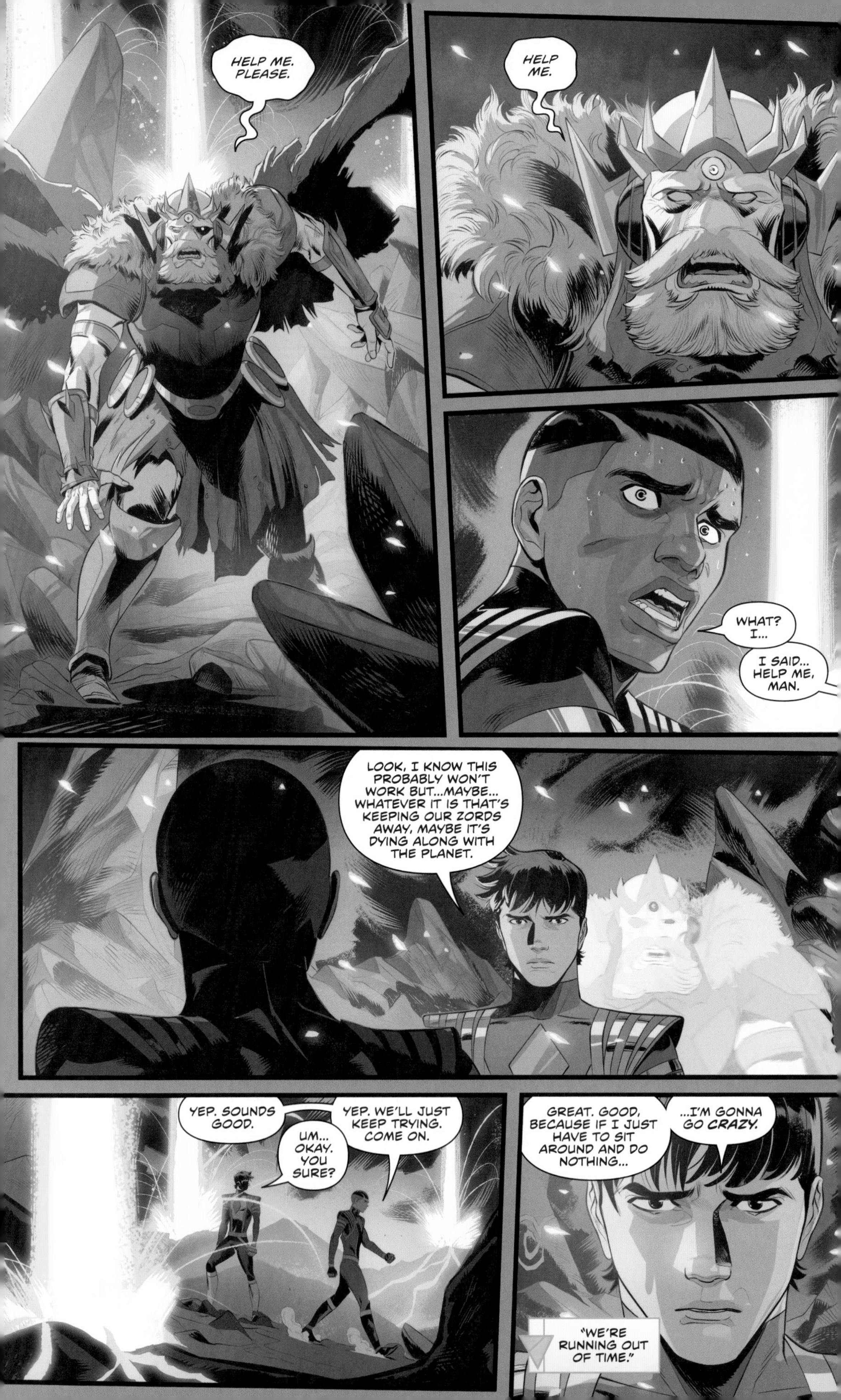
HELP ME. PLEASE.
HELP ME.
WHAT? I...
I SAID... HELP ME, MAN.
LOOK, I KNOW THIS PROBABLY WON'T WORK BUT...MAYBE... WHATEVER IT IS THAT'S KEEPING OUR ZORDS AWAY, MAYBE IT'S DYING ALONG WITH THE PLANET.
YEP. SOUNDS GOOD.
YEP. WE'LL JUST KEEP TRYING. COME ON.
UM... OKAY. YOU SURE?
GREAT. GOOD, BECAUSE IF I JUST HAVE TO SIT AROUND AND DO NOTHING...
...I'M GONNA GO CRAZY.
"WE'RE RUNNING OUT OF TIME."

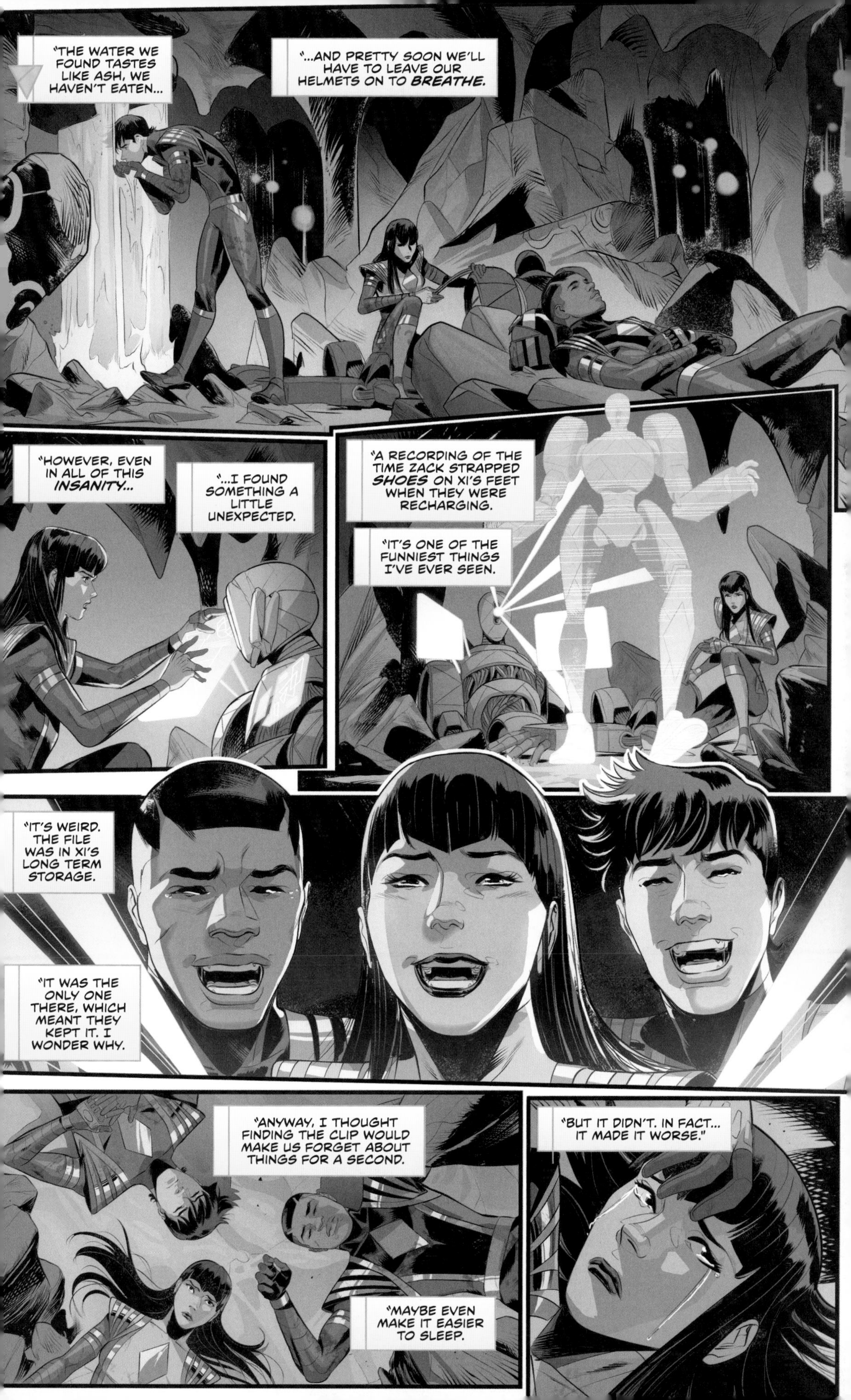
"THE WATER WE FOUND TASTES LIKE ASH, WE HAVEN'T EATEN...
"...AND PRETTY SOON WE'LL HAVE TO LEAVE OUR HELMETS ON TO BREATHE.
"HOWEVER, EVEN IN ALL OF THIS INSANITY...
"...I FOUND SOMETHING A LITTLE UNEXPECTED.
"A RECORDING OF THE TIME ZACK STRAPPED SHOES ON XI'S FEET WHEN THEY WERE RECHARGING.
"IT'S ONE OF THE FUNNIEST THINGS I'VE EVER SEEN.
"IT'S WEIRD. THE FILE WAS IN XI'S LONG TERM STORAGE.
"IT WAS THE ONLY ONE THERE, WHICH MEANT THEY KEPT IT. I WONDER WHY.
"ANYWAY, I THOUGHT FINDING THE CLIP WOULD MAKE US FORGET ABOUT THINGS FOR A SECOND.
"MAYBE EVEN MAKE IT EASIER TO SLEEP.
"BUT IT DIDN'T. IN FACT... IT MADE IT WORSE."

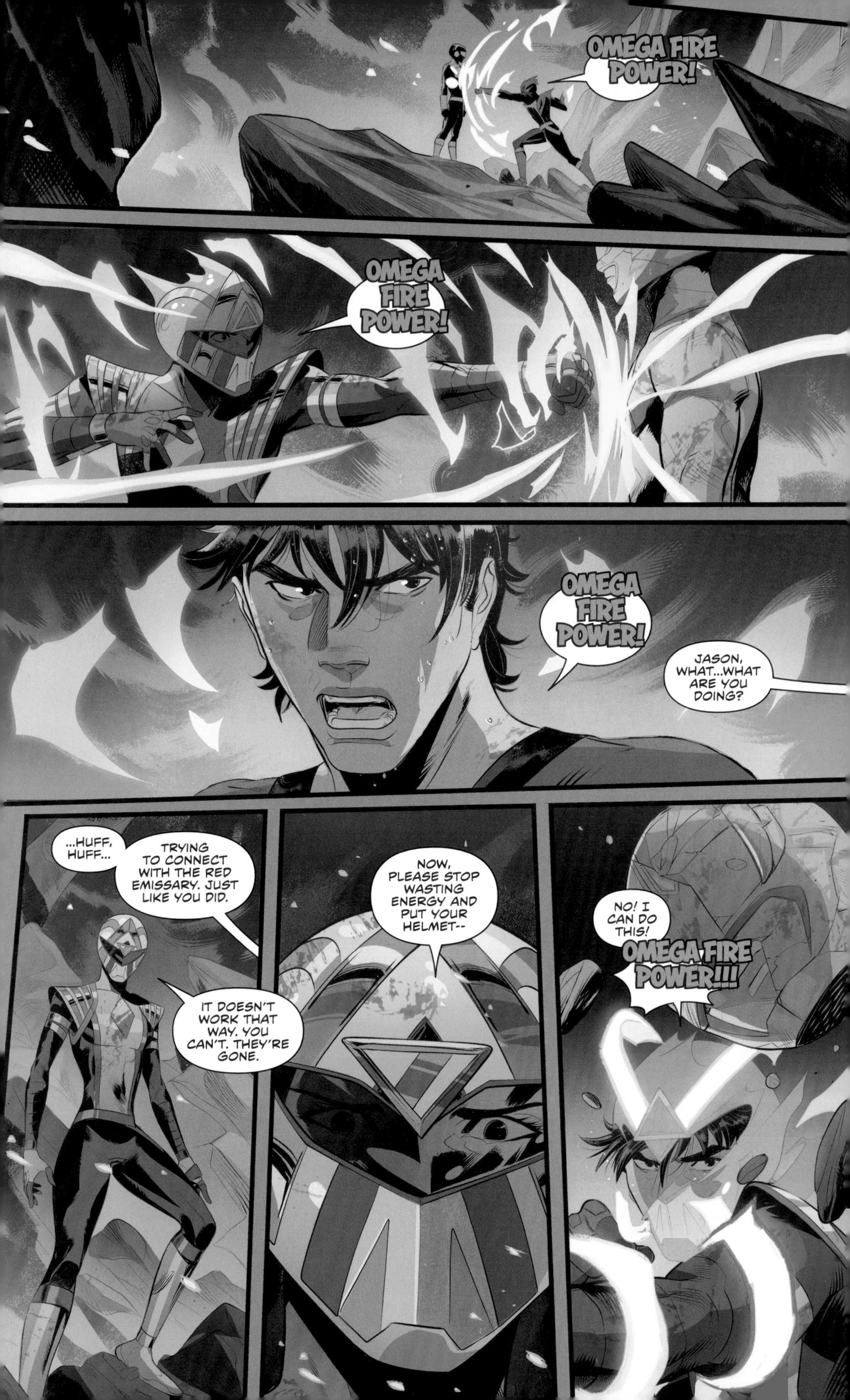
OMEGA FIRE POWER!
OMEGA FIRE POWER!
OMEGA FIRE POWER!
JASON, WHAT...WHAT ARE YOU DOING?
...HUFF, HUFF...
TRYING TO CONNECT WITH THE RED EMISSARY. JUST LIKE YOU DID.
IT DOESN'T WORK THAT WAY. YOU CAN'T. THEY'RE GONE.
NOW, PLEASE STOP WASTING ENERGY AND PUT YOUR HELMET--
NO! I CAN DO THIS!
OMEGA FIRE POWER!!!

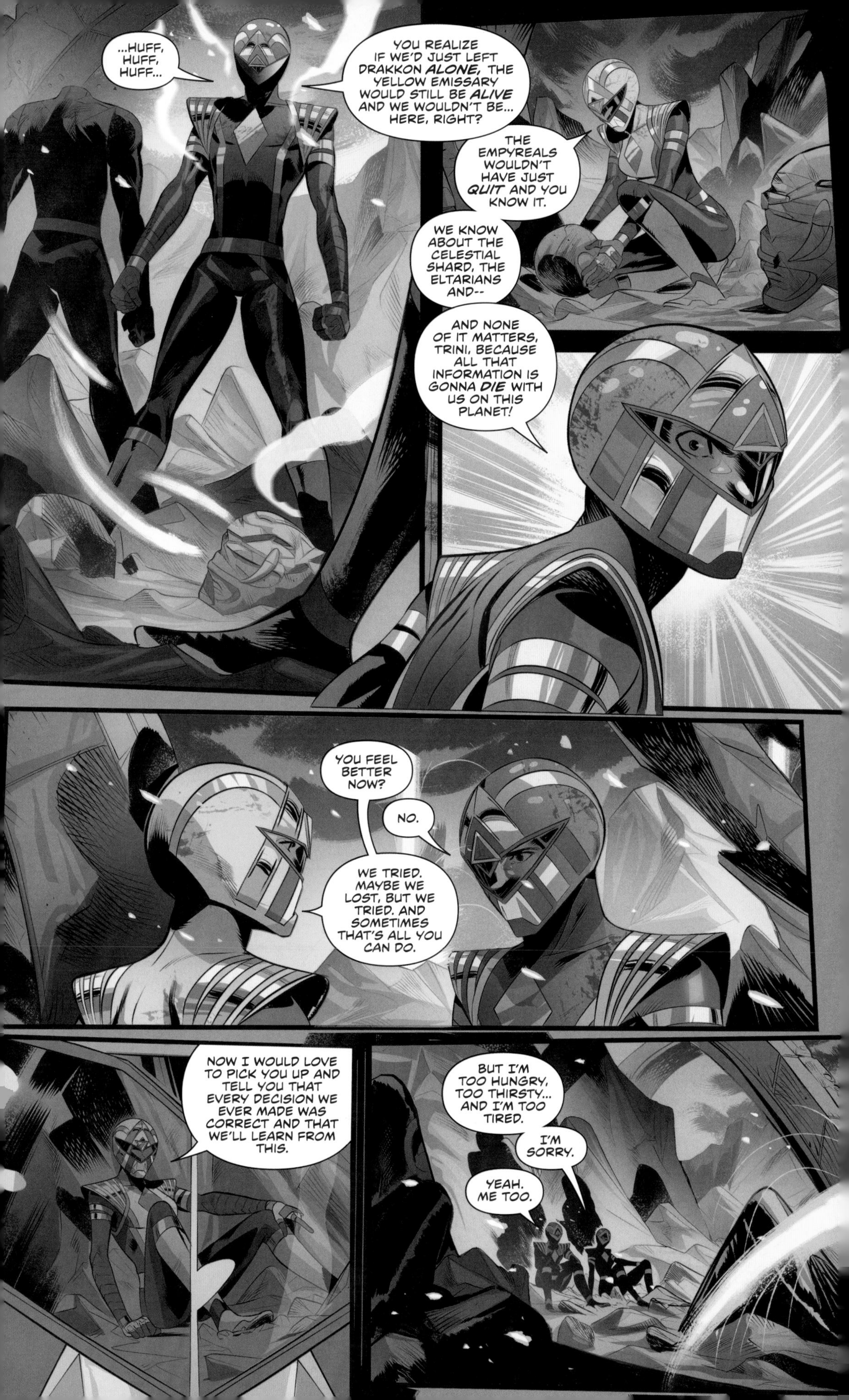
...HUFF, HUFF, HUFF...
YOU REALIZE IF WE'D JUST LEFT DRAKKON ALONE, THE YELLOW EMISSARY WOULD STILL BE ALIVE AND WE WOULDN'T BE... HERE, RIGHT?
THE EMPYREALS WOULDN'T HAVE JUST QUIT AND YOU KNOW IT.
WE KNOW ABOUT THE CELESTIAL SHARD, THE ELTARIANS AND--
AND NONE OF IT MATTERS, TRINI, BECAUSE ALL THAT INFORMATION IS GONNA DIE WITH US ON THIS PLANET!
YOU FEEL BETTER NOW?
NO.
WE TRIED. MAYBE WE LOST, BUT WE TRIED. AND SOMETIMES THAT'S ALL YOU CAN DO.
NOW I WOULD LOVE TO PICK YOU UP AND TELL YOU THAT EVERY DECISION WE EVER MADE WAS CORRECT AND THAT WE'LL LEARN FROM THIS.
BUT I'M TOO HUNGRY, TOO THIRSTY... AND I'M TOO TIRED.
I'M SORRY.
YEAH. ME TOO.

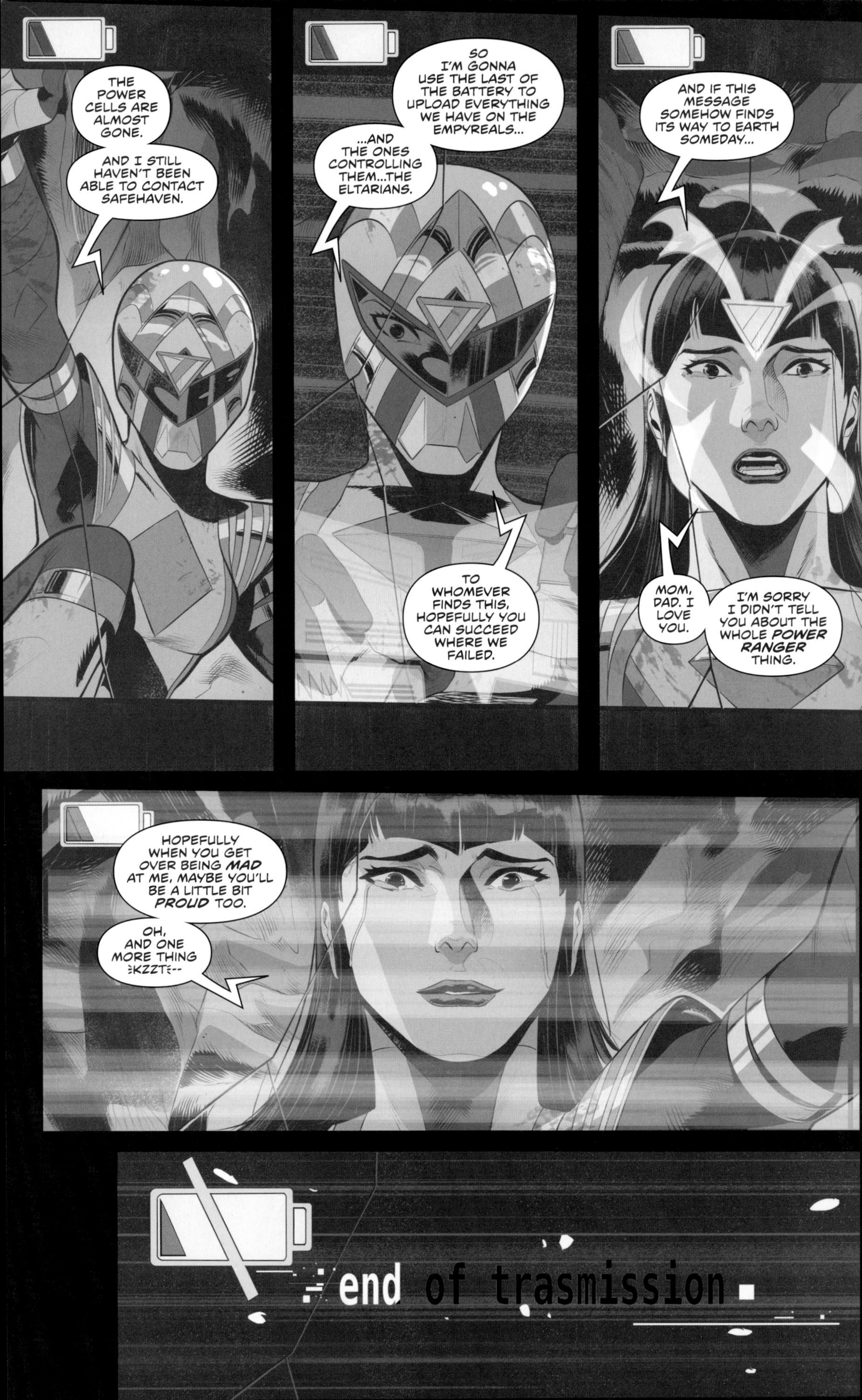

THE POWER CELLS ARE ALMOST GONE.
AND I STILL HAVEN'T BEEN ABLE TO CONTACT SAFEHAVEN.
SO I'M GONNA USE THE LAST OF THE BATTERY TO UPLOAD EVERYTHING WE HAVE ON THE EMPYREALS...
...AND THE ONES CONTROLLING THEM...THE ELTARIANS.
TO WHOMEVER FINDS THIS, HOPEFULLY YOU CAN SUCCEED WHERE WE FAILED.
AND IF THIS MESSAGE SOMEHOW FINDS ITS WAY TO EARTH SOMEDAY...
MOM, DAD. I LOVE YOU.
I'M SORRY I DIDN'T TELL YOU ABOUT THE WHOLE POWER RANGER THING.
HOPEFULLY WHEN YOU GET OVER BEING MAD AT ME, MAYBE YOU'LL BE A LITTLE BIT PROUD TOO.
OH, AND ONE MORE THING KZZT--
end of trasmission

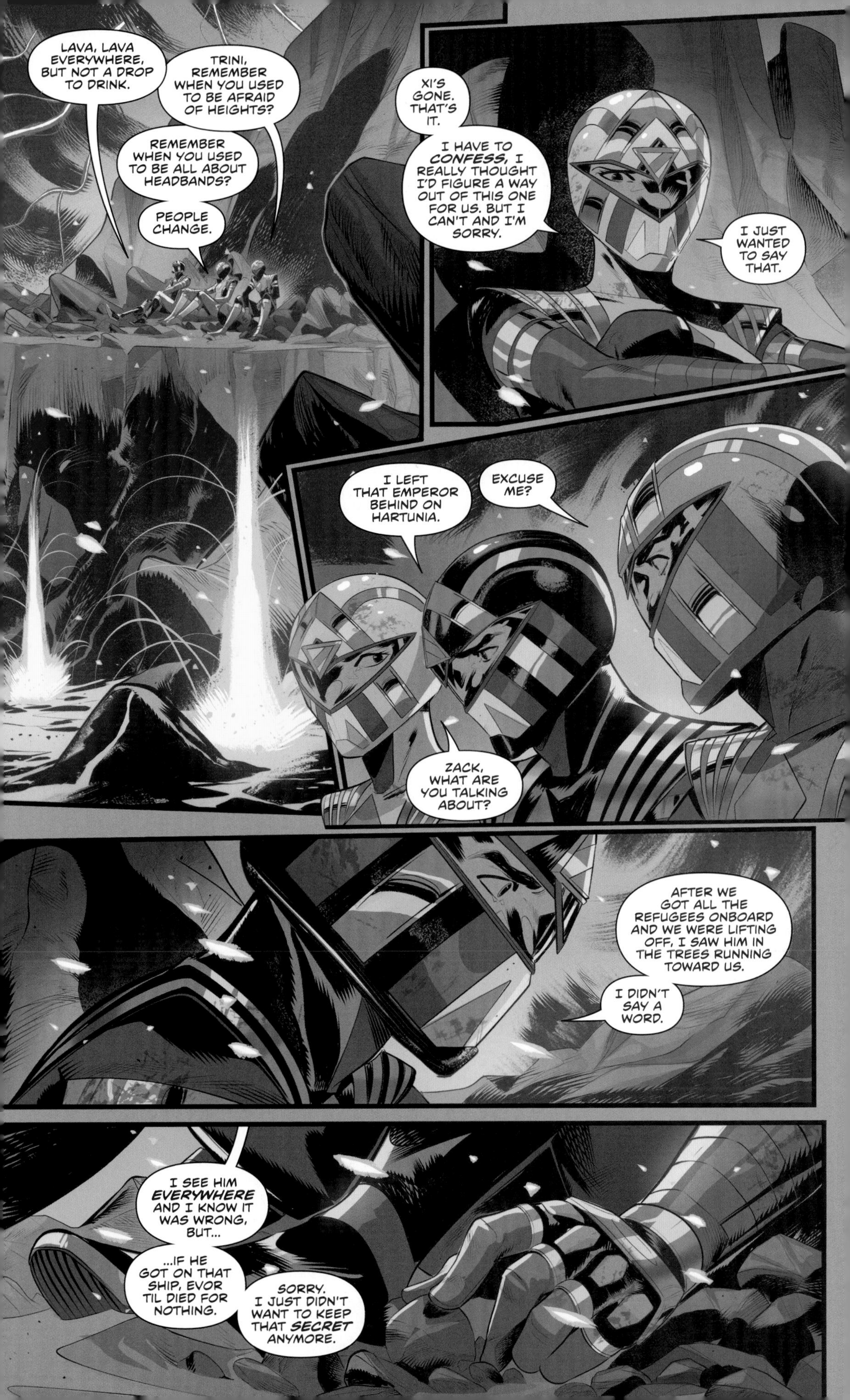
LAVA, LAVA EVERYWHERE, BUT NOT A DROP TO DRINK.
TRINI, REMEMBER WHEN YOU USED TO BE AFRAID OF HEIGHTS?
REMEMBER WHEN YOU USED TO BE ALL ABOUT HEADBANDS?
PEOPLE CHANGE.
XI'S GONE. THAT'S IT.
I HAVE TO *CONFESS,* I REALLY THOUGHT I'D FIGURE A WAY OUT OF THIS ONE FOR US. BUT I CAN'T AND I'M SORRY.
I JUST WANTED TO SAY THAT.
I LEFT THAT EMPEROR BEHIND ON HARTUNIA.
EXCUSE ME?
ZACK, WHAT ARE YOU TALKING ABOUT?
AFTER WE GOT ALL THE REFUGEES ONBOARD AND WE WERE LIFTING OFF, I SAW HIM IN THE TREES RUNNING TOWARD US.
I DIDN'T SAY A WORD.
I SEE HIM *EVERYWHERE* AND I KNOW IT WAS WRONG, BUT...
...IF HE GOT ON THAT SHIP, EVOR TIL DIED FOR NOTHING.
SORRY. I JUST DIDN'T WANT TO KEEP THAT *SECRET* ANYMORE.

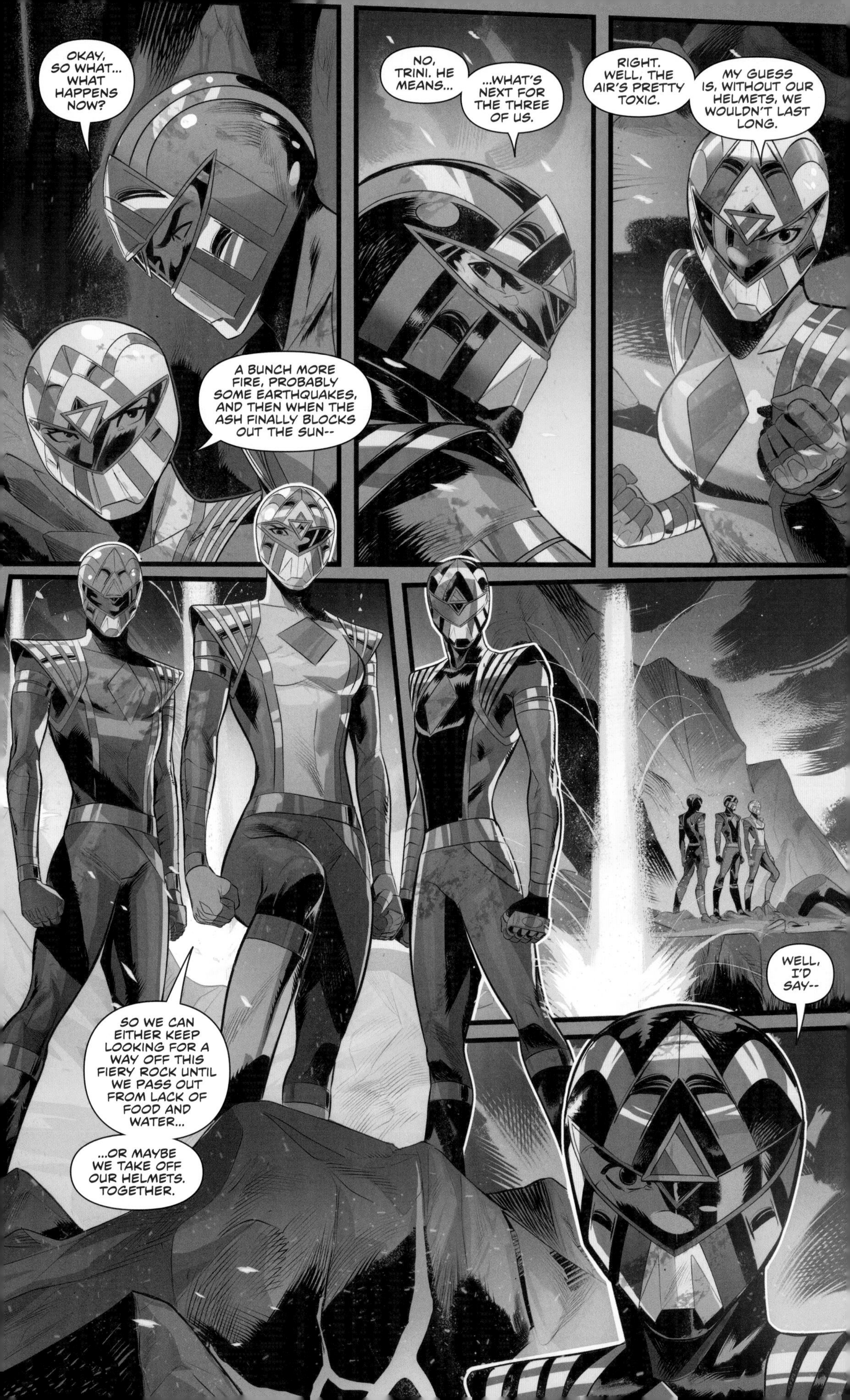

OKAY, SO WHAT... WHAT HAPPENS NOW?
A BUNCH MORE FIRE, PROBABLY SOME EARTHQUAKES, AND THEN WHEN THE ASH FINALLY BLOCKS OUT THE SUN--
NO, TRINI. HE MEANS...
...WHAT'S NEXT FOR THE THREE OF US.
RIGHT. WELL, THE AIR'S PRETTY TOXIC.
MY GUESS IS, WITHOUT OUR HELMETS, WE WOULDN'T LAST LONG.
WELL, I'D SAY--
SO WE CAN EITHER KEEP LOOKING FOR A WAY OFF THIS FIERY ROCK UNTIL WE PASS OUT FROM LACK OF FOOD AND WATER...
...OR MAYBE WE TAKE OFF OUR HELMETS. TOGETHER.

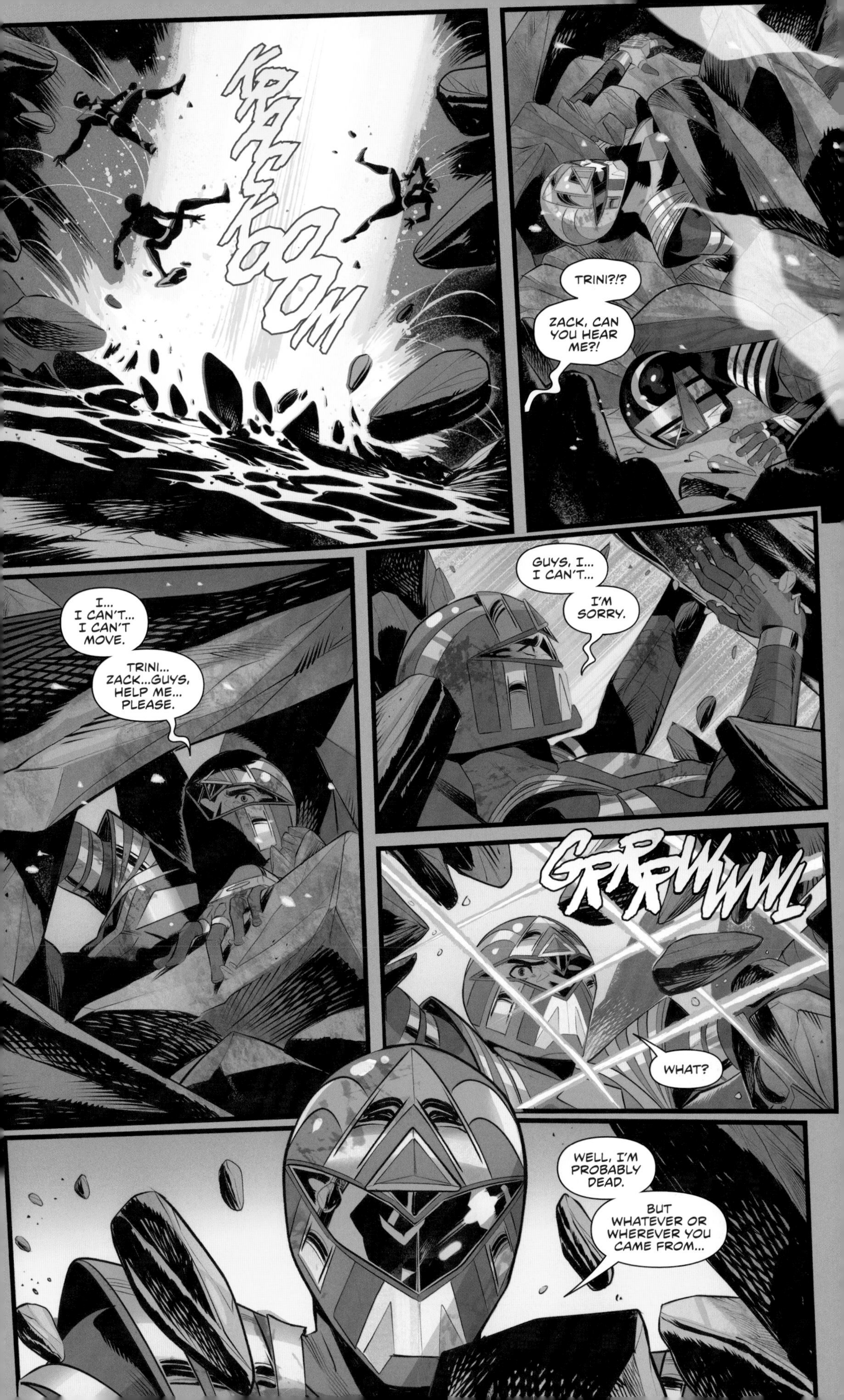
KRA-KOOOM
TRINI?!?
ZACK, CAN YOU HEAR ME?!
I... I CAN'T... I CAN'T MOVE.
TRINI... ZACK...GUYS, HELP ME... PLEASE.
GUYS, I... I CAN'T...
I'M SORRY.
GRRRWWWL
WHAT?
WELL, I'M PROBABLY DEAD.
BUT WHATEVER OR WHEREVER YOU CAME FROM...

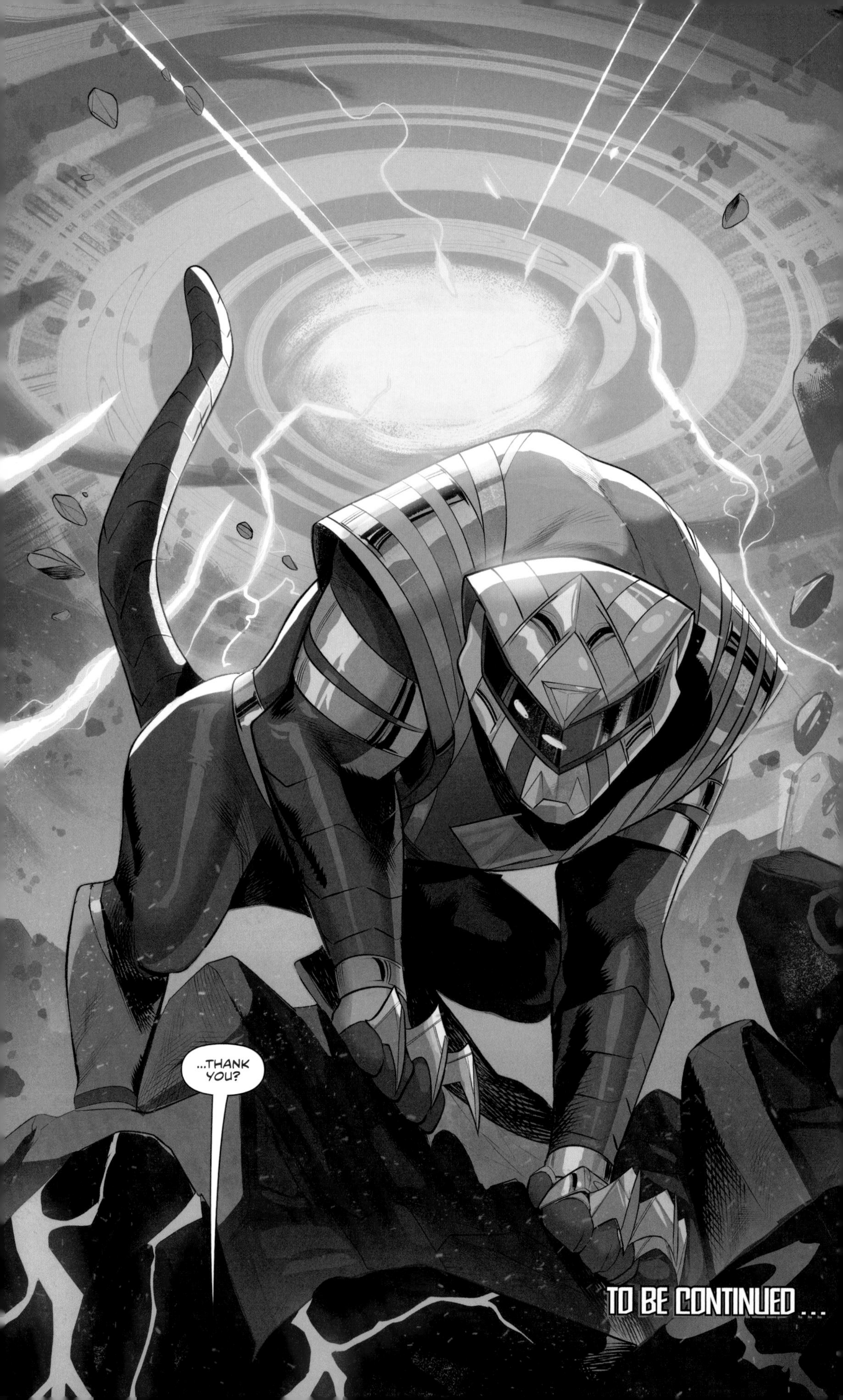
...THANK YOU?
TO BE CONTINUED . . .

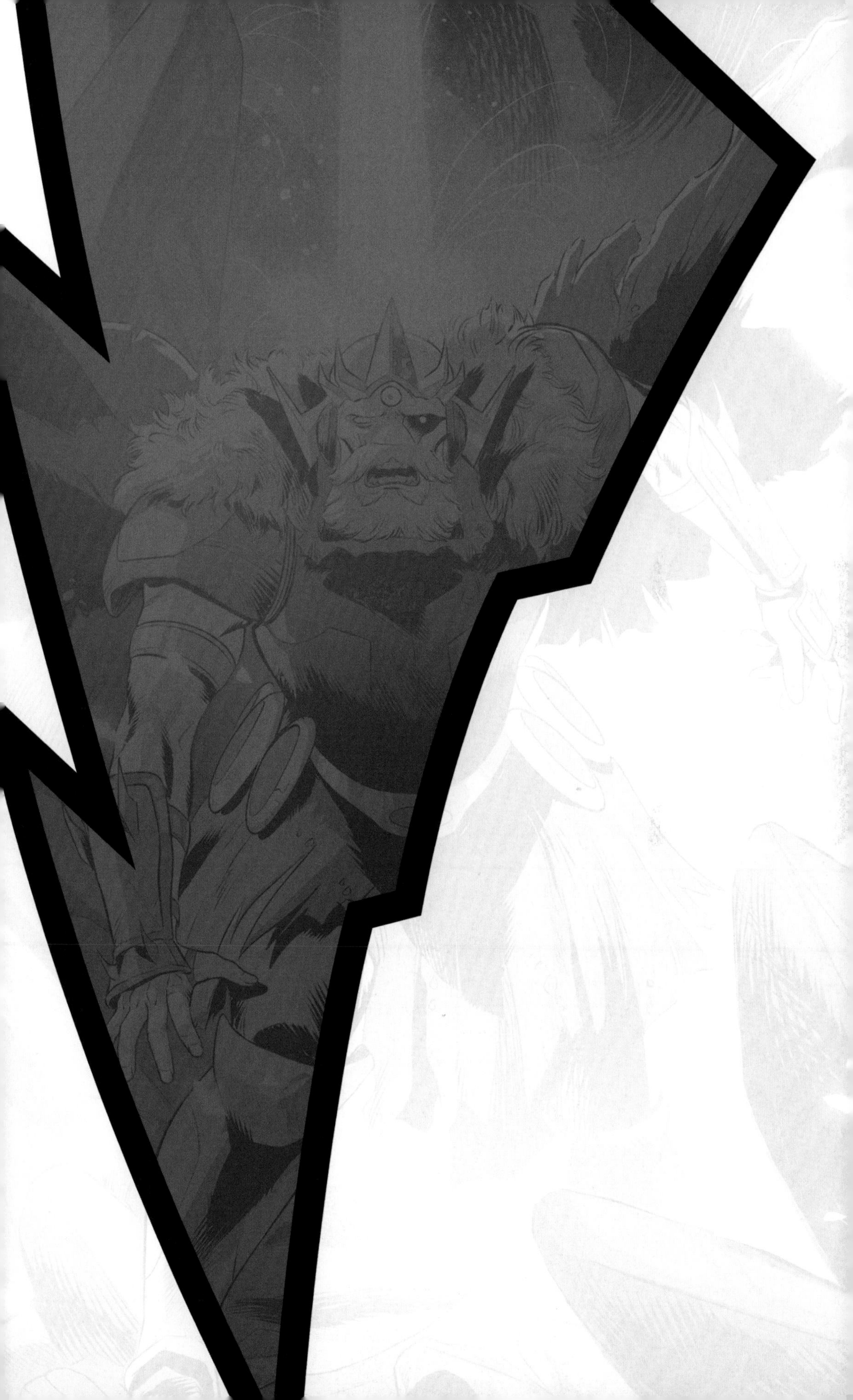

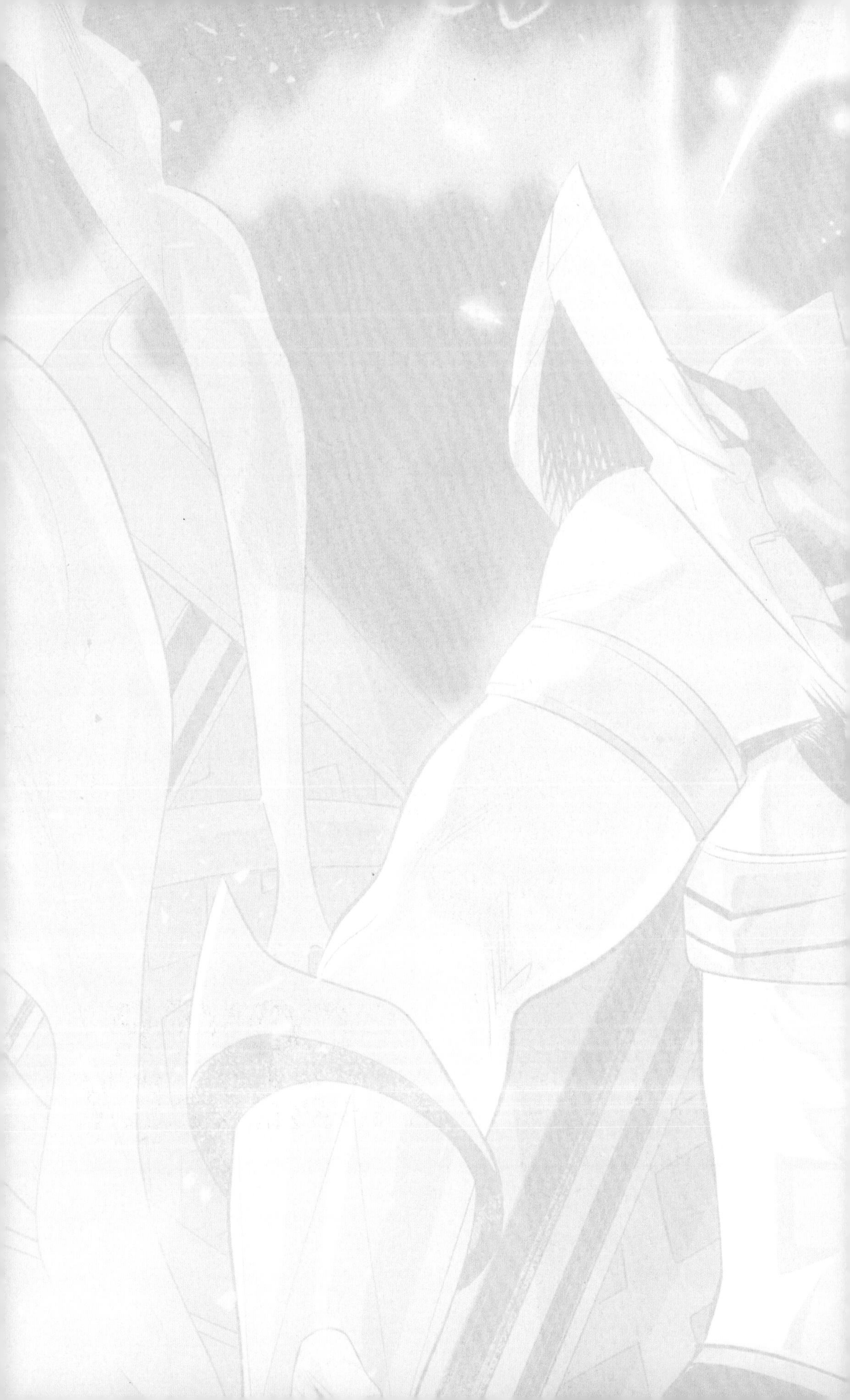

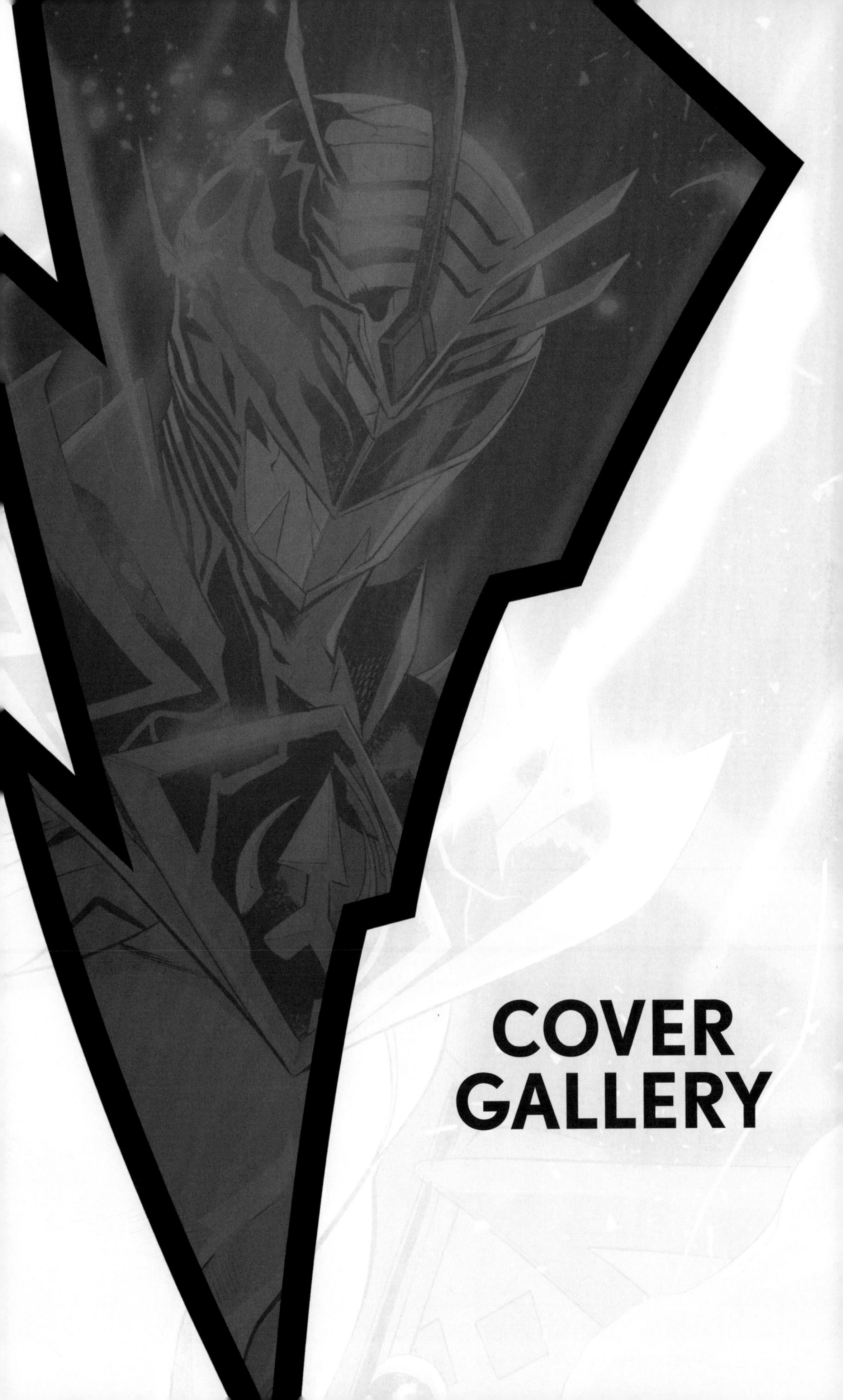

COVER GALLERY

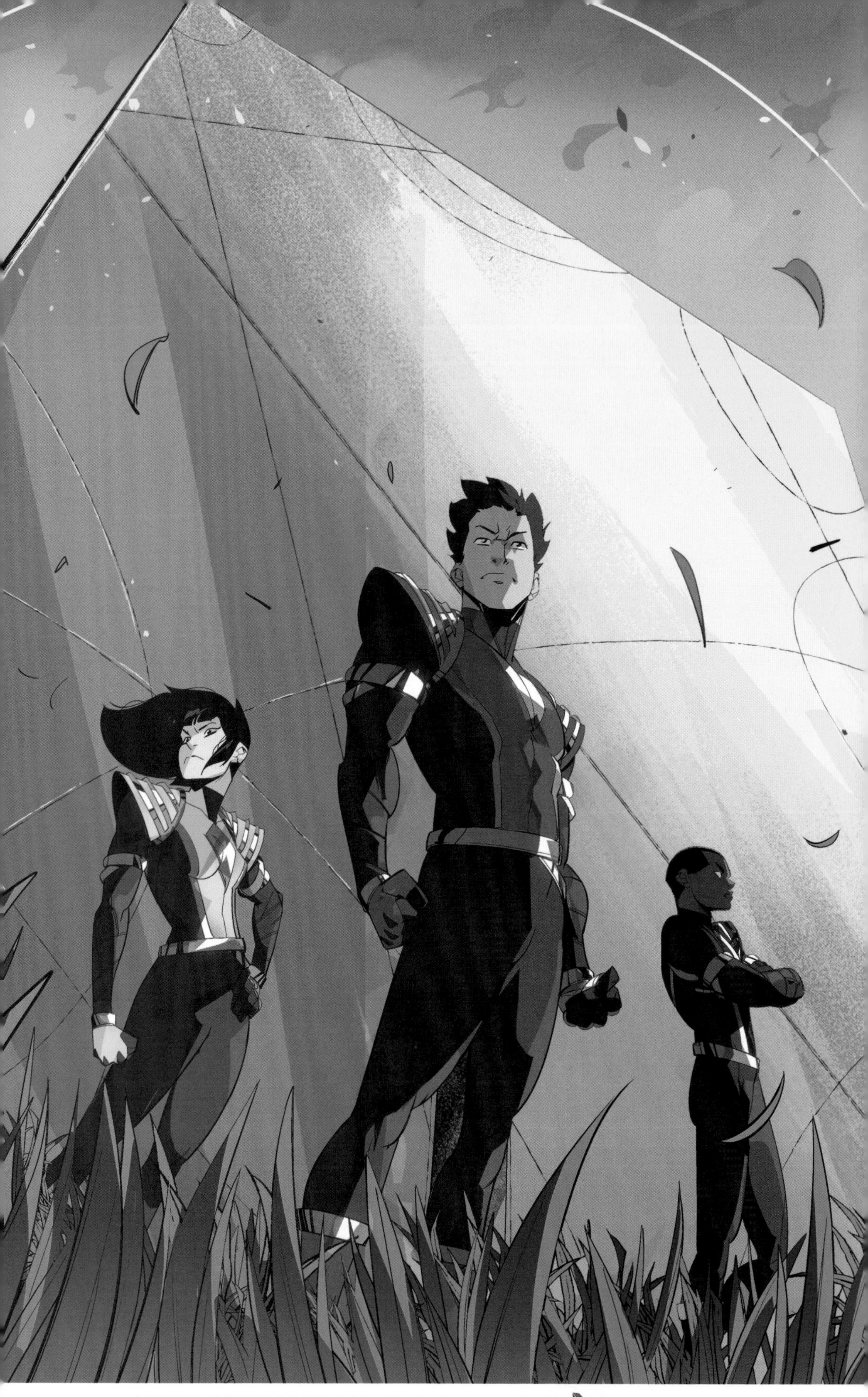

DANIELE DI NICUOLO WITH COLORS BY **WALTER BAIAMONTE** ISSUE #9 VARIANT COVER

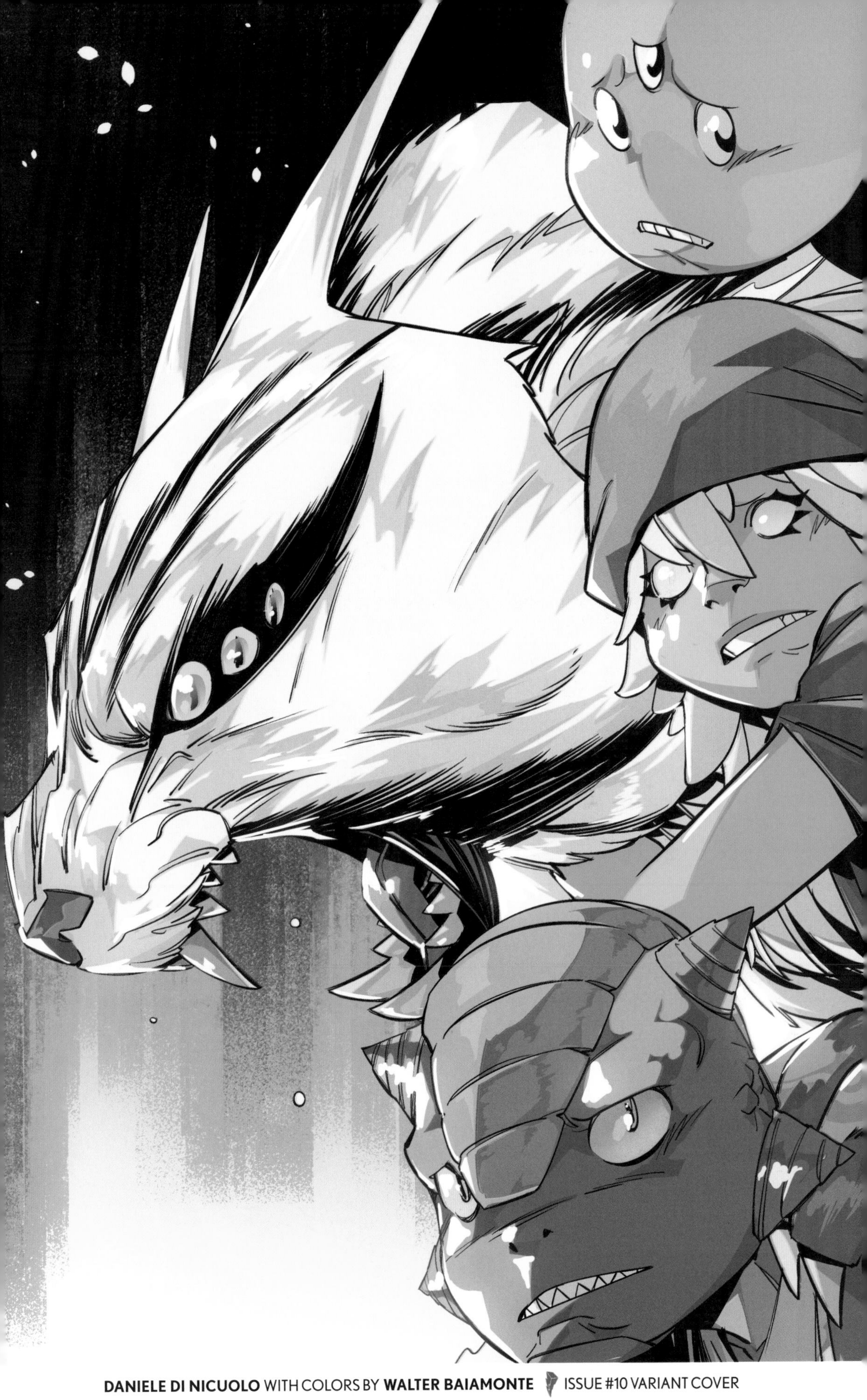

DANIELE DI NICUOLO WITH COLORS BY **WALTER BAIAMONTE** ISSUE #10 VARIANT COVER

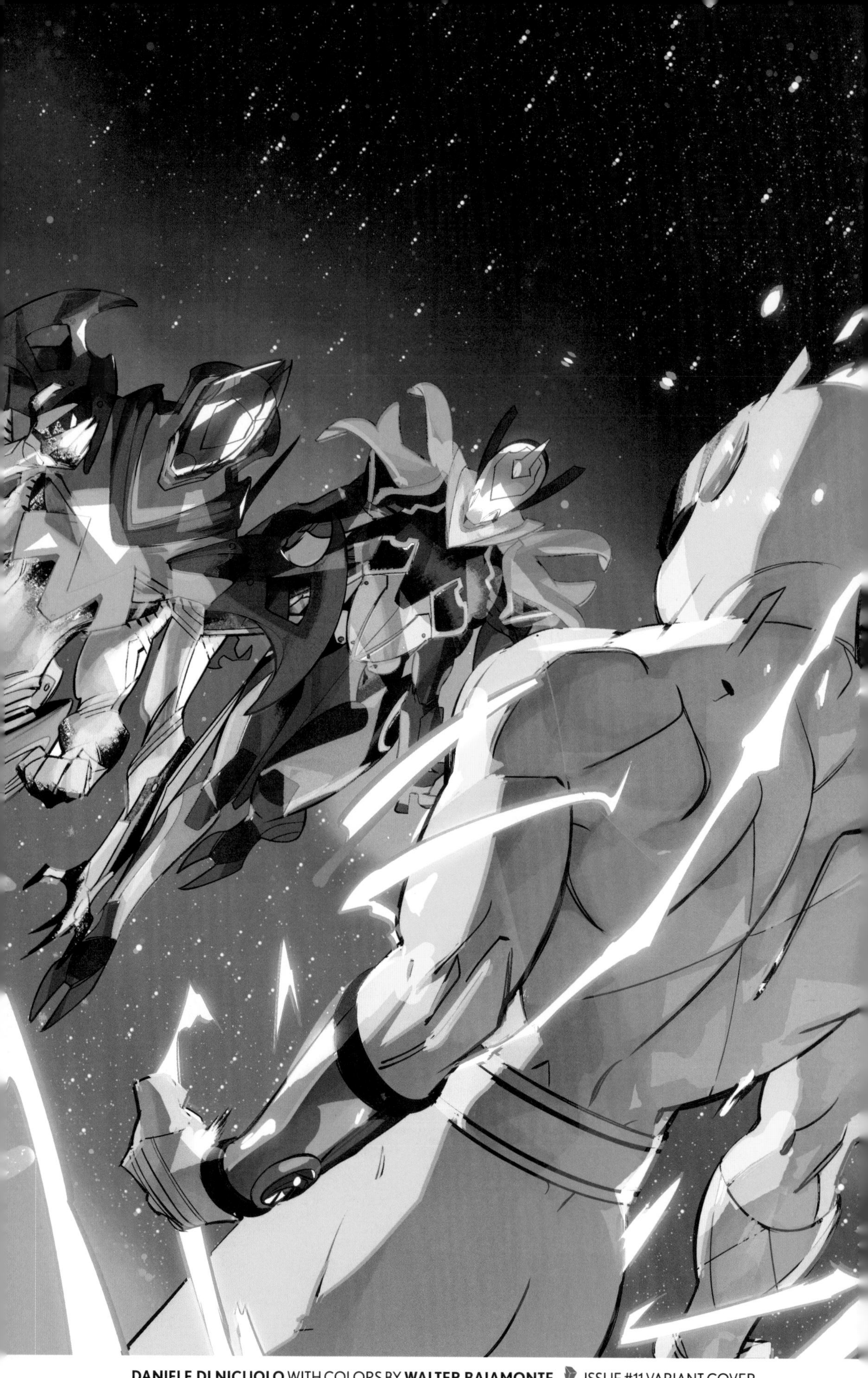

DANIELE DI NICUOLO WITH COLORS BY **WALTER BAIAMONTE** ISSUE #11 VARIANT COVER

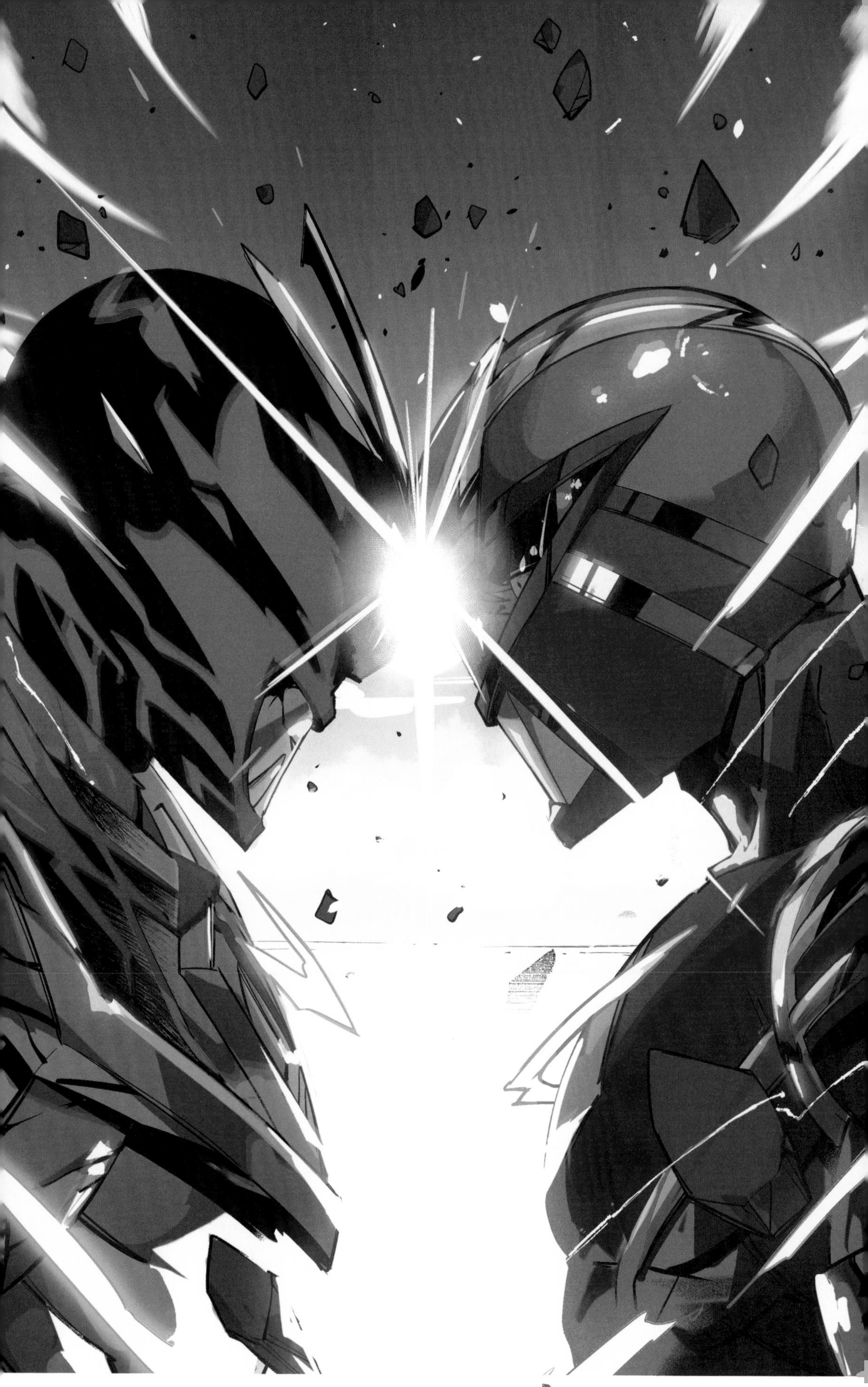

DANIELE DI NICUOLO WITH COLORS BY **WALTER BAIAMONTE** ISSUE #12 VARIANT COVER

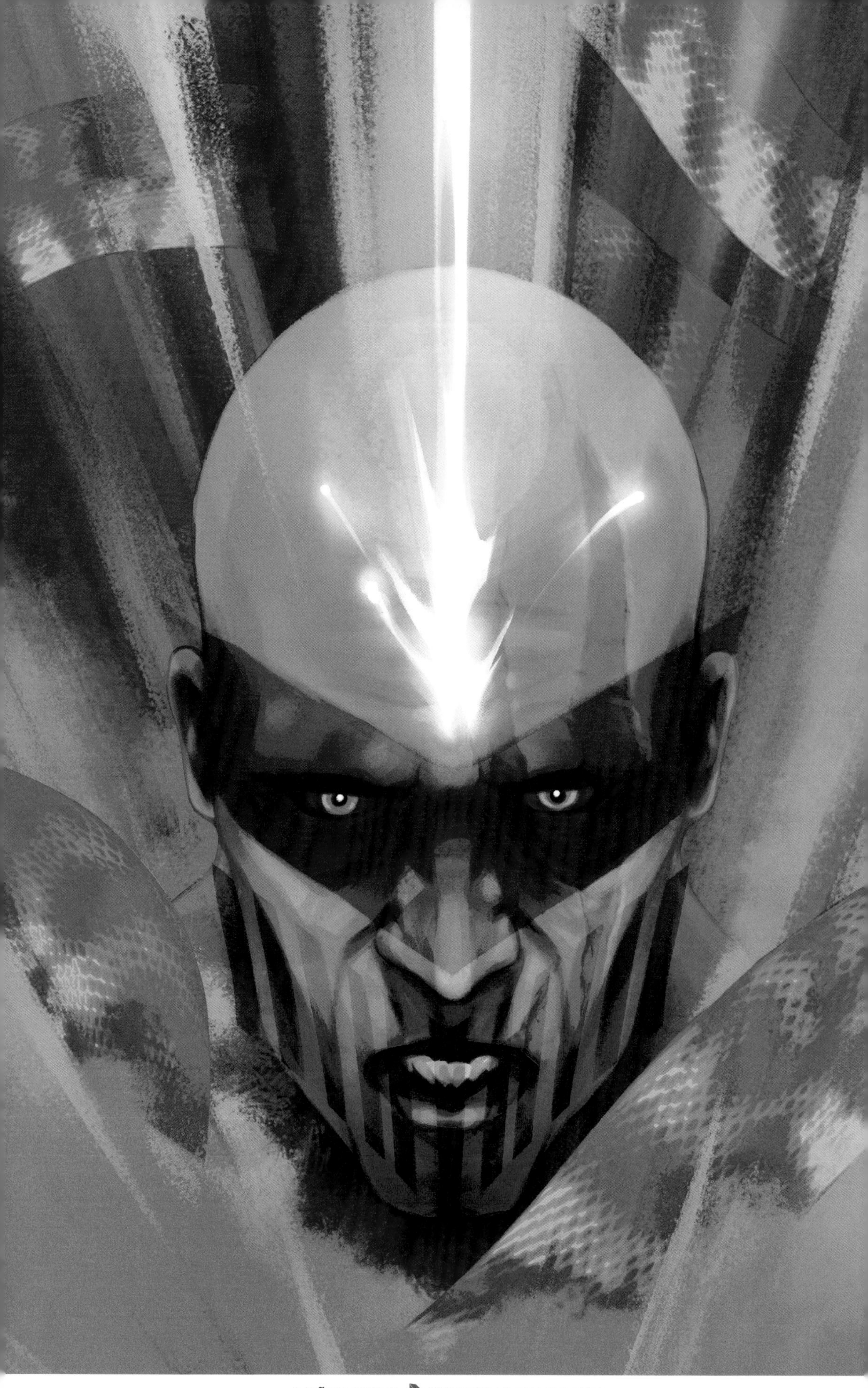

GOÑI MONTES ISSUE #10 VARIANT COVER

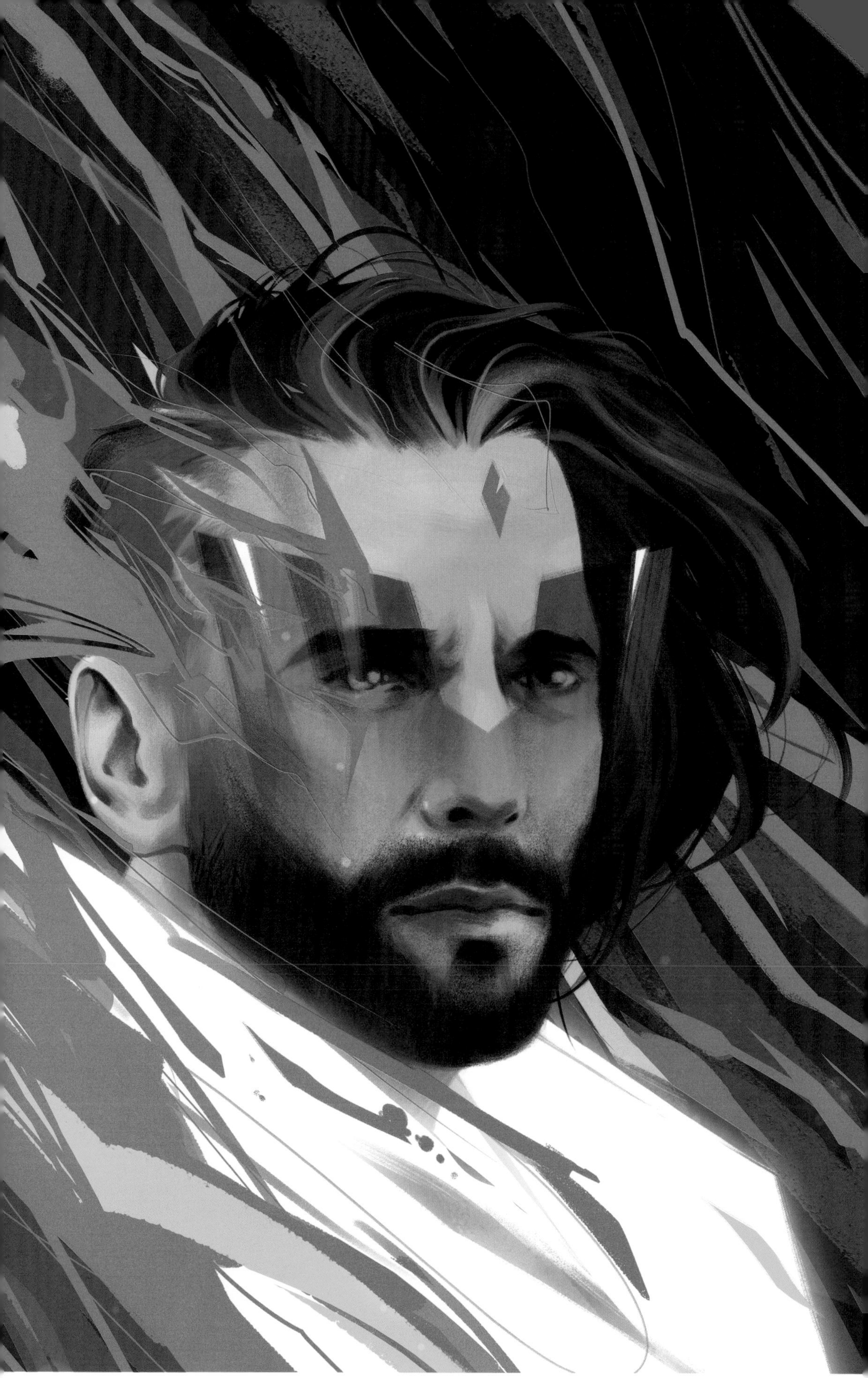

GOÑI MONTES | ISSUE #12 VARIANT COVER

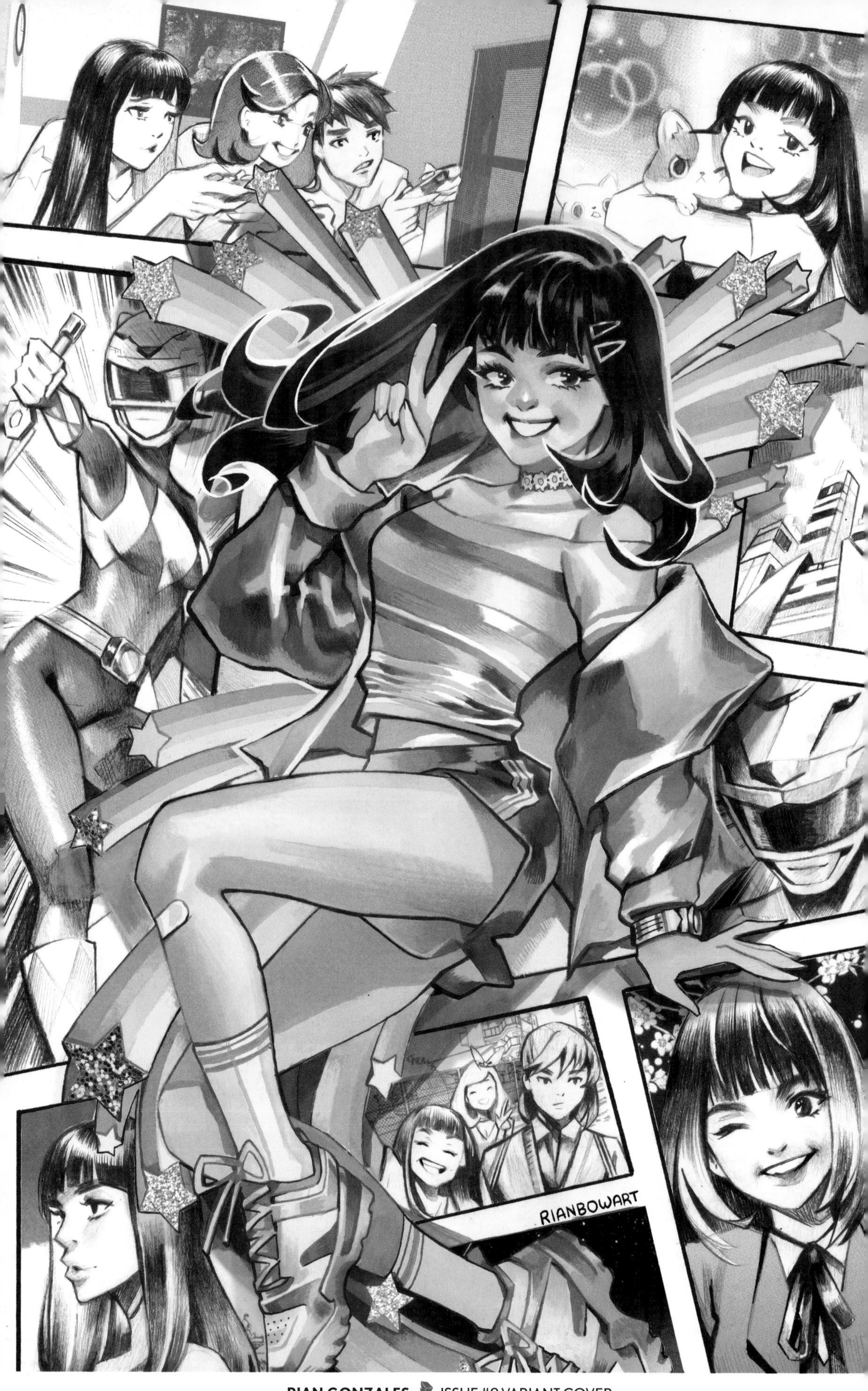
RIANBOWART

RIAN GONZALES ISSUE #9 VARIANT COVER

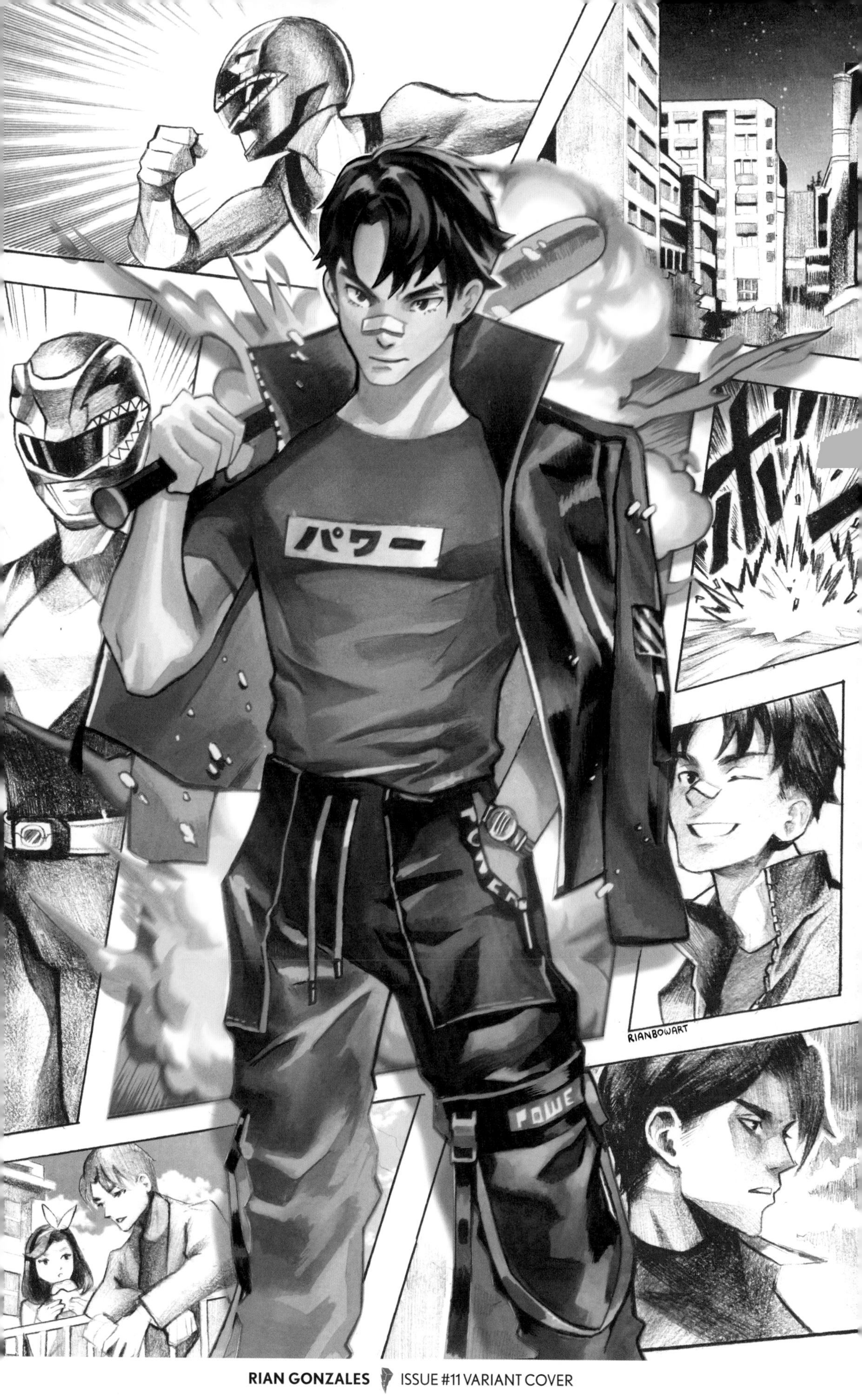
パワー
POWE
RIANBOWART

RIAN GONZALES ISSUE #11 VARIANT COVER

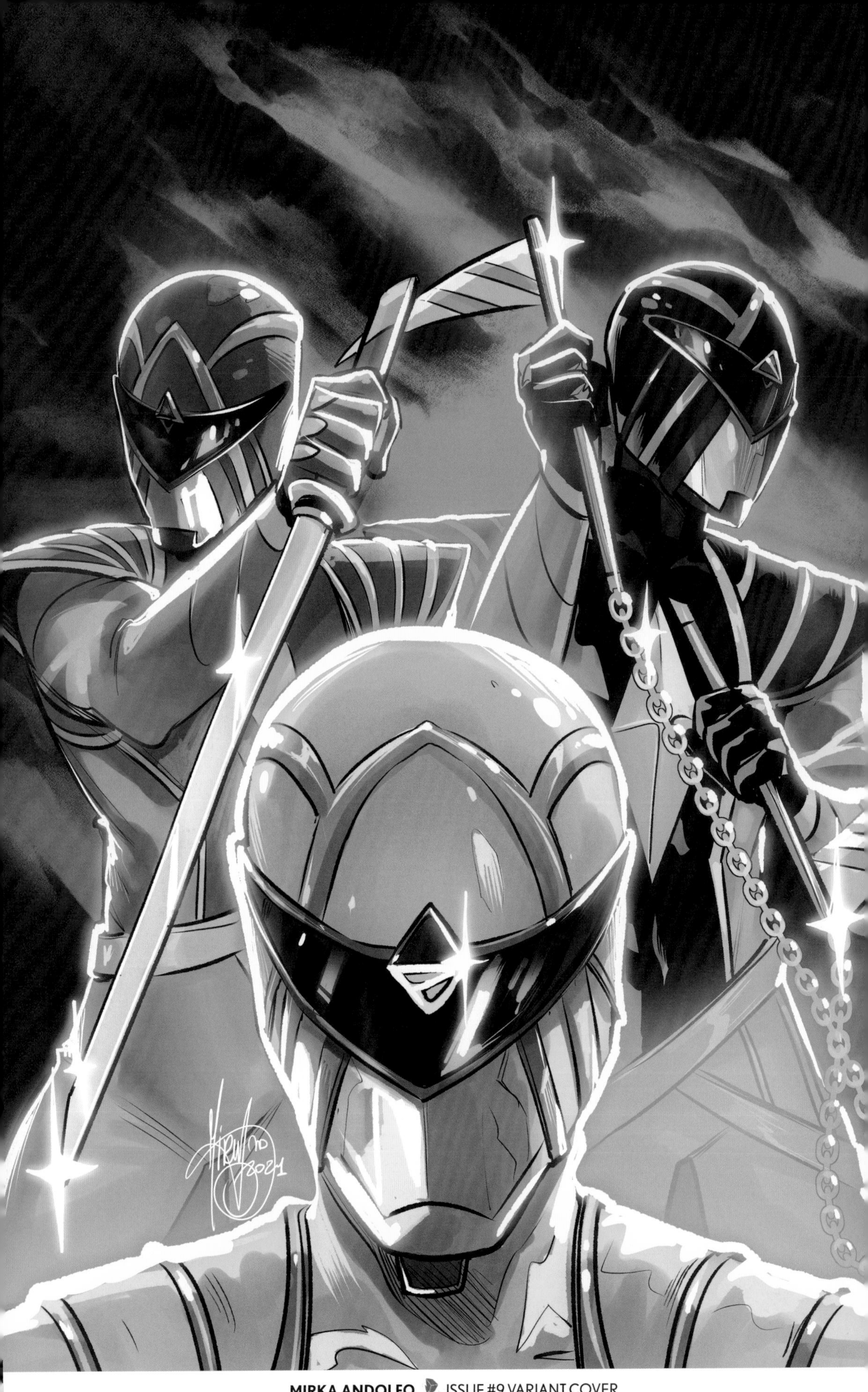

MIRKA ANDOLFO | ISSUE #9 VARIANT COVER

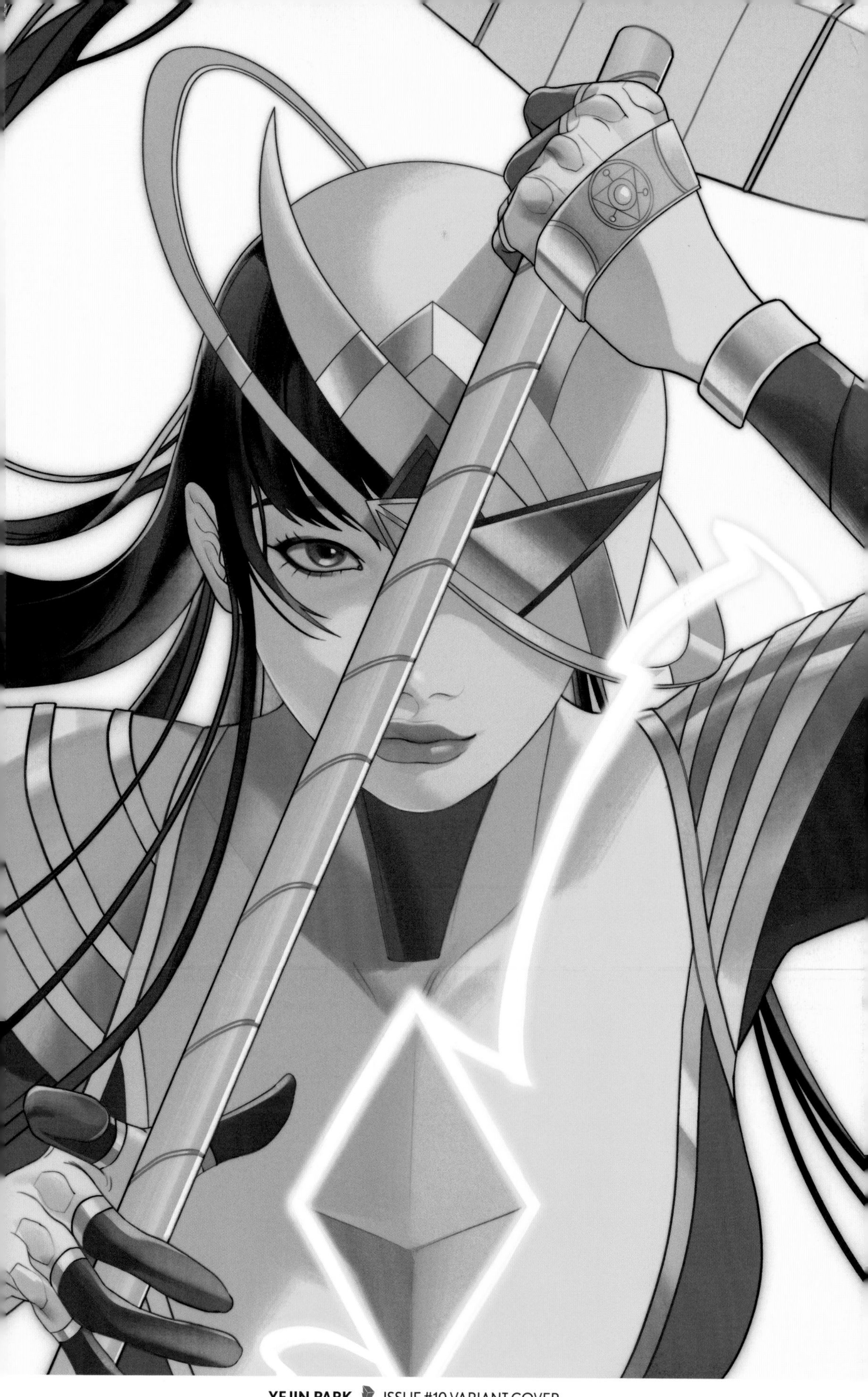

YEJIN PARK ISSUE #10 VARIANT COVER

DISCOVER MORE POWER RANGERS!

Mighty Morphin Power Rangers
Kyle Higgins, Hendry Prasetya, Matt Herms
Volume 1
ISBN: 978-1-60886-893-3 | $19.99
Volume 2
ISBN: 978-1-60886-942-8 | $16.99
Volume 3
ISBN: 978-1-60886-977-0 | $16.99
Volume 4
ISBN: 978-1-68415-031-1 | $16.99

Mighty Morphin Power Rangers: Pink
Kelly Thompson, Brenden Fletcher, Tini Howard, Daniele Di Nicuolo
ISBN: 978-1-60886-952-7 | $19.99

Saban's Go Go Power Rangers
Ryan Parrott, Dan Mora
Volume 1
ISBN: 978-1-68415-193-6 | $16.99

Saban's Power Rangers: Aftershock
Ryan Parrott, Lucas Werneck
ISBN: 978-1-60886-937-4 | $14.99

Mighty Morphin Power Rangers Poster Book
Goñi Montes, Jamal Campbell, Joe Quinones
ISBN: 978-1-60886-966-4 | $19.99

Mighty Morphin Power Rangers Adult Coloring Book
Goñi Montes, Jamal Campbell, Hendry Prasetya
ISBN: 978-1-60886-955-8 | $16.99

Mighty Morphin Power Rangers Year One: Deluxe HC
Kyle Higgins, Hendry Prasetya, Steve Orlando
ISBN: 978-1-68415-012-0 | $75.00

AVAILABLE AT YOUR LOCAL COMICS SHOP AND BOOKSTORE
Find a comic shop near you at www.comicshoplocator.com
WWW.BOOM-STUDIOS.COM